MEDICINAL PLANTS

DISTRIBUTION, UTILIZATION AND SIGNIFICANCE

ENV BOOKS SERIES

MEDICINAL PLANTS

DISTRIBUTION, UTILIZATION AND SIGNIFICANCE

Editors

Dr. Pankaj Sharma

Sr. Scientific Professional
Himachal Pradesh State Biodiversity Board
Himachal Pradesh State Council for Science, Technology & Environment
B-34, SDA Complex, Kasumpti, Shimla - 171 009
Himachal Pradesh, (India)

Dr. Pawan Kumar 'Bharti'

Vice President (Executive)
Society for Environment, Health, Awareness of nutrition & Toxicology (SEHAT)
1775, Sohan Ganj, Near Clock Tower, Delhi-7 (India)
E-mail: *gurupawanbharti@rediffmail.com*

Dr. Narayan Singh

Manager
CSR-TERI, Dalash, Kullu
Himachal Pradesh, India

DPH

DISCOVERY PUBLISHING HOUSE PVT. LTD.
NEW DELHI-110 002

Published by:
Tilak Wasan

DISCOVERY PUBLISHING HOUSE PVT. LTD.
4383/4B, Ansari Road, Darya Ganj
New Delhi-110 002 (India)
Phone : +91-11-23279245, 43596064-65
Fax : +91-11-23253475
E-mail : discoverypublishinghouse@gmail.com
sales@discoverypublishinggroup.com
web : www.discoverypublishinggroup.com

First Edition: **2015**

ISBN: 978-93-5056-734-0

Medicinal Plants: *Distribution, Utilization and Significance*

Printed at:
Infinity Imaging Systems
Delhi

ENV Books Series, India

Calls lengthy and error free chapters for further volumes of books on various environmental issues. (Send your manuscripts to envbooks@gmail.com)

Founding Editor **(*Editor-in-Chief*)**

Dr. Pawan Kumar 'Bharti'
Society for Environment, Health, Awareness of Nutrition & Toxicology (SEHAT-India), 1775, Sohanganj, Near Clock Tower, Delhi-7, India
E-mail: *gurupawanbharti@rediffmail.com*

Other titles by Editor-in-Chief:

1. **Advances in Agriculture and Ecology (2013)**
   Bharti, P.K.; Chauhan, A. and Ezeaku Peter Ikemefuna (eds.)
   (ISBN: 978-93-5056-362-5).
2. **Advances in Biotechnology and Ecological Sciences (2013)**
   Bharti, P.K., Chauhan, A. and Ray, J. (eds.)
   (ISBN: 978-93-5056-358-8).
3. **Agriculture and Environmental Biotechnology (2014)**
   Bharti, P.K. and Chauhan, A. (eds.)
   (ISBN: 978-93-5056-479-0).
4. **Agriculture Ecology and Environment (2014)**
   Bharti, P.K. and Olubukola O. Babalola (eds.)
   (ISBN: 978-93-5056-480-6).
5. **Agro-forestry and Climate Change (2014)**
   Bharti, Pawan K. and Singh, Narayan (eds.)
   (ISBN: 978-93-5056-514-8).
6. **Aquaculture and Fisheries Environment (2014)**
   Gupta, S.K. and Pawan K. Bharti (eds.)
   (ISBN: 978-93-5056-408-0).
7. **Aquatic Environment and Toxicology (2013)**
   Bharti, Pawan K. (ed.)
   (ISBN: 978-93-5056-236-9).

8. **Aquatic Biodiversity and Pollution (2013)**
Bharti, P.K.; Chauhan, A. and Kaoud, H.A.H. (eds.)
(ISBN: 978-93-5056-359-5).

9. **Aquatic Ecology and Biotechnology (2014)**
Bharti, P.K. and Zaki, M.S.A. (eds.)
(ISBN: 978-93-5056-451-6).

10. **Biodiversity of Aquatic Ecosystem:**
Significance, Threat and Conservation **(2013)**
Bharti, P.K. and Kaoud, H.A.H. (eds.)
(ISBN: 978-93-5056-297-0).

11. **Clean Technologies and Environmental Protection (2015)**
Chauhan, A.; Sharma, S. and Bharti, P.K. (eds.)
(ISBN: 978-93-5056-731-9).

12. **Climate Change and Agriculture (2012)**
Bharti, P.K. and Chauhan, Avnish (eds.)
(ISBN: 978-93-5056-148-5).

13. **Climate Change and Biodiversity (2013)**
Bharti, P.K. and Chauhan, Avnish (eds.)
(ISBN: 978-93-5056-360-1).

14. **Conservation and Cultivation of Medicinal Plants (2015)**
Bharti, P.K. and Singh, Narayan (eds.)
(ISBN: 978-93-5056-740-1).

15. **Eco-toxicology and Eco-technology (2013)**
Bharti, P.K. and Zaki, M. (eds.)
(ISBN: 978-93-5056-313-7).

16. **Environmental Biotechnology and Application (2013)**
Bharti, P.K. and Chauhan, Avnish (eds.)
(ISBN: 978-93-5056-262-8).

17. **Environmental Conservation and Biotechnology (2014)**
Chauhan, A. and P.K. Bharti (eds.)
(ISBN: 978-93-5056-512-4).

18. **Environmental Health and Problems (2013)**
Bharti, P.K. and Gajananda, Kh. (eds.)
(ISBN: 978-93-5056-263-5).

19. **Environmental Pollution and Biodiversity (2012)**
Bharti, P.K.; Chauhan, Avnish and Kumar, P. (eds.)
(ISBN: 978-93-5056-149-2).

20. **Fisheries and Toxicology (2014)**
Zaki, M.S.A.; Bharti, P.K. and Chauhan, A. (eds.)
(ISBN: 978-93-5056-452-3).

21. **Freshwater Ecosystem and Xenobiotics (2013)**
    Bharti, P.K.; Zaki, M. and Chauhan, A. (eds.)
    (ISBN: 978-93-5056-299-4).

22. **Limnology and Aquatic Science (2015)**
    Sharma, S. and Bharti, P.K. (eds.)
    (ISBN: 978-93-5056-735-7).

23. **Microbial Applications and Environment (2014)**
    Bharti, Pawan K. (ed.)
    (ISBN: 978-93-5056-515-5).

24. **Microbial Ecology and Habitat (2014)**
    Bharti, Pawan K. (ed.)
    (ISBN: 978-93-5056-514-8).

25. **Prakriti me Aushadhi (*in Hindi*) (2012)**
    Singh, J.R.; Bharti, P.K. and Bharti, B.
    (ISBN: 978-93-5056-200-0).

26. **Seed Technology, Plant Growth and Cropping System (2015)**
    Tyagi, P.K. and Bharti, P.K. (eds.)
    (ISBN: 978-93-5056-738-8).

27. **Soil Contamination and Conservation (2015)**
    Ezeaku, P.I. and Bharti, P.K. (eds.)
    (ISBN: 978-93-5056-737-1).

28. **Soil Quality and Contamination (2013)**
    Bharti, P.K. and Chauhan, Avnish (eds.)
    (ISBN: 978-93-5056-361-8).

29. **Waste Disposal and Management (2015)**
    Bharti, P.K.; Tabassum, B. and Bajaj, P. (eds.)
    (ISBN: 978-93-5056-729-6).

30. **Water Resources and Agriculture (2014)**
    Bharti, P.K. and Ezeaku Peter Ikemefuna (eds.)
    (ISBN: 978-93-5056-481-3).

Preface

The diversity of life exists on earth and each life form has its own needs for existence. Greater biodiversity leads to better productivity and better nutrient retention in ecosystem which leads to greater ecosystem stability. Global biodiversity is being lost at an unprecedented rate, as a consequence of human induced environmental change. Since 1966 the International Union for Conservation of Nature and Natural Resources (IUCN) has evaluated species conservation status worldwide and today the IUCN Red Lists have become one of the most important information sources about the conservation status of world's flora and fauna worldwide. Evaluating species conservation status is one of the main tools for establishing conservation priorities and management policies. A species global conservation status, however, is not necessarily the same as the conservation status on a regional scale. Some species that are threatened on a global scale may not be threatened on a regional scale, and species that are not threatened on a global scale might be threatened in some part of their range. Some species may be declining fast across their ranges on average but may be locally stable or even increasing. Furthermore, knowing the regional status of species is important for several reasons and loss of population and genetic diversity is a major concern. When a species is protected on a regional scale, conservation of its genetic diversity is promoted. Regional scale extinction of one species can provoke a cascade of extinctions, causing a change in species composition and in ecosystems processes. The extinction of a species is the result of local extinctions of its populations. Degradation and fragmentation of >70% of the original habitats placed Himalaya in the list of Global Biodiversity Hotspots.

The Indian Himalayan Region (IHR), is very well known for its diverse bio-geographic and eco-climatic features and is the richest bio-physical resources for its indigenous cultural groups, which live in harmony with their natural surroundings. In the IHR, attempts have been made to identify the threatened plants by various workers. Under the current scenario, about

20% of all species are expected to be lost within 30 years and 50% or more by the end of 21st century. In the IHR, over exploitation and habitat degradation are the two major factors responsible for decrease in population of the species.

Himachal Pradesh is the green, biomass rich state and regions also hosts variations in topographical features resulting diverse climatic and habitat conditions by virtue of this the state has overwhelming richness, representativeness and unique biodiversity. Furthermore, the state also has diversity of ethnic groups, inhabiting in different remote and difficult terrains depends on various bio-resources to meet out their daily needs for the sustenance. Among other bio-resources, the region is also well recognized for a plethora of medicinal plants, wild edibles and other non-timber forest products. The region is therefore, rightly recognized as a cultural landscape, where culture and biological diversity are mutually supportive. The overall biodiversity of the State has not been thoroughly studied. However, various individual studies have been conducted by numerous workers, covering various groups of organisms and various aspects of biodiversity. These studies are generally scattered and mostly not available to all those interested in biodiversity of the State.

Apart from the contributions of the authors to various aspects of Indian Himalayan medicinal plants, this volume includes recommendations covering future issues and priorities for the research and development on this important group of plants. Editors hope that this publication will be of immense help to researcher, students, teachers, conservationists, policy makers/planners, foresters, farmers and other interested to undertake studies/work on medicinal plants.

–Editors

(envbooks@gmail.com)

Contents

Pages: **1-16**

MEDICINAL PLANTS: *DISTRIBUTION, UTILIZATION AND SIGNIFICANCE*

Edited by: **Dr. Pankaj Sharma; Dr. Pawan Kumar 'Bharti'** and **Dr. Narayan Singh**

ISBN: 978-93-5056-734-0

Edition: **2015**

Published by: **Discovery Publishing House Pvt. Ltd., New Delhi (India)**

1

Diversity, Indigenous Uses, Conservation Prioritization and Current Status of Medicinal Plants in Himachal Pradesh

A Case Study from Chandra Valley

Pankaj Sharma[1]*; S.S. Samant[2] and Manohar Lal[2]

ABSTRACT

The value of medicinal plants in habitual healthcare practices provides clues to latest areas of research and in biodiversity conservation is nowglowing. However, information on the uses of plants for medicine is deficient from interior areas of Himalaya. Chandra valley in Lahaul & Spiti district in Himachal Pradesh, India is known for specific topography, severe climate and unique vegetation. The valley in Himachal Pradesh, part of Cold Desert Biosphere Reserve, is rich in medicinal plants, and local people practice theTibetan System of Medicine. Keeping this in view the present study has been conducted to study the diversity, indigenous uses, threat categorization and conservation prioritization of medicinal plants in Chandra valley of Lahaul

[1] Himachal Pradesh State Biodiversity Board, Himachal Pradesh State Council for Science, Technology & Environment, 34, SDA Complex, Kasumpti, Shimla-171 009, Himachal Pradesh, (India).

[2] G.B. Pant Institute of Himalayan Environment and Development, Himachal Unit, Mohal-Kullu - 175 126, Himachal Pradesh, (India).

& Spiti district in Himachal Pradesh, North Western Himalaya. A total of 261 species of medicinal plants belonging to 50 families and 168 generawere recorded and used by the inhabitants of the area.These medicinal plants comprise of 5 trees, 231 herbs, 23 shrubs and 02 ferns. From the total, 146 medicinal plants were native, 2 endemic and 17 were near endemic. Maximum medicinal plants were reported in the altitudinal zone, 3100-3800m and decreased with increasingaltitude in the study area. These species have been also analyze for their nativity, endemism and rarity, and are prioritized for cultivation. An area-specific threat categorization of species is very important for short or long termmanagement planning. In present study such an attempt in the study area, using information on different attributes was initiated. The occurrence of critically endangered, endangered and vulnerable medicinal plants indicates high anthropogenic demands on these species. The over-exploitation, habitat degradation and changing environmental conditions may lead to the extinction within a few years. Therefore, regular monitoring of population and habitats, development of conventional protocol, establishment of species *in-situ* conditions and associated habitats and replication of this approach in other parts of Indian Himalayan Region have been suggested.

Key words: Diversity, indigenous uses, native, endemic, threat categorization, conservation prioritization, Chandra valley

INTRODUCTION

In worldwide, millions of people rely on medicinal plants for primary health care, income generation and livelihood options. The medicinal properties of plants coveramarvellousinvolvement in the origin and advancement of many conventional herbal therapies. The Indian Himalayan Region (IHR) comprises of five biogeographic provinces, covers approximately an area of 591 thousand km^2 (Rodgers and Panwar 1988) and extending from Jammu & Kashmir in the North-West to the Arunachal Pradesh in the East. IHR one of the mega hot spot of biological diversity (Myers 2000) is a source of a great diversity of food, fuel, fodder, timber, dye and medicinal plants. It comprises about 18% of India and is more than 2,800 km long and 220 to 300 km wide, with altitudes from 200–8000 m (Anonymous 1992). The IHR alone supports about 8,000 species of angiosperms (40% endemics), 44 species of gymnosperms (15.91% endemics), 600 species of pteridophytes (25% endemics), 1,737 species of bryophytes (32.53% endemics), 1,159 species of lichens (11.22% endemics) and 6,900 species of fungi (27.39% endemics) (Singh and Hajra 1996; Samant et al. 2007 a). There are over 816 tree species, 675 edibles and nearly 1,748 species of medicinal value with various traditional and modern therapeutic uses found in the IHR (Samant et al. 1998). 118 species of medicinal plants yielding essential oils, 279 species of fodder, 155 sacred plants (Samant and Pant 2003) and 121 rare-endangered plants (Samant et al. 2007a).This has adversely affected thevery existence of a number of plants of high commercial value (Farooquee and Saxena 1996). Further, with theincreasing world demand and renewed global interest in traditional ethnopharmacy coupled with the increasingpreference for natural substances in the health care system, the natural stock of medicinal plants of the IHR isunder tremendous pressure (Samant et al. 1998; Kala et. al. 2006; Singh et al. 2009; Rana and Samant 2011).In India over 2,500 species of ethnobotanical uses areknown (Jain 1991). The verysurvival of these resources is now under threat from rapidlyexpanding human population and concomitant environmentaldegradation occurring at a fast pace.

A large number of studies have been carried out on medicinal plants of the IHR (Jain 1991; Samant et al. 1998, 2000, 2007 a&b; Rai et al. 2000; Samant and Pal 2003; Kala 2000; Rana and Samant, 2009, 2010, 2011). However, in Himachal Pradesh studies of medicinal plants are fragmentary and mainly focus on inventory (Bhattacharya and Uniyal 1982; Chauhan 1988, 1999; Kapahi 1990; Badola 2001; Sood et al. 2001; Badola and Pal 2003; Kala 2006; Uniyal et al. 2006), although a few studies haveaddressed diversity, distribution patterns, nativity, endemism, rarity and conservation prioritization of medicinal plants (Samant et al. 2007 a&b). Himachal Pradesh has 643 medicinal plants, out of which 269 are native, 374 non-native, 17 endemic, 131 near endemic, 12 criticallyendangered, 21 endangered, 27 vulnerable, two near threatenedand three data deficient (Samant et al. 2007a).The Lahaul & Spiti district of the State is rich in medicinal plant diversity. Very few studies are available on medicinal plants and there are no integrated studies.There is plenty scope for the promotion of medicinal plant cultivation and conservation and as such an integrated study on diverse parameters of the medicinal plants has not been carried out so far. Therefore, the study conducted in Chandra valley in Lahaul & Spiti district of the State.

Medicinal plants are worn in the Ayurvedic, Unani and other traditional systems of medicineand in plant based pharmaceutical industries. The Tibetan system of medicine is also depends on Himalayan species (Samant et al. 1998). Estimates indicate that at least 90% of medicinal plant species are extracted from the wild (Anonymous 2000); and that 69% of the material is collected through destructive harvesting, which suggests that medicinal plants are significantly threatened (Dhar et al. 2000). Tremendous anthropogenic pressures have been identified as the main causes of decline in the population and accessibility of the medicinal plants in the Himalayan region (Samant et al. 1998). With the increasing demand and renewed global interest in the healthcare system, the natural stock of medicinalplants of Himachal Pradesh is under terrific pressure (Samant et al. 1998). To provide the information essential to shore up further action, this paper brings together existing information with results from current field surveys.

STUDY AREA

Chandra valley (3,100-5,000m) in Lahaul & Spiti districtof the Cold Desert Biosphere Reserve in Himachal Pradesh (Map). The valley is a unique socio-physical unitand covers an area of 2, 590 km^2 (Pandey, 1993). It is surrounded by the main Himalayan ranges on the North, the mid Himalayan range or Pir-Panjal on the South, the Kunjum range which separates Lahaul from Spiti on the East and the off-shoot of the Pir-Panjal range on the West. The valley is approachable from Rohtang Pass (3978 m) by road to Lahaul from Kullu and Kunjum Pass (4740 m) road to Lahaul from Spiti. It started from source of the Chandra River *i.e.*, Chandratal at Baralacha (4891m) and flows in South Westerly direction till ends after meeting with Bhaga river at Tandi. Locally this valley is known as Tinan/Rangloi valley. The Valley is very well known for the glaciers. The notable glaciers are SamundraTapu, Bara Shigri, Lord Gepan, Sissu, Sonapari, Kulti, Shiti, Brende, Neelghar and Anghar. The various nallah such as Pagal, Shooling, Kulti, Koksar, Sissu, Ropsang, Neelgar, Mooling and Gawadi and many small streams drain into the Chandra river. The valley represents two prominent lakes i.e., Chandertal and Sissutal. The soil contains the properties of Schistose and Calcareous Group. The climate of the area is dry temperate to alpine types, which shows distinct seasons. The rainy season receives rainfall which varies between 10 mm to 300 mm yr^{-1} depending upon the part of the valley. The winter season is comparatively a large period i.e., starts from November and ends by April. During this period, heavy snow fall occurs in the area. The snowfall varies from 3-12 feet. The vegetation of the Chandra valley is mainly comprises of sub-alpine and alpine types. *Pinuswallichiana, Piceasmithiana, Abiespindrow, Salix* spp. and *Betulautilis* forests are found in patches in the East facing of the valley. The residents of the area are Hindu,Buddhist or mixture of the two. They are largely dependenton local biodiversity for their subsistence.

METHODS

Surveys, Data Collection and Analysis

The 22 villages namely (Jagle,Gramphu, Koksar, Teling, Sissu, Thorang, Shashen, Shooling, Ropsang, Khorpani, Khangsar, Sheltu, Goundhla, Phugtal, Yangla, Dalang, Yuramurthi, Murtichang, Mooling, Shipting, Bargul, Gwadi) and surroundings areas of the Chandra valley (3,100-5,000m) were surveyed in different seasons, i.e. winter, summer and rainy for three years (2007-2010) to assess the medicinal plant diversity and generate information on utilization of medicinal plants by the inhabitants of the area. Participatory Rural Appraisal (PRA) followed for information generation on medicinal plants.

Also, local knowledgeable persons including *Vaidhyas* were interviewed. Information generated on the indigenous uses and commercial values. Among the knowledgeable persons, one person was hired to collect medicinal plants from the natural habitat(s). The specimens of each species were collected and identified with the help of floras, and research papers (Collett 1902;

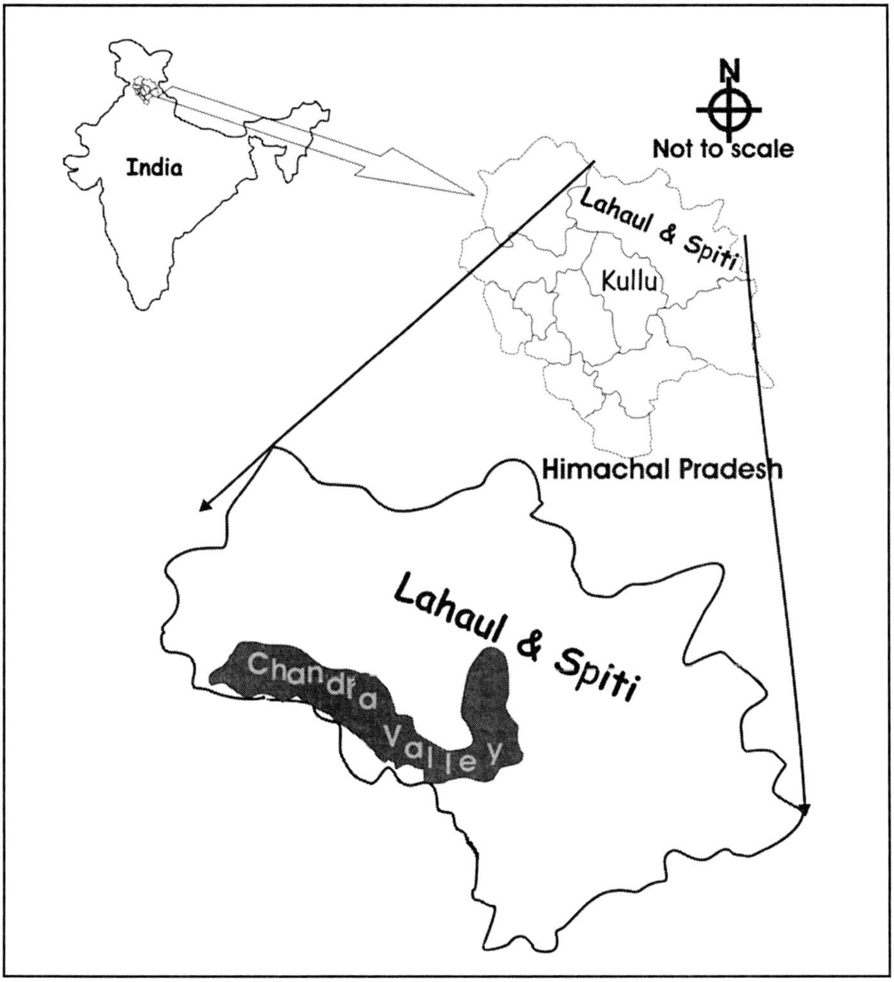

Map Study Area

Polunin and Stainton 1984, 1987; Aswal & Mehrotra 1994; Dhaliwal and Sharma 1999, 1997; Singh and Rawat 2000; Khullar 1994, 2000). Information on locality, altitudinal range, life form, habitat and other morphological characters was collected for each species. The data were compiled and analyzed for diversity and distribution pattern of the species following Samant and Dhar, 1997 and Samant et al. 1998.

Nativity, Endemism, Threat Categorization and Conservation Prioritization

The nativity of species represents the primary evidence or origin, following Anonymous (1883-1970) and Samant et al. (1998). Endemism of a species was identified on distribution range of the species and following Dhar and Samant (1993) and Samant et al. (1998). Species confined to the IHR were considered as endemic, and those with a distribution extending to neighbouring countries (Himalayan region of Afghanistan, Pakistan, Tibet,

Nepal, Bhutan and adjacent states of the IHR) were considered as near endemics. The threat categories of the medicinal plants were identified using seven attributes (i.e. habitat preference, distribution range, availability, use value, trade value, extraction and nativity and endemic species) and following (Samant et al. 1998; Ved et al. 2003) and IUCN criteria. Species with a combination of these criteria (serial number 1, 2 and 3) were given marks accordingly. Species with score >55 were identified as critically endangered; 51-54 as endangered; 46-50 as vulnerable; 40-45 as near threatened; and <40 as least concern (Table 1.1).

RESULTS

Diversity and Distribution Patterns

In total, 261 species of medicinal plants belonging to 168 genera and 50 families were recorded. Of these, 5 species were trees, 23 shrubs, 231 herbsand 02 ferns (Figure 1.1). The families Asteraceae (51 spp.), Apiaceae (16 spp.), Fabaceae and Polygonaceae (15 spp. each), Lamiaceae (13 spp.), Ranunculaceae (11 spp.), Gentianaceae, Boraginaceae and Rosaceae (9 spp. each), Brassicaceae and Scophulariaceae (8 spp. each), Caryophyllaceae (7 spp.), Alliaceae, Campanulaceae, Caprifoliaceae, Ericaceae and Orchidaceae (5 spp. each), Geraniaceae and Cupressaceae (4 spp. each), Fumariaceae, Liliaceae, Poaceae, Plantaginaceae, Balsaminaceae, Primulaceae, Solanaceae and Velerianaceae (3 spp. each), were rich in medicinal plants.Among the genera, *Artemisia* (11 spp.), *Polygonum* (7 spp.), *Astragalus* and *Saussurea* (6 spp. each), *Nepeta* (5 spp.), *Allium, Swertia, Pedicularis, Juniperus, Geranium, Selinum* and *Rheum* (4 spp. each), *Anaphalis, Aster, Erigeron, Impatiens, Silene, Rhododendron, Corydalis, Polygonatum, Plantago, Anemone* and *Thalictrum* (3 spp. each) were dominant. A total of 17 families were monotypic. Maximum medicinal plant species (177 spp.) were reported in the altitudinal zone, 3100-3800mfollowed by (84 spp.) altitudinal zone, 3801-5000 and decreased with increasing altitude. All the species were recorded from 15 different habitats.

Utilization Pattern, Indigenous Uses and Phytochemistry

Diverse parts of the medicinal plant species were used in treatments of diseases/ailments of different body parts such as skin, bones, bronchitis, ears, eyes, head, kidney, intestine, liver, lungs, muscles, teeth, throat, etc. Maximum species used for Cold & Cough (31 spp.), followed byStomachache (29 spp.), Skin disease (25 spp.),Headache (23 spp.), Rheumatism (22 spp.), Diarrhoea Blood purifier (21 spp.), (15 spp.) and Asthma (11 spp.) problems. The indigenous uses of the species have been given in (Table 1.2).

Among the parts used of medicinal plants, roots (66 spp.), leaves (73 spp.), whole plants (72 spp.), aerial part (70 spp.), flower (32 spp.), seeds (17 spp.), stems (13 spp.), fruits (16 spp.), bark (9 spp.), bulb (5 spp.), rhizomes (4 spp.), inflorescences (4 spp.), tubers (4 spp.), fronds (2 spp.), gum, ashes of plants, twigs, disc floret and wood (1 spp. each) were used by the inhabitants of the Chandra valley (Figure 1.2). Amongst the medicinal plants,

Table 1.1: Criteria Used for Prioritization of Medicinal Plants for Conservation in Chandra Valley, Himachal Pradesh

Serial No.	Habitat	Distribution	Availability	Use Value	Trade Value	Extraction	Nativity and Endemism	Score
1.	2	<500	Low	> 10	High	Commercial	Native & Endemic	10
2.	3-4	500-1000	Moderate	5-10	Medium	Self use	Native/Endemic	6
3.	5	>1000	High	<5	Low	No use	Non-native	2

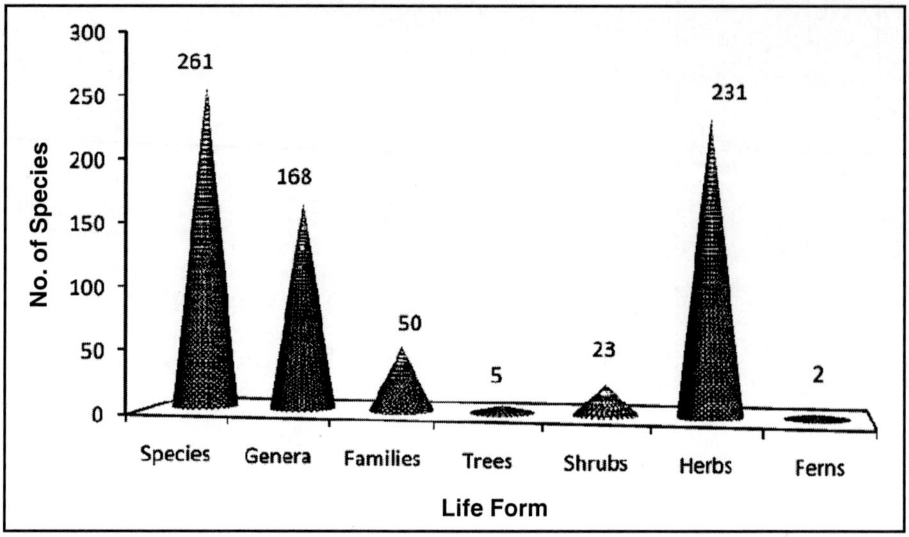

Fig. 1.1: Distribution of Medicinal Plants in Chandra Valley, Himachal Pradesh

Aconitum heterophyllum, A. violaceum, Angelica glauca, Arnebiaeuchroma, Betulautilis, Bergeniastracheyi, Buniumpersicum, Carumcarvi, Dactylorhizahatagirea, Ephedra gerardiana, Hippophaerhamnoides, H. salicifolia, Hypericumperforatum, Hyssopusofficinalis, Hyoscyamusniger, Inularacemosa, Juglansregia, Juniperuspolycarpos, Jurinellamacrocephala, Podophyllumhexandrum, Picrorhizakurrooa, Rheum australe, R. webbianum, Rhododendron anthopogon, Saussureacostus, S. gossypiphora and *Taraxacumofficinale* were most preferred for indigenous use and tradepurposes.Of the total medicinal plant species, phytochemistry of 43 species is known and 218 species require detailed phytochemical investigation.

Nativity and Endemism

Of the total species recorded, 146 species were native to the Himalayan region, while 115 species were non-native, from different domains of the world. Two species were endemic restricted to the IHR (*Angelica glauca* and *Delphinium cashmirianum*) and 17 species were identified as near-endemics. The number of native, endemic and near-endemic species appears to increase along an altitudinal gradient irrespective of the total species richness.

Threat Categorization and Conservation Prioritization

15 species were identified as critically endangered, 12 as endangered, 25 as vulnerable, 17 species as near threatened and 193 as of least concern (Table 1.3). The species identified as critically endangered, endangered and vulnerable have been prioritized for conservation. Among these 70 prioritized medicinal plants 23 species were highly scored and posses high prioritization score, based on their demand and market potential (Fig. 1.3).

Table 1.2: Medicinal Plants Species Used in Various Diseases/Ailments by the Inhabitants of Chandra Valley, Himachal Pradesh

Common Ailments	No. of Species	Medicinal Plant Species
Cold & Cough	31	*Carumcarvi, Pimpinelladiversifolia, Achilleamillefolium, Echinopscornigerus,Erigeron alpines, Saussureagnaphalodes, S. taraxacifolia, Cynoglossumlanceolatum, Cannabis sativa, Rhodiolaheterodonta, Gaultheria trichophylla, Rhododendron lepidotum, R. campanulatum, R. anthopogon, Nepetadiscolor, N. floccosa, Thymus linearis, Dactylorhizahatagirea, Bistortaaffinis, B. amplexicaule, Sorbusaucuparia, Aconitum heterophyllum, Delphinium cashmirianum, Peducularispectinata, Picrorhizakurrooa, Lagotiskunawurensis, Hyoscyamusniger, Viola biflora, Nardostachys grandiflora, Juniperusindica, Ephedra gerardiana*
Stomachache	29	*Angelica glauca, Bupleurumcandollii, Carumcarvi, Cortiadepressa, Pimpinelladiversifolia, Erigeron multiradiatus, Inularacemosa, Saussureacostus, Berberisjaeschkeana, Barbarea intermedia, Rhodiolaheterodonta, R. anthopogon, Parochetuscommunis, Gentianacoronata, G. tenella, Swertiaalternifolia, Geranium nepalense, G. himalayense, G. pratense, Nepetalongibracteata, Eragrostis minor, Rumexnepalensis, Plantago major, Androsacerotundifolia, Rosa webbiana, Aconitum violaceum, Delphinium cashmirianum, Solanumnigrum, Juniperuspolycarpos*
Skin disease	25	*Bupleurumcandollii, Seliniumvaginatum, Artemesiamacrocephala, Crepismulticaulis, Jurinellamacrocephala, Prenanthesbrunoniana, S. costus, S. albescens, S. gosyipiphora, Berberisjaeschkeana, Codonopsisclematidea, Cannabis sativa, R. campanulatum, Hippophaesalicifolia, Astralagusrhizanthus, Corydalis govaniana, Thymus linearis, Podophyllumhaxandrum, Polygonumrecumbens, Galiumasperifolium, Verbascumthapsus, Lagotiscashmeriana, Viola biflora, Valerianahardwickii, Adiantumvenustum*
Diarrhoea	15	*Allium stracheyi, A. victorialis, Lindelofialongiflora, Capsella bursa-pastoris, Origanumvulgare, Bistortaaffinis, Polygonumparonychioides, P. plebium, P. somdevae, Plantagohimalaica, Geumelatum, Aconitum heterophyllum, Picrorhizakurrooa, Verbascumthapsus, Solanumnigrum*

(Table Contd...)

Common Ailments	No. of Species	Medicinal Plant Species
Rheumatism	22	*Carumcarvi, Cortiadepressa, Ferula jaeschkeana, Artemesiamacrocephala, Chrysanthemum pyrethroides, Inularacemosa, S. costus, S. gosyipiphora, Thlaspiarvense, Codonopsisclematidea, R. campanulatum, Corydalis meifolia, C. govaniana, Gentianellamoorcroftiana, Hyssopusofficinalis, Dactylorhizahatagirea, Anemone obtusiloba, Aconotumviolaceum, Pedicularisbicornuta, Solanumnigrum, Myricariagermanica, Ephedra gerardiana*
Headache	22	*Bupleurumcandollii, Inula grandiflora, I. racemosa, Taraxacumofficinale, Tanacetumdolichophyllum, S. costus, S. taraxacifolia, Cerastiumcerastoides, Saginasaginoides, Loniceraspinosa, Cuscutareflexa, R. campanulatum, Corydalis meifolia, Geranium pretense,Polygonumsomdeve, Plantagohimalaica, Primuladenticulata, Anemone rivularis, Aquilegia fragrans, Delphinium cashmirianum, Juniperusindica, Ephedra gerardiana*
Blood purifier	21	*Artemesia maritime, Erigeron bellidioides, Inularacemosa, Taraxacumofficinale, S. costus, Berberisjaeschkeana, Onosma hispida, Capsella bursa-pastoris, Astragalusnivalis, Gentianellamoorcroftiana, Jaeschkeaoligosperma, Nepetafloccosa, Polygonatumcirrhifolium, Dactylorhizahatagirea, Epipactishelleborine, Goodyerarepens, P. recumbens, P. tortuosum, Populusciliata, Nardostachys grandiflora, Ephedra gerardiana*
Asthma	11	*Selinumconiifolium, I. racemosa,S. costus, Sonchuswightianus, Loniceraspinosa, Rheum australe, Picrorhizakurrooa, Verbascumthapsus, Hyoscyamusniger, J. polycarpos, Ephedra gerardiana*

Table 1.3: Status of Threatened Species in Chandra Valley, Himachal Pradesh

Critically Endangered	Endangered	Vulnerable	Near Threatened
Angelica glauca, Jurinellamacrocephala, Corydalis govaniana, Meconopsisaculeata, Aconitum heterophyllum, A. violaceum, Picrorhizakurrooa, Nardostachys grandiflora, Valerianahardwickii, Arnebiaeuchroma, Rheum australe, Saussureaobvallata, S. gosyipiphora, Juniperusrecurva, Arnebiabenthamii	*Inula grandiflora, Allium carolinianum, Cortiadepressa, Selinumtenuifolium, Artemisia sieversiana, Prenanthesbrunoniana, Viburnum cotinifolium, Swertiaalternifolia, S. ciliata, S. petiolata, Nepetaeriostachya, Origanumvulgare, Polygonatumverticillatum, Plantagodepressa, Myricariagermanica, Juniperusindica*	*Valerianajatamansi, Heracleumthomsonii, Allium humile, A. stracheyi, A. victorialis, Buniumpersicum, Carumcarvi, Heracleumcandicans, Selinumconiifolium, Saussoreaalbescens, Inularacemosa, Rhododendron campanulatum, Hippophaesalicifolia, Corydalis meifolia, Swertiacordata, Hyssopusofficinalis, Polygonatumcirrhifolium, Plantagohimalaica, Bergeniastracheyi, Viola biflora, Juniperuscommunis, J. polycarpos, Rhododendron lepidotum, R. anthopogon, Hippophaerhamnoides* sub sp. *turkastanica*	*Allium wallichii, Corydalis vaginans, Ferula jaeschkeana, Berberisjaeschkeana, Jaeschkeaoligosperma, Dactylorhizahatagirea, Podophyllumhaxandrum, Rheum moorcroftiana, R. webbianum, Saussureacostus, Ephedra gerardiana, Betulautilis*

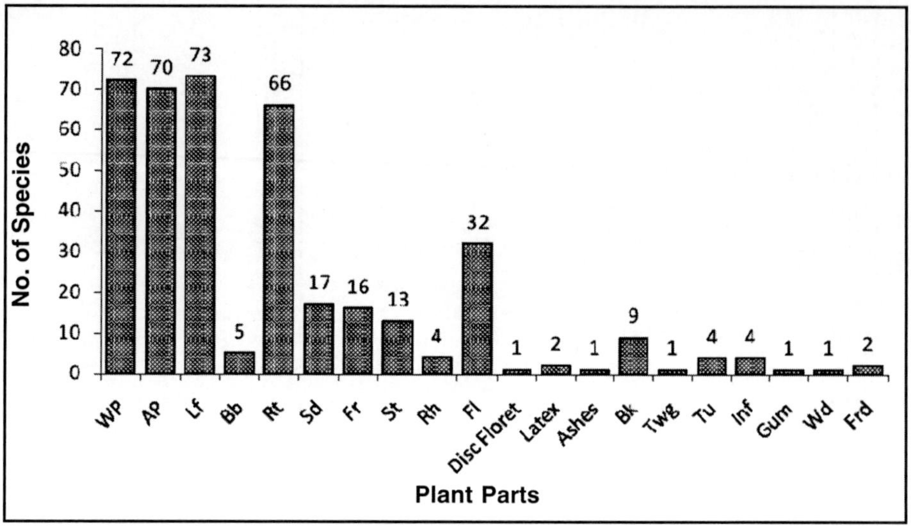

Fig. 1.2 Parts used in Different Ailments/Diseases by the Inhabitants of Chandra Valley, Himachal Pradesh

Abbreviations used: Rt=Root; Lf= Leaf; Fl= Flower; Sd= Seed; St= Stem; Wp= Whole Plant, Wd= Wood; Bb= Bulb; Bk= Bark; Fr= Fruit; Rh= Rhizome; Ap=Aerial part; Inf=Inflorescence; Tu=Tuber; Frd=Frond; Ashes=Ashes oftwig

The medicinal plants prioritized for conservation were critically endangered, endangered and vulnerable categories species – *Aconitum heterophyllum, Aconitum violaceum, Allium wallichii, Angelica glauca, Arnebiaeuchroma, Bergeniastracheyi, Betulautilis, Buniumpersicum, Carumcarvi, Corydalis govaniana, Dactylorhizahatagirea, Ephedra gerardiana, Ferula jaeschkeana, Heracleumthomsonii, Hippophaesalicifolia, Inularacemosa, Jurinellamacrocephala, Picrorhizakurrooa, Podophyllumhexandrum, Rheum australe, Rheum moorcroftiana, Saussureacostus* and *Valerianajatamansi* were recommended for commercial cultivation in the Chandra valley based on their market potential (Table 1.3).

DISCUSSION

The IHR is well known for its diversity of Medicinal plants (Jain 1991; Samant et al. 1998, 2001, 2007, 2009; Singh et al., 2009; Pant et al., 2009; Ranaand Samant, 2011). However, studies on medicinal plants at catchment, watershed and valley specific are not available. Therefore, the present study provides comprehensive baseline catalogue on diversity, distribution pattern, nativity, endemism, rarity, utilization patters, indigenous uses, part/s used and phytochemistry of medicinal plants inChandra valley of Himachal Pradesh, North western Himalaya.

The occurrence of 261 species of medicinal plants in the area indicates that its environmental conditions, particularly, shady moist and forest habitats, are suitable for growth and development of such species. The habitats require regular monitoring to understand the dynamics of the vegetation.

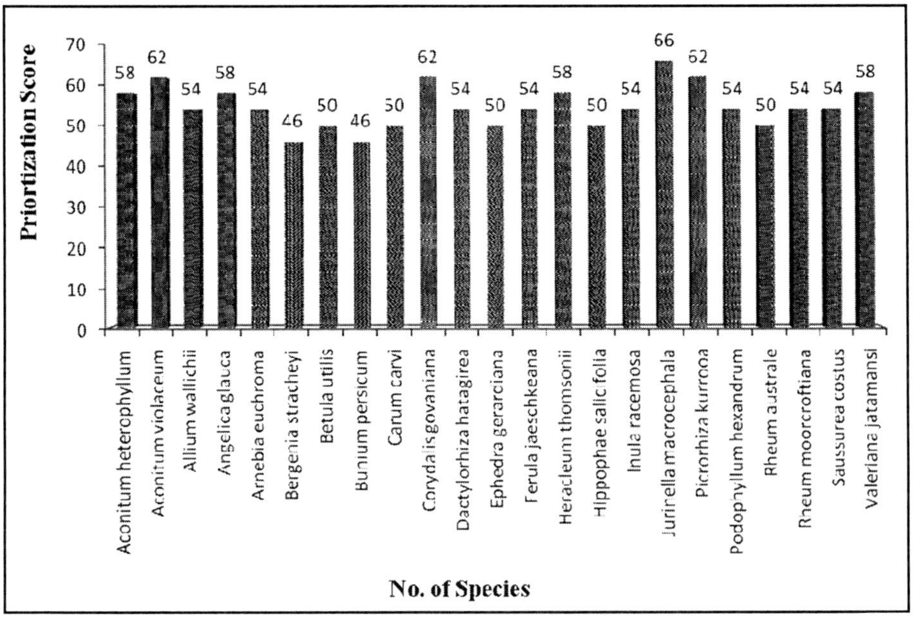

Fig. 1.3: Prioritization Score of Different Prioritized Medicinal Plant Species for the Chandra Valley, Himachal Pradesh

The altitudinal range 3100-3800m has the most vegetation medicinal plants. The occurrence of 55.9% of native species, 6.5% of near endemic species and 0.8% of endemic species shows the high significance of the area. Habitat degradation and over exploitation of these species may lead to their early extinction in the area. The over exploitation of medicinal plants parts such as roots, rhizomes, tubers, inflorescences, fruits, oils, bark, seeds, etc. may lead to poor regeneration and extinction of these species in near future.

Biodiversity loss is one of the world's most pressing crises with many species declining to critically low levels and with significant numbers going extinct. At the same time there is growing awareness of how biodiversity supports human livelihoods. An area specific threat categorization of species is most important for short or long term management planning. The present study represents such an approach in this area, using information on different attributes. Cultivation of such medicinal plants in the surrounding villages and other private lands may condense the extinction pressure on the wild habitats. Identification of active ingredients would help identifying the potential species for marketing. Regular populations and habitats monitoring of native, endemic and threatened medicinal plants using ecological methods and notification of key areas as medicinal plants conservation areas (MPCAs) for *in situ* conservation, with the involvement of the State Forest Department and inhabitants of the area have been suggested. Besides these, mass reproduction using conventional methods, establishment and maintenance of herbal gardens and medicinal plant nurseries for *ex situ* conservation and ensuring the availability of quality planting material for cultivation, together with education and awareness programmes for large scale cultivation area suggested.

REFERENCES

Anonymous. 1883-1970. Index Kewensis Plantarum Phanerogamarum Vol. 1-2 (1883-1885) and 15 Suppl. (1886-1970). Clarendron Press, Oxford.

Anonymous. 1992. Action Plan for Himalaya. G.B. Pant Institute of Himalayan Environment & Development, Kosi-Katarmal, Almora.

Anonymous. 2000. Report of the Task Force on Conservation & Sustainable use of Medicinal Plants. Government of India Planning Commission.

Aswal BS, Mehrotra BN. 1994. Flora of Lahaul-Spiti (A Cold Desert in North-West Himalaya). Bishen Singh Mahendra Pal Singh, Dehradun.

Badola HK. 2001. Medicinal Plant Diversity of Himachal Pradesh. In: Samant SS, Dhar U, Palni LMS (eds.) Himalayan Medicinal Plants: Potential and Prospects. Gyandodaya Prakashan, Nainital (India). pp. 87-116.

Badola HK, Pal M. 2003. Threatened Medicinal Plants and Their Conservation in Himachal Himalaya. Indian For. 129: 55-68.

Bhattacharya UC, Uniyal B.P. 1982. A Botanical Tour to Pangi and Trilokinath in Upper Chenab. J Bombay Nat Hist Soc. 79: 57-78.

Chauhan NS. 1988. Ethnobotanical study of Medicinal Plants of Himachal Pradesh. In: Kaushik P. (ed.) Indigenous Medicinal Plants: Today & Tomorrow Printers & Publishers, New Delhi. pp. 187-198.

Chauhan NS. 1999. Medicinal and Aromatic Plants of Himachal Pradesh. Indus Publishing Company, New Delhi, India.

Collett H. 1902. Flora Simlensis.Thacker Spink. & Co. Calcutta and Simla, Reprinted. Bishen Singh Mahendra Pal Singh, Dehradun.

Dhar U, Samant SS 1993. Endemic Diversity of Indian Himalaya. I. Ranunculaceae and II. Paeoniaceae. J Biogeography 20: 659-668.

Dhar U, Rawal RS, Upreti J. 2000. Setting Priorities for Conservation of Medicinal Plants - A Case Study in the Indian Himalaya. Biol Cons. 95: 57-65.

Dhaliwal DS, Sharma M. 1997. Phytogeographic Comments on the Flora of Kullu District. In: Sharma TA, Saini SS, Trivedi ML, Sharma M. (eds.) Current Researches in Plant Sciences 1: 169-175; Vols. I-II. Bishen Singh Mahendra Pal Singh, Dehradun.

Dhaliwal DS, Sharma M. 1999. Flora of Kullu District (Himachal Pradesh). Bishen Singh Mahendra Pal Singh, Dehra Dun.

Farooquee NA, Saxena KG. 1996. Conservation and Utilization of Medicinal Plants in High Hills of the Central Himalayas. Env Cons. 23 (1): 75-80.

Jain SK. 1991. Dictionary of Indian Folk Medicine and Ethnobotany. Deep Publications, New Delhi.

Kala CP. 2000. Status and Conservation of Rare and Endangered Medicinal Plants in the Indian Trans-Himalaya. Biol Cons. 93(1): 371-379.

Kala CP. 2006. Medicinal Plants of the High Altitude Cold Desert in India: Diversity, Distribution and Traditional Uses. Int J Bio Sci & Man. 2(1): 43-56.

Kapahi BK. 1990. Ethnobotanical Investigations in Lahaul (Himachal Pradesh). J Eco Taxon Bot. 14: 49-55.

Khullar SP.1994. An Illustrated Fern Flora of the West Himalaya Vol. I. International Book Distributors, Dehradun.

Khullar, S.P. 2000. An Illustrated Fern Flora of the West Himalaya Vol. II. International Book Distributors Dehradun.

Myers N, Muttermeier RA, Muttermeier CA, Da Fonseca ABG, Kent J. 2000. Biodiversity Hotspots for Conservation Priorities. Nature. 403: 853-858.

Pandey, CB. 1993. Working Plan for the Lahaul Forest Division. Department of Forest Farming & Conservation, Himachal Pradesh.

Pant S, Samant SS, Arya SC. 2009. Diversity and Indigenous Household Remedies of the Inhabitants Surrounding Mornaula Reserve Forest in West Himalaya. Ind J Trad Know. 8 (4): 606-610.

Polunin O, Stainton A. 1984. Flowers of the Himalaya. Oxford University Press, Delhi.

Polunin O, Stainton A. 1987. Concise Flowers of the Himalaya. Oxford University Press, Delhi.

Rai LK, Prasad P, Sharma E. 2000. Conservation Threats to Some Important Plants of the Sikkim Himalaya. BioCons. 93:27-33.

Rana MS, Samant SS. 2009. Prioritization of Habitats and Communities for Conservation in the Indian Himalayan Region: A State of the Art Approach from Manali Wildlife Sanctuary. Curr Sci. 97(3): 326-335.

Rana MS, Samant SS. 2010. Threat Categorization and Conservation of Floristic Diversity in the Indian Himalayan Region: A state of Art Approach from Manali Wildlife Sanctuary. JN at Cons. 18: 159-169.

Rana MS, Samant SS. 2011. Diversity, Indigenous Uses and Conservation Status of Medicinal Plants in Manali Wildlife Sanctuary, Northwestern Himalaya. Ind J Trad Know. 10 (3): 439-459.

Rodger WA, Panwar WS. 1988. Planning a Wildlife Protected Area Network in India. Vol. 1 & 2. Wildlife Institute of India, Dehradun.

Samant SS, Dhar U. 1997. Diversity, Endemism and Economic Potential of Wild Edible Plants of Indian Himalaya. Int. J Sustain Dev World Ecol. 4: 179-191.

Samant SS, Dhar U, Palni LMS. 1998. Medicinal Plants of Indian Himalaya: Diversity Distribution Potential Values. Nainital: Gyanodaya Prakashan.

Samant SS, Palni LMS. 2000. Diversity, Distribution and Indigenous Uses of Essential Oil Yielding Plants of Indian Himalayan Region. J Med & Arom Plant Sci. 22: 671-687.

Samant SS, Pal M. 2003. Diversity and Conservation Status of Medicinal Plants in Uttaranchal State. Ind Fores.129 (9): 1090-1108.

Samant SS, Pant S. 2003. Diversity, Distribution Pattern and Traditional Knowledge of the Sacred Plants in Indian Himalayan Region. Ind J For. 26 (3): 222-234.

Samant SS, Pant S, Singh M, Lal M, Singh A, Sharma A, Bhandari S. 2007a. Medicinal Plants in Himachal Pradesh, North Western Himalaya, India. Int J Bio Sci & Mangt. 3(4): 234-251.

Samant SS, Butola JS, Sharma A. 2007b. Assessment of Diversity, Distribution, Conservation Status and Preparation of Management Plan for the Medicinal Plants in the Catchment Area of Parbati Hydro-Electric Project Stage III in North Western Himalaya. J Mount Sci.4 (1): 34-56.

Singh DK, Hajra PK. 1996. Floristic Diversity. In: Gujral GS, Sharma V eds. Biodiversity Status in the Himalaya. New Delhi: British Council. pp. 23-38.

Singh SK, Rawat GS. 2000. Flora of Great Himalayan National Park, Himachal Pradesh. Bishen Singh Mahendra Pal Singh, Dehradun.

Singh A, Lal M, Samant SS. 2009. Diversity, Indigenous Uses and Conservation Prioritization of Medicinal Plants in Lahaul Valley, Proposed Cold Desert Biosphere Reserve, India. Int J Bio Sci & Manag. 5(3): 132-154.

Sood SK, Nath R, Kalia DC. 2001. Ethnobotany of Cold Desert Tribes of Lahaul-Spiti (NW Himalaya). Deep Publications, New Delhi.

Uniyal SK, Singh KN, Jamwal P, Lal B. 2006. Traditional Use of Medicinal Plants Among the Tribal Communities of Chota Bhangal, Western Himalaya. J Ethno & Ethnomed. 2: 14.

Ved DK, Kinhal GA, Ravikumar K, Prabhakaran V, Ghate U, Vijaya Shankar R, Indresha JH. 2003. Conservation Assessment and Management Prioritization for the Medicinal Plants of Jammu & Kashmir, Himachal Pradesh & Uttaranchal. Foundation for Revitalisation of Local Health Traditions, Bangalore, India.

MEDICINAL PLANTS: *DISTRIBUTION, UTILIZATION AND SIGNIFICANCE*
Edited by: Dr. Pankaj Sharma; Dr. Pawan Kumar 'Bharti' and Dr. Narayan Singh
ISBN: 978-93-5056-734-0
Edition: 2015
Published by: Discovery Publishing House Pvt. Ltd., New Delhi (India)

2

Status and Conservation of Medicinal Plants in a Central Part of Himachal Pradesh, North West Himalaya

Sakshi Bhandari Rana1[1]*; Man S. Rana[2] and S.S. Samant[3]

ABSTRACT

Medicinal plants are invaluable and indispensable resources of Himalaya. Their proper documentation and conservation status needs an immediate attention. This paper documents the medicinal plants found in rich yet unexplored central part of Himachal Pradesh. Total 298 species (Angiosperms: 284; Gymnosperms: 04; and Pteridophytes: 10) of medicinal plants belonging to 94 families and 205 genera were recorded. Maximum number of medicinal plants was reported in the altitudinal zone 1801-2800m and it showed a decreasing pattern with the increasing altitude.Use pattern is undoubtedly an asset to local inhabitants, but it also largely affects the survival rate of the medicinal plants as mostly roots/rhizomes/bark/whole plant is extracted. Total 17 species should be concentrated to conserve the species in its natural habitat so as to minimize the loss to ecosystem.People's participation in conservation programme should be encouraged to maximum level so as to minimize the loss of this valuable plant diversity.

Key words: Diversity, Medicinal Plants, Conservation, Use Value, Threatened Categories.

INTRODUCTION

The bioresources of any region particularly of biodiversity hotspots like Himalaya are considered a global heritage and invaluable reservoir for sustainable development. The Indian Himalayan Region (IHR) is a rich reservoir of fauna and floristic resources, of which medicinal plants form an essential part. From the IHR, 1748 species of medicinal plants have been recorded (Samant et. al., 1998). Himachal Pradesh situated in the North Western part of IHR contains a multitude of floristic diversity, which is of great medicinal significance. These medicinal plants are the richest resource of our traditional medicines, phytopharmaceuticals, modern allopathic drugs and household remedies (Handa, 1991). The perusal of available literature showed that in general, in Himachal Pradesh, a large number of studies have been conducted on medicinal plants (Jain, 1991; Singh, 1993; Chauhan, 1999; Sood *et. al*., 2001; Badola and Aitken, 2003; Pandey *et al*., 2004; Uniyal *et al*., 2006; Chandrashekhar, 2007; Singh *et al*., 2009; etc.). However, the central part of Himachal Pradesh which is rich in biodiversity is still unexplored or underexplored.

Most of the medicinal principle chemicals available in the industries nowadays are extracted from wild plants (Anonymous 1997); and almost 69% of the material is collected through destructive harvesting, which suggests that medicinal plants are significantly under threat (Dhar *et al*. 2000). With increasing demand and renewed global interest in traditional ethnopharmacy, coupled with the increasing preference for natural substances in the healthcare system, the natural stock of medicinal plants of Himachal Pradesh is under tremendous pressure (Samant *et al*. 1998).Decline in population and availability of medicinal plants in the Himalayan region is caused due to excessive anthropogenic pressures and unscientific extraction (Samant *et al*. 1998). Keeping in view the economic value, future potential and status of the medicinal plants this study has focused on: (a) assessing the diversity and distribution; (b) use value; and (c) assess status of threatened

The study area (31° 27.79′-31°33.98′N Latitudes and 76° 59.46′-77° 03.21′ E Longitudes) comprises the stretch of the district from Chailchowk to Kamrunag via Ruhanda (Fig. 2.1). The area covered is approximately 558 Km². It is a mountainous region with acuteunevenness of terrain from 1300m amsl at Chailchowk to 3050m amsl at Kamrunag peak.

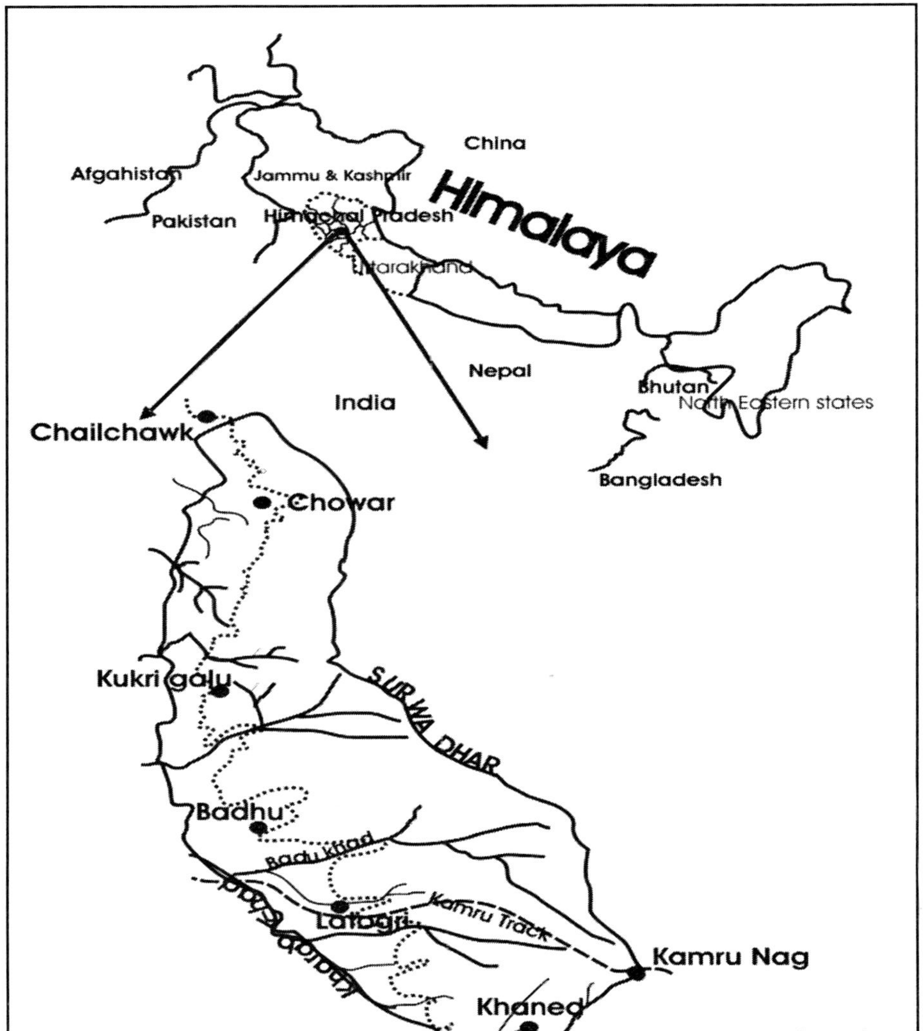

Bilaspur and Hamirpur districts. Population in this arealives in small villages and houses scattered across the hills and valleys. The representativevillages of the study area are Kaflu, Ratheri, Dhagwain, Matogalu, Kutachi, Sanjala, Badhu,Bharmot, Shillnu, Shakoor, Ruhanda and Khanad. The geology of the area comprises of Granite Gneiss, Leucogranite, Phyllite, Quartazenite, Minor Limestone, Pebbly Quartzite, Slate, Grit, Streaky and Banded Gneisses, and Schists. The area has a sub-tropical/mild temperate climate in the Chailchowk region which changes to typical temperate and sub-alpineclimate types as one move to Kamrunag region. Altogether, the climate is temperate with well-marked three seasons viz., summer (mid April–mid June), rainy (monsoon) (mid June-September) and winter (October-March) seasons. The higher reaches of Rohanda andKamrunag hills get precipitation in the form of snow during the winter season. Climatically the area is unique; the temperature ranges between -4°C to 38°C.

METHODOLOGY

Khanad, Ruhanda, Shakoor, Shillnu, Bharmot, Badhu, Sanjala, Kutachai, Matogalu, Dhagwan, Kaflu, and Ratheri, the representative villages located in different altitudes in the study area were selected to generate information on resource utilization pattern of the inhabitants. Local *Vaidhyas* and knowledgeable persons from each village were interviewed, irrespective of their age or gender. The interviews were mostly individual, except in some cases, where several people participated at the same time. Interviews did not follow a previously-defined strict questionnaire; it consisted of open and semistructured questions, which encouraged the interviewees spontaneous participation. The language used with the informants was the local dialect of the study area *viz.* Mandyali and in some cases, Hindi also.

As part of the interviews, among the village experts, one person was hired to survey and collect the samples of the economically important plants from the natural habitats for further identification. Information on botanical binomial, local name of the plant, plant part used to cure the ailment and the ailment for which it is used, altitudinal range, habit, habitat/s, and use values was gathered. Fresh samples of the useful species were collected and identified with the help of local and regional floras (Chowdhery and Wadhawa, 1984; Aswal and Mehrotra, 1994; Dhaliwal and Sharma, 1999; Singh and Rawat, 2000; Khullar, 1994, 2000, *etc.*). Information on mode of utilization of medicinal plants was collected. Regarding the external use of the plant, the most common is as poultice and as ointment, prepared by macerating the useful part to

is another popular method of preparation for oral administration in the present investigated area.

The indigenous uses are based on the surveys, however in the case of medicinal plants information on indigenous uses has also been updated with the help of existing secondary information (Jain, 1991; Samant and Palni, 2000; Samant *et al.*, 2001, 2007). Some of the species of medicinal plants are not used by the inhabitants, but their uses as medicine are known from other parts of the State and IHR. Such species have also been included under medicinal plants. The information was compiled and analysed for the utilization pattern following Samant *et al.* 2007.

Threat categories of the species were identified based on habitat preference, population size, distribution range and use values and following IUCN criteria (Ved *et.al.* 2003).

RESULTS

Diversity and Distribution of Medicinal Plants

Total 298 species (Angiosperms: 284; Gymnosperms: 04; and Pteridophytes: 10) of medicinal plants belonging to 94 families and 205 genera were recorded (Table 2.1). The dominant families were Asteraceae (32 spp.); Lamiaceae (24 spp.); Rosaceae (16 spp.); Ranunculaceae (14 spp.); Fabaceae and Orchidaceae (11 spp. each). Among genera, *Rubus* and *Desmodium* (05spp, each); *Plectranthus, Persicaria* and*Berberis* (04 spp., each); were the dominant.

ALTITUDINAL DISTRIBUTION

Maximum number of medicinal plants (224 species) was reported in the altitudinal zone, 1801-2800m followed by <1800m zone (192 species) and >2800m zone (74 species) (Fig. 2.2). Some important species of the altitudinal zone, <1800m were *Cinnamomumtamala, Myricaesculenta, Rhododendron arboreum,Centellaasiatica, Acoruscalamus,Vitexnegundo, Berberislycium, Royleacinerea, Zanthoxylumarmatum, etc.* and altitudinal zone, 1801-2800m *Dioscoreadeltoidea, Thymus linearis, Berberisaristata, Hedychiumspicatum, Polygonatumverticillatum, Bergenialigulata, Origanumvulgare, Skimmialaureola, Viola canescens, etc*. and of >2800m were *Morinalongifolia, Podophyllumhexandrum, Taxusbaccata* sub sp. *wallichiana, Selinumvaginatum, Dactylorhizahatagirea,* etc.

USE AND COMMERCIAL VALUE

Indigenous practices of the plant resources for medicine and various other purposes are very popular in the present investigated area (Fig. 2.3).

and flower petals of *Rhododendron arboreum* in headache, fever, wounds and nose bleeding. Among the medicinal plants, *Cinnamomumtamala*, *Dactylorrhizahatagirea*, *Thymus linearis*, *Hedychiumspicatum*, *Viola canescens*, *Zanthoxylumarmatum*, *Selinumtenuifolium*, *Ajugabracteosa*, *Valerianajatamansi*, and *Taxusbaccata* subsp. *wallichiana* were highly preferred.

Among the preferred medicinal plants, whole plant of *Valerianajatamansi*, bark of *Cinnamomumtamala*, leaves of *Taxusbaccata* subsp. *wallichiana*, rhizome of *Hedychiumspicatum*, root of *Berberislycium* and fruits of *Myricaesculenta* were traded by the inhabitants in large scale to earn their livelihood (Table 2.1).

THREATENED MEDICINAL PLANTS

Among the total medicinal plants, 03 species have been categorized as Critically Endangered; Endangered (08 spp.); and Vulnerable (06 spp.); forHimachal Pradesh and total 04 species; Endangered (03 spp.) and Vulnerable (01 spp.) wereunder global threat categories by IUCN, whereas 02 species *i.e.*, *Berberisaristata* (Rare) and *Dioscoreadeltoidea* (Vulnerable) have been recorded in the Red Data Book of Indian Plants (NayarandSastry 1987, 1988, 1990).

DISCUSSION

Medicinal plants form an integral part of everyday life of almost every individual in the mountainous region. In fact it is being said in Indian Ayurveda that everything green is medicine. Ever increasing human and livestock populations are exerting pressure on forest resources and livelihoods as a result of resource shortages (Chetrriand Sharma, 2006). In fact, the spread of weeds has also taken away much of the fodder resources as such obnoxious weeds cannot be grazed (Srivastava, 2002). This condition is particularly predominant in the lower altitudes of the study area causing habitat degradation. Due to habitat degradation and over exploitation, population of the medicinal plant species is decreasing at an alarming rate (Kala 2000; Samant *et al.*, 2000, 2006). The present study provides comprehensive information on diversity, distribution and utilization patterns, indigenous uses, species preference of the medicinal plants in the study area. Such type of baseline information on the useful species is very much required to know the population status of the species in wild, and identify their economic and conservation aspects.

Occurrence of 298 medicinally important species (Angiosperms: 284; Gymnosperms: 04; and Pteridophytes: 10) belonging to 94 families and 205

ersity Distribution and Uses of Medicinal Plants in the Study Area

	Local Name	AR(m)	HF	Part (s) Used	Uses
	2	3	4	5	6
*a*Medik.	Basunti	1300-1500	Sh	Rt, Fl, Fr, Lf, Wd	Antipyretic, anthelmintic, antiseptic, antispasmodic, asthma, bronchitis, cold, congestion, cough, dislocation of joints, eczema, malaria, pulmonary problems, rheumatism, swelling
.	–	1300-2000	H	WP	Anaemia, body pain, headache, swelling in legs, toothache
*a*L.	Putkanda	1300-2500	H	WP	Asthma, boils, bronchitis, cold, cough, dysentery, germicide, headache, laxative leucoderma, piles, pneumonia, rheumatism, scabies, skin diseases, sore, stomachache, tonic, toothache, whooping cough, wounds, veterinary diseases
	Putkanda	1300-2000	H	WP	Blisters in mouth, cholera, scorpion sting, swelling, whooping cough
Moq.	–	1600-2000	H	Lf, Sd	Emetic, abortifacient
h) Moq.	–	1300-2200	H	Rt, Lf	Skin diseases
na Sw.	Kakare	1300-2200	T	Fr	expectorant, cough, asthma, fever, appetite, irritability c the stomach
	Titri	1300-2200	T	Fr, Wd	Gastric problem, skin diseases

(Table Contd..

	2	3	4	5	6
e					
*umfalcatum*L.		1600-3050	H	Rt	Abdominal inflammation, fever, liver complain
asiatica(L.) Urb.	Brahmi	1300-1600	H	WP	Antihelmintic, brain tonic, cholera, cough, diarr diuretic, dysentery, eczema, eye complaints, fe gastric problems, headache, leprosy, liver comp nervine diseases, respiratory diseases, skin dise stomachache, syphilis, tumor, boils, urine com wounds.
*umcandicans*L.	Badiyacha	1800-2800	H	Lf, Rt	Leucoderma, menstrual complaints
*tylejavanica*Thunb.	–	1300-2000	H	Lf	Dysentery, indigestion, fever
laacuminata Cl.	–	2000-3050	H	WP	Dysentery
*ifolia*DC.	–	1500-2500	H	Rt	Cold, cough, digestive disorder
*enuifolium*Wall.	Bhutkeshi	2800-3050	H	WP	Incense, insecticidal, nervine tonic, sedative
*alamus*L.	Barin/Bauch	1300-2200	H	Rh, St, Lf	Abdominal pain, asthma, bodyache, bronchitis, cough, cuts, dysentery, epilepsy, fever, headacl hysteria, inflammation, malaria, pain in neck, sl diseases, snake bite, stomachache, teething in cl tonic, veterinary medicine
*ajacqmontii*Bl.	–	2200-3050	H	Bb	Ringworm and other skin diseases
sum(Wall.) Schott	Biskaphar	1300-2200	H	WP	Veterinary diseases
eae					
*ichemirica*Dcne.	–	2500-3050	H	Rt	Dysentery, gastric complaints, vomiting
*epalensis*Koch.	Mathodi, Grumru	1300-2500	Sh	Fr, Lf	Cold cough, stimulant, diaphoretic, cathartic, rheumatism

(Table

	2	3	4	5	6
*ta*Br.	–	1800-2500	Sh	WP	Purgative, eczema, colic, ulcers
anii	–	1300-1800	Sh	WP	Rickets
Vt.	–	1800-2500	Sh	WP	Cold, eye complaints, gonorrohea
*s*Buch.	Sansarpali	2000-2800	H	Tu, AP	Urinary problems
l.	Sansarpali	1300-1700	H	Tu	Anthelmintic, aphrodisiac, rheumatism, bleeding from nose, cough, dysentery, febrifuge, gastric complaints, gonohorrea, headache, menustral complaints, snake bite stomachache, tonic, urine complaints
*n*L.	Fye	1800-3050	H	WP	Cold, diaphtheria, epilepsy, fever, gastric complaints, hysteria, piles, stimulant, tonic, toothache,ulcer
*des*L.		1300-2000	H	Lf, Rt, Sd, Fr, Fl	Antilithic for kidney stone, antiseptic, boils, burns, cancer, cuts, diarrohea, headache, leprosy, muscular pain, piles, ringworn, scabies, snake bite, sores, swellings, tumor, uterine disorders, hair problems, wounds
C.	Durwa	2000-3050	H	Rt	Stomachache
n)	–	2000-3050	H	Rt	Colic
*a*Hk.f.	–	1800-2700	H	Fl	Antibacterial, checks bleeding
ns.) Cl.	–	1500-3050	H	WP, Lf	Diuretic

(Table Contd

	2	3	4	5	6
*appa*L.	–	2000-3050	H	Rt	Gastric, burns
a nilagirica(Cl.)	Kubsh	1300-2700	H	Lf, Rt, Sd	Abscess, analgesic, anthelmintic, antiseptic, as complaints, epilepsy, febrifuge, headache, nerv disorders, skin diseases, sores, stomachache, tc wounds, insect repellant
*flora*Roxb. n	–	1300-2200	H	Lf, Rt, Sd	Carminative, wormifuge, throat problems
*rghiana*Bess.	Drubaha	2000-3050	H	Lf	Pimple, Sores
*ternata*Merr.	–	1300-1600	H	Fr, Lf, Fl, Rt	Apetizer, cough, cuts, inflammation, snake bite toothache, ulcers
L.	–	1500-2200	H	WP	Cough, cuts, ear and eye complaints, headache, inflammation, leprosy, skin diseases, snake bit wounds
aciniata(Roxb.) DC.	–	1300-2000	H	WP	Blood purifier
la minima (L.). Asch		1300-1700	H	Lf	Opthalmia, toothache
wallichii DC.	–	1800-2500	H	WP	headache, pneumonia
*tricta*Willd.	–	1300-2200	H	WP	Bone fracture, swelling
*linepurpurea*Kuntz	–	1300-1800	H	WP	Headache, intermittent fever, stomachache
*ı bonariensis*L.	–	1300-1700	H	Lf	Rheumatism, mouth, throat and skin diseases
radiatus (DC.) Cl.	–	1300-2200	H	WP	Tonic, renal and stomach pain
ium adenophorum	–	1300-2200	Sh	Lf	Cuts, injuries, wounds, stomachache
*gaparviflora*Cav.	–	1500-2500	H	Lf	Snake bite, Bleeding
gossypina(Royle)	–	1300-2500	H	Rt	Blood pressure, gastric disorders

(Table

	2	3	4	5	6
*ucum*DC.	Goiphul, Brunn	1300-2200	H	WP	Cuts, wounds
	Gorbagare	1300-2500	H	Lf	Skin diseases, postnatal care
	Gadush	1600-2500	H	Lf	Headache, urinary complaints
alla azz.	–	2200-2800	H	Sd, Lf	Carminative, wounds, colic
*moides*DC.	–	2500-3050	H	WP	Inflammation of mouth, sore throat
	–	2000-3050	H	AP	Insect bites, ringworm diseases, earache
*ea*L.	–	1800-2800	H	WP	Anthelmintic, antifungal, anti-inflammatory, carminative diuretic, febrifuge
	–	1300-2200	H	Lf	Cuts, injuries
	–	1300-1800	H	Lf, La	Febrifuge, jaundice, galactogogue, liver complaints, tonic
*lis*Webb.	–	1300-2800	H	WP	Blisters, blood purifier, bowel complaints, diuretic, dysentery, gastric, ulcer, headache, kidney diseases, live complaints, tonic, wounds
*fera*Royle	–	2200-3050	H	Sd, Fl	Cooling, tonic
	–	1600-2700	H	Sd, AP	Cough, cold, rheumatism
	–	1300-2600	H	Sd, WP	Mucilaginous substance of the stem in abortion
	–	1500-2000	H	Lf	Bristles on tongue, ulcer in mouth
C.	Kasmal	1800-2800	Sh	WP	Antidote to snake bite, malaria, piles
x DC.	Kasmal	1300-1700	Sh	WP	Antidote to snake bite, eye complaints, malaria, piles
neid.	Kasmal	2700-3050	Sh	Rt, Fr	Astringent, blood purifier, diuretic, eye diseases, jaundice, skin diseases

(Table Contd.

	2	3	4	5	6
*n*Royle	Kasmal	1300-2200	Sh	Rt, Fr	Jaundice, eye diseases
eae					
*palensis*D.Don	Kosh	1300-2200	T	Rt, Lf, Bk	Cuts, wounds, diarrohoea, dysentery, stomacha
(Spach) Endl.	Kosh, Kunish	1600-2500	T	Lf, St	Cuts, wounds, stomachache
eae					
*ceiba*L.	Semal	1300-1600	T	Rt, Bk	Abdominal pain, acne, aphrodisiac, diarrohea, c dysentery
aceae					
ssumglochidiatum Benth.	–	1300-3050	H	Rt	Dyspepsia, digestive disorders
nicum(Hornem.) xLehm.	–	1300-2200	H	Lf, Rt	Asthma, cough, vomiting
iceae					
bursa-pastoris lik	–	1300-3050	H	WP	Blood pressure, dropsy
*rvense*L.	–	1300-2500	H	WP	Wounds, cuts, Pulmonary infection, swelling
ulaceae					
*psisovata*Benth.	–	2800-3050	H	Lf	Swollen joints
aceae					
s sativa L.	Bijya	1300-2000	H	Lf, Bk, Sd, Fr, Fl, St	Anthelmentic, appetizer, bowel complaints, col convulsions, cramps, epilepsy, cuts, dyspepsia, complaints, eye diseases, gonohorrea, laxative, nervine stimulant, piles, skin diseases, sleep pi
liaceae					
*n cotinifolium*Don	Dab	1600-2500	Sh	Lf, Fr, Bk	Menorrhoea
*sum*D.Don	Tilenal	2200-3050	Sh	Bk,Wd, St	Menorrhoea

(Table

	2	3	4	5	6
:dgew.	–	1300-2100	H	WP	Asthma, burns, cold, dysentery, headache, hay fever, insect bites, laxative, sores, pneumonia, skin diseases, snake bite, stomachache, vomiting, wounds
:odes	–	1700-2700	H	WP	Backache, bodyache, headache, renal pain, cough
) Vill.	Bariyala	1300-2000	H	WP	Bone fracture
sWall.	Chopru	1700-2200	T	Rt, Bk, Lf	Dysentery, eye diseases, headache
um L.	–	1300-2500	H	Lf, Sd	To revive taste, skin diseases, urine complaints
*sa*Bl.	–	1300-2000	H	WP	On insect stings
..)D.Don	–	1500-2000	H	Rt	Veterinary diseases
s Wall.	Fanai	1300-2000	Sh	St, Lf, Fr	Emetic
*:spidata*Lour.	–	1300-2300	H	Lf, Rt, Sd, Fr	Burns, diarrohoea, dysentery, fever, pneumonia, rheumatism, snake bite, vomiting
:b.	–	1300-2200	H	WP	Bodyache, burns, cuts, swelling of legs, veterinary diseases
*a*L.	Tardi	1300-2000	H	Tu	Abdominal pain, boils, bone fracture, dysentery, piles, jaundice
ex Kunth	–	1600-2800	H	Tu	Dysentery, piles

(Table Contd..

	2	3	4	5	6
ceae					
ongifolia Wall. ex DC.	–	2900-3050	H	Rt	Boils
ceae					
cuminata R.Br.	Bakli/ Banchaula	1300-2000	T	Bk, Fr, Wd	Sores on tongue
aceae					
isconferta Roxb.	Geai	1300-1800	Sh	Fl, Fr	Sores, ulcer
ae					
valifolia (Wall.) Drude	Airean, Ehran	1300-2000	T	WP	Boils, pimples, skin diseases, wormifuge, wounds
ndron arboreum Sm.	Brash	1400-2200	T	Fl, Lf	Dysentery, fever, headache, rheumatism, woun bleeding
biaceae					
iapilosa L.	–	2000-3050	H	WP	Fistular sores
philippensis Mull.	Kambal	1300-1500	T	Sd, Fr	Blisters, Boils, Skin diseases, Snake bite
ommunis L.	Arand	1300-1600	Sh	Sd, Rt, Lf, Fr	Antidote, burns, constipation, contraceptive, d gum troubles, headache, heat stroke, injury, inte worms, joint pain, laxative, muscular pain, purg sciatica, skin diseases, sores
nsigne Trin.	Dudhla	1300-1900	T	La	Germicidal
e					
ia albida Heyne	–	1300-1800	H	Rt	Purgative
umelegans DC.	Chagla, Kathi	1300-2500	Sh	AP, Rt, Wd	Epilepsy, carminative
eticum (L.) DC.	Chagla	1300-2200	Sh	WP	Antidote to snake venom, cough, dysentery, ey fever, tonic, vomiting

(Table

	2	3	4	5	6
hunb.) DC.	–	1300-2000	H	Rt	Abortifacient
ll.	–	1300-1600	H	Rt, Lf, Fr	Rheumatism, wounds
	–	1600-2500	H	WP	Abdominal pain, cold, cough, fever, snake bite
*a*Roxb.	–	1300-1700	Sh	Rt, Lf	Ulcer, neck swelling
	–	1300-2000	H	Rt, Lf	Epilepsy
*ha*Wall.	Kali Kathi	1600-2800	Sh	Lf, Wd	Veterinary diseases, urinary probleml
*nis*Buch.	–	1800-2800	H	Fl	Stomach disorders, earache
A.Rich.	–	2000-2800	H	Rt, Sd	Cholera, ulcers
sley	–	1300-1800	H	WP	Diarrhoea, fever, liver complaints
ne.	–	1800-2500	H	WP	Headache, intermittent fever
	–	2800-3050	H	WP	Headache, fever
*a*Buch.	–	1600-2400	H	WP	Malarial fever
Wall.ex Cl.	Charaite	2000-3050	H	WP	Anthelmintic, antiperiodic, appetitzer, laxative
	Charaite	2000-2600	H	WP	Fever
se Sw.	Jibrughass	1500-2500	H	Rt	Cuts, jaundice, toothache, ulcer, wounds, stomach complaints
*um*Thunb.	–	1600-2600	H	WP	Skin diseases
hoisy	Kharau	1300-2200	Sh	Lf, Fl	Wounds, boils

(Table Contd.

	2	3	4	5	6
*ratum*L.	–	1900-2400	H	Rt	Wounds, boils
*m*Buch.-Ham.	BaniWakra	1800-2500	Sh	Sd, Lf	Food poisoning, abortifacient
laceae					
*goorchioides*Gaertn.	–	1300-2000	H	Rh	Aphrodisiac, alterative, appetizer, useful in pile and colic disorders
*aurea*Lour.	–	1600-2000	H	WP	Injuries, swelling
eae					
*acteosa*Wall. exBenth.	Neel kanth	1300-2600	H	Lf	Ascariasis
*diumumbrosum*Koch.	–	1300-2700	H	WP	Astringent, carminative, heart tonic
*okiaoppositifolia*Sm.	Banse	1300-1700	Sh	Lf	Cough, sores, wounds
iaflava(Benth.) Benth.	Jaunkra	1600-2000	H	Lf	Ointment
osa(Don) Rehd.	Bothi,	1600-2200	H	Lf, Fr, Sd	Relieve sciatica
lifera Benth.	–	1600-2700	H	Lf, Inf	Internal burns
longifolia (L.) Huds.	Podina	1300-3050	H	Lf, WP	Antiseptic, carminative, stimulant, wounds
ata L.	–	1300-1800	H	Lf	Indigestion, malarial fever
eria biflora Buch.-Ham.	–	1300-2100	H	Lf	Cold, gastroenteritis
oyleana Stew.	–	2000-2800	H	WP	Cerebral tonic, Mental Disorders
m vulgare L.	Bantulsi	1600-3000	H	WP	fever, hysteria, influenza, menstrual complaint stimulant, tonic
bracteosa Royle	–	2000-3050	H	Fl	Eye diseases
1.					
thus coesta Buch. x D.Don	Chichri	2000-2500	H	Lf	Gastric complaints
Spr.	–	1300-1500	H	Sd	Rheumatism, tonic
us Wall.	–	1500-2600	Sh	Lf	Fever

(Table

	2	3	4	5	6
	–	2000-2600	H	Lf	Cuts,wounds
ıalense	–	1800-2300	Sh	Lf	Cuts, fever
L.	Patindu	2000-2800	H	WP	Breathing problems, lung complaints, cerebral complaint cold, fever, gastric complaints, headache, liver complaint
ll.	Karnai titpoti	1300-1700	Sh	Lf, Rt	Blood purifier, fever, pimples, tonsils
).	Guadra	1300-2200	H	Rt, Lf, Fl	Astringent, colic, cold, cough
Vall. ex Benth.	–	2000-3050	H	Rt	Astringent, emetic
	–	1400-2200	H	Lf, Rt	Wounds, cold, cough
ns Buch.	–	1300-2100	H	Lf, Fl	Dysentery, vomiting
enth.	Ban jira	2000-3050	H	WP	Anthelmintic, eye disorders, postnatal problems, liver complaints, skin diseases, stomach ache
ala	–	1300-1600	T	Bk, Lf	Heart & throat complaints
(D.Don) Hara	Pangain, Paror	1800-2800	T	Fr, Lf	Scabies, eczema
ifolium	Salam-Mishri	2500-3050	H	Tu	Aphrodisiac, blood purifier, cuts, wounds
.) Al.	Salam-Mishri	2000-3050	H	Tu	Aphrodisiac, appetite, nervine tonic, tonic
a Dumort.	Piyan	1300-1800	H	AP	Mouth sores
	Rhini	1300-2000	Sh	WP	Abortifacient, antifertility, bodyache, spleen complaints

(Table Contd.

	2	3	4	5	6
eae					
dia fruticosa (L.) Kurz.	Dhwe	1400-1700	Sh	St, Fl, Rt	Bone fracture, burns, cholera, cough, dropsy, dy fever, haemorrhage, injuries, mennorhoea, musc nausea, night blindness, fever, rheumatism, skin small pox, sores, spleen complaints, sprain, ulce veterinary sore
ae					
*rticillata*L.	–	1300-2000	H	WP	Cough, emollient pectoral complaints, piles, ulc complaints
data (Burm.f.) Borss.	–	2000-2300	H	WP	Abortifacient, cooling, cuts, pain in back, snake
bata L.	–	1300-1600	Sh	Rt, St	Diarrhoea, dysentery, rheumatism, body pain
ceae					
lebbek Benth.	Siris	1300-1500	T	Fl, Sd, Bk, Rt, Lf	Diarrhoea, dysentery, gonorrhea, eye sores, nigh blindness, piles
maceae					
stellata Buch Don	Kubsh	1400-2000	Sh	Rt, Lf	Cough, digestion, dysentery, nose bleeding, snake bite, wounds, stomachache, toot
ae					
edarach L.	Darek	1300-1700	T	Lf, Fr, Sd	Skin diseases, rheumatism, antiseptic, wormicid abortifacient
liata Roem.	Tooni, Tun	1300-1600	T	Bk, Fr, Lf	Antiseptic, dysentery, bronchitis, fever, gastric
a (Royle) Roem.	Darlein	1400-2200	T	St	Antiseptic, gastric troubles
rmaceae					
elos pariera L.	–	1300-2000	H	WP	tonic, diuretic & antilithic, astringent, dropsy, u diseases
a glabra (Roxb.) Miers.	–	1300-1600	H	Tu	Asthma, dysentery, fever

(Table

	2	3	4	5	6
sk.	Fegra	1300-1800	T	Fr, Lf	Digestive disorders
		1300-2000	T	Fr, La	Dysentery, indigestion, laxative
	Pipal	1300-1500	T	Lf, Fr, Bk	Abortifacient, asthma, blisters, boils, ulcer, cholera, dysentery, fever, haematuria, laxative, rheumatism, scabie skin diseases, small pox, snake bite, sores in mouth, tonic toothache, urinary complaints, whooping cough
Buch.-	Kaphal	1400-2400	T	Bk, Fr, Wd	Asthma, cholera, cough, fever, indigestion, malaria, rheumatism
L.	Kanaru	1600-2500	Sh	AP	Colic pain, vermifuge
num Wall.	Banmalti	1500-2000	Sh	Lf	Cuts, wounds
	Banmalti	1600-3050	Sh	Fl, Lf, Rt	Skin diseases, blood diseases, heart problems
	Banmalti	1800-2900	Sh	Fl, Lf, Rt	Ringworm
folium L.	–	1800-3050	H	WP	Abdominal pain, hepatic, intestinal and renal complaints
*ta*Lindl.	–	1500-2500	H	Lf	Sores, eczema
girea	–	2900-3050	H	Tu	Astringent, bone fracture, expectorant, tonic, wound
ne (L.)	–	1600-2200	H	Lf, Rh	Fever, aphrodisiac
(L.) R.Br.	–	2400-2800	H	AP	Syphilis, blood purifier
orthii Hk.f.	–	2000-2800	H	Tu	Blood purifier, tonic

(Table Contd.

	2	3	4	5	6
nedia Don	Sirab	1600-2000	H	Tu	Tonic
nata Hk.f. ex Collett	–	1300-1500	H	Tu	Flatulence
um lanceum x Swartz.	–	1800-3050	H	Bb	Urinary diseases
acuminata Don	–	1600-2200	H	Lf, Rt	Tonic
fera (Lindl.) Kuntze	–	2800-3050	H	Bb	Tonic
nepalense D.Don	–	1600-2500	H	Tu	Malaria, dysentery and tonic
ceae					
rniculata L.	Malori	1300-2200	H	WP	Appetizer, cooling, cough, cuts, dysentery, epile complaints, fever, jaundice
ia Hk.f.	–	1500-2500	H	WP	Cuts, dysentery, fever, insect bite, scurvy, skin di stomachache, wart
aceae					
e mexicana L.	–	1300-1500	H	Sd, Rt	Emetic, wormicide, leucorrhoea
iaceae					
a nubicola Royle	–	2700-3050	H	Tu	Food poisoning, snake bite
caceae					
ca acinosa Roxb.	Zharka	2000-2500	H	Lf	Body pain
naceae					
himalaica Pilg.	Isabgol	2900-3050	H	Sd	Dysentery, chronic fever, rheumatism, cough, col
lata L.	Isabgol	2000-2800	H	Lf	Blood purifier
utica L.	Mushkneti	1400-2500	H	WP	Mouth sores
lla nepalensis Trin.	Garein	1300-2000	H	WP	Ointment

(Table

	2	3	4	5	6
ini	Dantu ghass	1300-1600	H	Lf	Rheumatism, skin diseases
(D) Pers.	Doob	1300-2500	H	WP	Cramps, dropsy, dysentery, hysteria, headache, menstrual complaints, piles, sores, tonic, urinary complaints, wound
ertn.	–	1300-1800	H	WP	Fever
ortus L.	Kumbri	1300-1700	H	WP	Asthma, dysentery, fever, muscular pain, piles, rabies, snake bite, toothache
a Raeusch.	–	1300-1900	H	AP, Rt	Antidote, fever, intestinal parasites, liver complaints, piles tonic
neum L.	Surah	1300-2000	H	Lf	Asthma, cholera
ndrum Royle	Ban Kakri	2900-3050	H	Fr, Rt, Sd	Cancer, cough, cuts, wounds, fever, gastric ulcers, hepatic diseases, purgative, skin diseases
ulis(D. Don)	–	1500-2600	H	Lf, Rt	Cough, dysentery, tonic
ys (Don) Hara	–	1600-2800	H	Lf	Insect bite
Moench	–	1300-2000	H	Rt, Fr, Lf	Lung disorders, rheumatism, typhoid, urine complaints
a (Buch. Gross	–	1300-2000	H	WP	Antidote in snake bite, insect sting, boils
n.	Nalora	1600-2000	H	Lf	Swelling
	–	1300-2200	H	WP	Cough, gastric problems
e ex Bab.	–	1800-2500	H	WP	Blood purifier, boils, skin diseases
Spr.	Malora	1800-3050	H	Lf, Rt	Boils, colic, cooling, diuretic, purgative, scurvy, swelling o muscles

(Table Contd.

	2	3	4	5	6
ıceae					
hia lobelioides Wall.	–	1600-2200	H	Lf	Snake bite
*denticulata*Sm.	Kauri	1800-3050	H	Fl, Lf	Diabetes, urinary ailments
eae					
ranatum L.	Daru	1300-1800	T	Fr	Stomach disorders, vomiting
ulaceae					
picata Wall. exRoyle	–	2200-2600	H	Rt	Asthma, eye complaints, rheumatism
e obtusiloba D.Don	–	2500-3050	H	Rt, Sd	Convulsions, menorrohoea, rheumatism, purgative
ris Buch.-Ham. ex DC.	Carbini	2200-3050	H	WP	Ear complaints, bone fracture
a Buch.-Ham. ex DC.	–	1800-2800	H	Rt, Lf	Ring worm, eczema
a pubiflora Wall. ex Royle	–	2500-3050	H	AP	Febrifuge
barbellata Edgew.	–	2800-3050	Sh	Lf, Rt	Skin diseases, sores, tumors
naniana DC.	–	1400-2000	Sh	Lf, Rt	Skin diseases, sores, tumors
na Buch.-Ham. ex DC.	–	1800-2600	Sh	Rt	Cold, cough
um denudatum Hk. f. & Th.	–	2700-3050	H	Rt	Antihelminthic, toothache, ulcer
um Wall. ex Royle	Kelulu	2800-3050	H	WP	Antidote, cuts, wounds, diarrhoea, fever
lus diffusus L.	–	1600-2800	H	WP	Boils
us Royle ex D.Don	–	2500-3050	H	AP	Anthelmentic, vermifuge
m foliolosum DC.	Mamiri	1500-2600	H	Rt	Abdominal pain, blood purifier, eye diseases, luec rheumatism
lum Edgew.	Katmeena	2600-3050	H	Rt	Diuretic, eye diseases, tonic
ıceae					
s purpureus Edgew.	–	1400-2000	Sh	Fr,Wd, Lf	Purgative
ter Wall.	–	1300-2200	Sh	Bk	Dysentery, diarrhoea
us Roxb.	Chathau	1400-2200	Sh	Fr, Lf, Wd	Emetic, purgative, infection of spleen

(Table

1	2	3	4	5	6
Ledeb.	Kanaula	1600-2800	H	AP, Rt	Cough, urinary problem
Focke	–	1600-2500	H	Lf,Fl, Fr, Rt	Cuts, eye diseases, swelling, ulcer on tongue, veterinary diseases
. ex G. Don	–	2800-3050	H	Rt	Astringent, dysentery
guinea Lodd.	–	2800-3050	H	Lf	Wounds, analgesic
Hk.f.	Dora	1800-3000	H	Rt	Astringent, tooth complaints, tonic
yle	Bekhal	1600-2600	Sh	Sd, Fr	Burns, cuts, rheumatism, wounds
Lindl.	–	2200-3050	Sh	Fl	Stomachache
	Kuja/Shami	1300-1800	Sh	Lf, Fr, Wd	Diarrhoea, ophthalmia, wounds
	–	2000-3050	Sh	Rt, Fr, Fl	Uterine diseases
ch.-Ham. ex Sm.	Akhaey	1500-2500	Sh	Fr, Rt	Diarrhoca
	Akha	1500-1800	Sh	Fr, Rt	Dysentery, malaria, stomachache, worms
n	Akha	2700-3050	Sh	Fr, Rt	Dysentery
	–	1800-2600	Sh	Fr	Stomachache
.	Kalanche, Kala akha	1500-2600	Sh	Lf, Fr	Diarrhoea, stomach disorder
Hor. ex Kuntz	–	2800-3050	H	Fr, Rt	Menorrhoea, antidote
.	–	2700-3050	Sh	Sd	Sores, wounds
ium L.	–	2200-3050	H	AP	Bronchitis, tonsils
olata Wall.	Bilan	1300-3050	Sh	Bk, Lf	Boils, Blisters in mouth
.		1300-2400	H	Rt, St	Tonic, astringent, antidote, dysentery

(Table Contd.

	2	3	4	5	6
ie					
ghausenia albiflora ichb.	Pissumar	2000-2900	H	Rt	Antiseptic, wounds
laureola (DC.) Zucc.	Ner	2500-3050	Sh	Lf	Tooth care, mouth wash
ylum armatum DC.	Tirmara, Trimbar	1300-1800	Sh	Fr, Sd	Cough, cholera, fever, eczema, itching, leucoderma, piles, rheumatism, tonic, tooth comp
aceae					
nia cordata Thunb.	–	1500-2000	H	Lf, Rt	Blood purifier, boils, sores, cholera, dysentery, s diseases, stomach complaints
gaceae					
ivularis Buch.-Ham. ex Don	–	1800-2800	H	Lf	Blood purifier, toothache
ligulata (Wall.) Engl.	Pashan-bhed	1500-2000	H	Lf, Rh	Asthma, boils, cuts, wounds, burns, fever, liver c piles, kidney stone, urine complaints
a parnassifolia D.Don	–	2800-3050	H	Rt	Vermifuge
ilariaceae					
ia himalaica Wettst.	–	2800-3050	H	Lf	Eye disorders
ergia indica Vatke.	–	1300-1800	H	Lf	Bronchitis, skin diseases, sore throat, toothache
ris pectinata Wall. ex Benth.	–	2500-3050	H	WP	Bodyache, sedative
dulcis L.	–	1500-1800	H	WP	Antiemetic, eye diseases, fever, gout, rheumatism urine complaints
ım thapsus L.	Gaddi Tamaku	1300-2800	H	Sd	Asthma, cough, inflammation, leucoderma, veterinary disease
iceae					
spera L.	–	1400-2000	Sh	Rt, Lf, St	Skin eruptions, sores, wounds
ceae					
nnoxia Mill.	–	1300-1600	H	Lf, Sd, Fr	Antihydrophobic, asthma, boils, rheumatism

(Table

	2	3	4	5	6
	Datura	1300-1700	H	Lf, Sd, Fr	Asthma, dislocation of joints, jaundice, rheumatism, stomach complaints, toothache
L.	–	1300-1800	H	WP	Eczema, itching, toothache, wounds, veterinary antihelminthic
L.	–	1300-1800	H	Fr	Asthma, fever, colic
	–	1400-2500	H	Fr, Lf, Fl, Sd	Antidote, boils, cough, dysentery, ear complaints, fever, eye complaints, skin diseases, urinary complaints
ch. & Wendl.	–	1300-2000	H	Fr, Rt	Asthma, blisters, boils, cough, toothache
sis (Lour.) Drace	Lodge	1500-2000	T	Bk, Lf	Astringent
Wall. ex Stued.	Kania/ Patrori	1800-2800	Sh	Rt, Lf	Intestinal complaints
lia Buch.-Ham.	Bihul	1300-1600	T	Lf, St, Fr, Bk	Skin diseases, fever, veterinary diseases
inum Kunth	–	2800-3050	H	Tu	Dysentery
ylla D.Don	Siar	1300-1800	Sh	Lf, St, Bk	Dysentery, eczema
Frost.	–	1300-2000	H	Rt	Dandruff, hair problems
dd.	–	1800-2600	H	Lf	Wounds
. ex Wedd.	Bicchu buti	1300-2300	H	WP, Lf	Antiseptic, dandruff, swelling
q. ex Wedd.	–	1300-2100	H	WP	Rheumatism, stomachache

(Table Contd.

	2	3	4	5	6
ıaceae					
a hardwickii Wall.	Nihani	2000-3050	H	WP	Skin diseases
ınsi Jones	Nihani	1300-3050	H	WP	Antidote to sting of insects, hysteria, neurosis, sk
ıceae					
eris foetida (Don) Robin	Rumri	1300-2000	Sh	Lf	Wounds
camara L.	Ujarru	1300-1500	H	Lf, Fr	Itching, ringworm, veterinary medicines
undo L.	Banha	1300-1600	T	Lf, Fr, Rt	Rheumatism, arthritis, sprains, anthelmentic, anal
ae					
'ora L.	Banafsha	2800-3050	H	Lf, Fl	Bronchitis, cold, cough
ens Wall.	Banafsha	1300-2500	H	Lf, Fl	Asthma, bronchitis, cold, cough, eye diseases
L.	Banafsha	1800-2600	H	Lf, Fl	Medicinal (Antipyretic, biliousness, cold, cough, diseases)
raceae					
racemosa Sm.	–	1300-1700	H	Rt	Headache
um spicatum am. ex Sm.	Ban haldi, Shau	1300-2200	H	Rh, Lf	Asthma, blood purifier, bronchitis, nausea
alpina Royle	–	2500-3050	H	Rt	Tonic, veterinary diseases
perms					
e					
ıdrow Spach.	Tosh	2200-3050	T	Lf, Wd	Rheumatism, ulcer
leodara x D. Don) G. Don	Kelo, Diar	1500-2300	T	Res, Lf, Wd	Antihelminthic, rheumatism, ulcers
xburghii Sarg.	Chir	1300-2200	T	Sd, Wd, Res	Boils, bone fracture, cracks in sole of feet, lepros diseases, snake bite, sprain, swelling, urine compl

(Table

	2	3	4	5	6
subsp. .) Pilger	Rakhala/ Talispatra	2400-3050	T	Bk, Lf, Wd	Anti cancerous
s-veneris L.	Barin	1300-2200	H	Frd, Lf	Bronchitis, cold, cough, fever, menstrual complaints, throat disorders
on	–	1800-3050	H	Frd	Fever
ntum	Linger	1300-1800	H	Frd	Constipation
tum (Thunb.)	–	2000-2800	H	Rt, WP	Dysentery
e *ata* C. Chr.	–	1300-1600	H	Rh	Cholera
	–	1800-2900	H	WP	Anthelmintic
Hauke	Khasra ghass	1300-2000	H	WP	Tooth complaints
	–	1800-3050	H	WP	Diuretic, haemostat, Dyspepsia
um (L.) Kuhn.	–	1600-2500	H	Rt, Frd, WP	Antelmintic, haemostat, cuts, wounds
	Puai	1500-2000	H	Frd	Medicinal (Wounds)

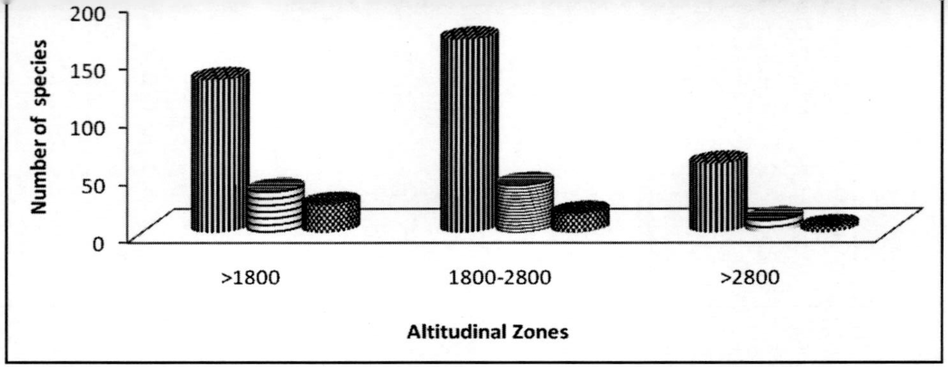

Fig. 2.2: Altitudinal Distribution of Medicinal Species in the Study Area

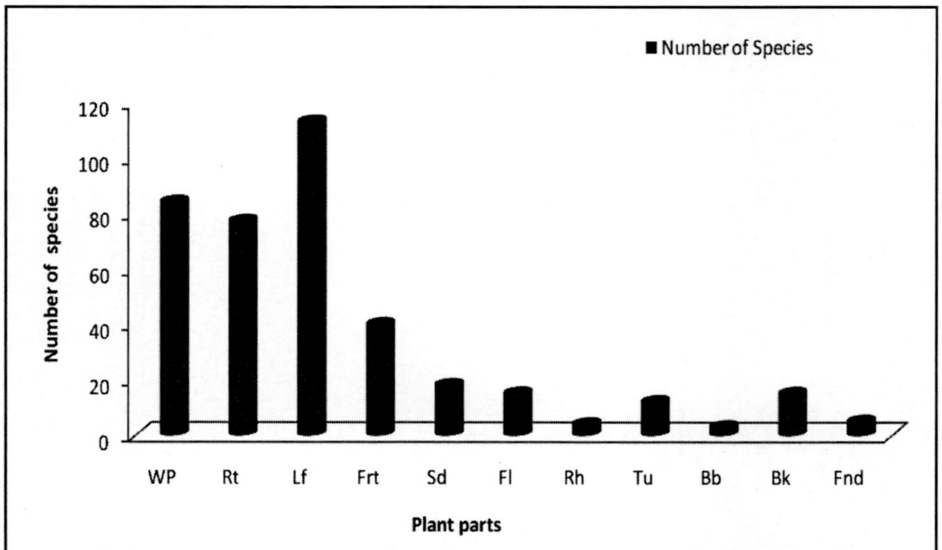

Fig. 2.3: Utilization Pattern of Plant Parts of Medicinal Species in the Study Area

Abbreviations used: WP=whole plant; Rt=root; Lf=leaf; Frt=fruit; Sd=seed;

spp.); Lamiaceae (24 spp.); Rosaceae (16 spp.); Ranunculaceae (14 spp.); Fabaceae and Orchidaceae (11 spp. each), these families are well represented in the flora of present investigated area (Sakshi, 2010) and contain some very common plants. As confirmed by Johns *et al.* (1990) the more common a plant is in an area, the greater the probability of its popular use. The parts of the plants most used for medicinal purposes are leaves (113spp.) and whole plant (88) and root (77 spp.).

According to Bonet*et al.*, (1999), the reason why leaves are used most is because they are easily accessible. The maximum number of economically important species was recorded in the altitudinal zone 1801-2800m. Generally diversity of the economically important species decreases with the increasing altitude.However, a lesser amount of number of species at lower altitudinal zone in the study is due to short altitudinal width of the zone *i.e*, 1300-1800m. The over exploitation of *Cinnamomumtamala*, *Dactylorhizahatagirea*, *Hedychiumspicatum*, *Dioscoreadeltcidea*, *Podophyllumhexandrum* etc. by the inhabitants from the natural habitats may lead to extinction of these species from the area in near future. Efforts should be concentrated to conserve the species in its natural habitat so as to minimize the loss to ecosystem.

Promotion for cultivation of such medicinal plants in the villages may also reduce the human pressure on the wild habitats. People's participation in conservation programme should be encouraged to maximum level so as to minimize the loss of this valuable plant diversity. In addition, identification of active ingredients would help identifying the potential species for marketing. Mass multiplication of the commercially viable medicinal plants through conventional (vegetative and seeds) and in-vitro (tissue culture) methods, establishment of these species in natural habitats and ex-situ conditions mainly cultivation in marginal lands of the inhabitants and capacity building of the inhabitants for the cultivation and sustainable utilization of medicinal plants have been suggested. The state medicinal plant board and forest department may implement the above suggestions for the development of medicinal plant sector. Such type of studies are also required in other parts of the Indian Himalayan Region so that comprehensive database of medicinal plants could be developed and utilized in identification and notification of medicinal plant conservation areas and develop location and region specific management plan.

EFERENCES

J.Ethnopharmaco. 68:145-168.

Chandrasekar, K. 2007. Newly Recorded Ethnomedicinal Plants from Pin Valley National Park, Himachal Pradesh. *J. Non-Timb. Forest Prod*. 14(4): 261-264.

Chauhan, N.S. 1999.*Medicinal and Aromatic Plants of Himachal Pradesh,* (Indus Publishing Company, New Delhi, India).

Chettri, N. and Sharma, E. 2006. Assessment of Natural Resources Uses Patterns: A Case Study Along a Trekking Corridor of Sikkim Himalaya, India. *Resources Energy Dev.* 3(1): 21-34.

Chowdhery, H.J.andWadhwa B.M.1984. *Flora of Himachal Pradesh,* Vols. 1-3, Botanical Survey of India, Calcutta.

Dhaliwal, D.S.and Sharma M. 1999. *Flora of Kullu District (Himachal Pradesh)*, Bishen Singh Mahendra Pal Singh, Dehra Dun.

Handa, S.S. 1991. Harnassing Ayurveda for Modern Drug Development. *ThePharmacos*. 30: 13-30.

Jain, S.K. 1991. *Dictionary of Indian Folk Medicine and Ethnobotany,* Deep Publications, New Delhi.

Johns, T., Kokwaro, J.O. and Kimanani, E.K. 1990. Herbal remedies of the Luo of Siaya District, Kenya: Establishing quantitative criteria for consensus. *Eco. Bot*. 44: 369-381.

Kala, C.P.2000. Status and Conservation of Rare and Endangered Medicinal Plants in the Indian Trans-Himalaya, *Biol Cons,* 93(1): 371-379.

Khullar, S.P. 1994. *An Illustrated Fern Flora of the West Himalaya,* Vol. I, International Book Distributors, Dehradun.

Khullar, S.P. 2000. *An Illustrated Fern Flora of the West Himalaya,* Vol. II. International Book Distributors Dehradun.

Nayar, M.P. and Sastry, A.R.K.1987, 1988 & 1990. *Red Data Book of Indian Plants*, Vol. I-III. Botanical Survey of India, Calcutta.

Pandey, M.M., Rawat, A.K.S. and Mehrotra, S. 2004. Enumeration of some Potential Economic Plants of Mandi District in Himachal Pradesh. *J. Eco. Bot. Tax*. 28(3): 552-555.

Sakshi. 2010. *Eco-ethnobotanical Assessment and Conservation Priorities of Floristic Diversity along an Altitudinal Gradient in Central Part of Himachal Pradesh*. Ph.D. Thesis. Kumaun University, Nainital.

Samant, S.S. and Palni, L.M.S. 2000. Diversity, Distribution and Indigenous Uses of Essential Oil Yielding Plants of Indian Himalayan Region, *J Med Arom Plant Sci,* 22: 671-684.

Samant, S.S., Butola, J.S. and Sharma, A. 2007. Assessment of Diversity, Distribution, Conservation Status and Preparation of Management Plan for Medicinal Plants in the Catchment Area of Parbati Hydro-electric Project Stage-III in North Western Himalaya, *J Mount Sci,* 4(1) (2007) 36-54.

Samant, S.S., Dhar, U.andPalni, L.M.S. 1998. *Medicinal Plants of Indian Himalaya: Diversity Distribution Potential Values,* GyanodayaPrakashan, Nainital.

Utilization Patterns in Askot Wildlife Sanctuary in Kumaon Himalaya, India, for Conservation and Management. *Environ. Cons.* 27(1): 5-13.

Samant, S.S., Dhar, U. and Palni, L.M.S. 2001. *Himalayan Medicinal Plants: Potential and Prospects.* Gyanodaya Prakashan, Nainital.

Samant, S.S., Rawal, R.S. and Dhar, U. 2006. Diversity, Extraction and Status of Fodder Species in Askot Wildlife Sanctuary, West Himalaya, India. *Int. J. Biod. Sci. Manag.* 2: 29-42.

Singh, S.K.and Rawat, G.S. 2000. *Flora of Great Himalayan National Park, Himachal Pradesh,* Bishen Singh Mahendra Pal Singh, Dehradun.

Singh, A., Lal, M., and Samant, S.S. 2009. Diversity, Indigenous Uses and Conservation Prioritization of Medicinal Plants in Lahaul Valley, Proposed Cold Desert Biosphere Reserve, India. *Int. J. Biod. Sci. Manag.* 5(3): 132-154.

Singh, P.B. 1993. Medicinal Plants of Ayruvedic Importance from Mandi District of Himachal Pradesh. *B.M.E.B.R.* 14: 126-136.

Sood, S.K., Nath, R. and Kalia, D.C. 2001. *Ethnobotany of Cold Desert Tribes of Lahaul–Spiti (N. W. Himalaya),* Deep Publications, New Delhi.

Srivastava, R.K. 2002. *Invasion of Exotic Weeds in the Natural Forest of Tropical India due to Forest Fires: A Threat to Biodiversity.* IFFN. No. 27-July, 90-92.

Uniyal, S.K., Singh, K.N., Jamwal, P.and Lal, B. 2006. Traditional Use of Medicinal Plants Among the Tribal Communities of Chhota Bhangal, Western Himalaya, *J Ethnobiol Ethnomed,* 2: 2-14.

Ved, D.K., Kinhal, G.A., Ravikumar, K., Prabhakaran, V., Ghate, U., Vijaya Shankar, R.and Indresha, J.H. *Conservation Assessment and Management Prioritization for the Medicinal Plants of Jammu & Kashmir, Himachal Pradesh & Uttaranchal,* Foundation for Revitalization of Local Health Traditions, Bangalore, India.

Pages: **48-72**

MEDICINAL PLANTS: ***DISTRIBUTION, UTILIZATION AND SIGNIFICANCE***

Edited by: **Dr. Pankaj Sharma; Dr. Pawan Kumar 'Bharti'** and **Dr. Narayan Singh**

ISBN: 978-93-5056-734-0

Edition: **2015**

Published by: **Discovery Publishing House Pvt. Ltd., New Delhi (India)**

3

A Case Study on Ethno-Botanical Herbs of Uttarakhand, Himalaya

Deeksha Nautiyal[1]; Jyoti Pandey[1]; Anjali Arya[1]; Meenakshi Jalal[2] and Brijendra Lal[1]

INTRODUCTION

Himalayan region is well known for having important medicinal plants; traditionally these plants have been used by local people for health care and now over exploited as international demand increased. Many of their medicinally important plants are threatened because of unsustainable harvesting. In India over 2,500 species of ethno-botanical use are known (Jain, 1991). The estimated 95% of medicinal plants collected in India are from the wild and process of collection is said to be destructive because of the use of parts, like roots, barks, wood and whole plants. An estimate of the parts used by *Ayurvedic* industries are: roots- 29.6%, leaves- 25.8%, bark- 13.5%, wood- 2.8%, whole plant- 16.3% and rhizome- 4% and rest: seeds, flowers etc (Mathoo, 2003). Research institutions and State Forest Departments have a larger role in sustainable development of medicinal plants. Efforts have to be made for preserving these plants *in-situ* by way of

[1] Research Scholar's.

[2] M.Sc Student, Department of Forestry & Environmental Science, Kumaun University, Nainital (Uttarakhand), India.

controlling over-exploitation, unscientific harvesting, protecting the plants in reserved forests and by enforcing legal channels so that endangered species do not become extinct.

An analysis of alpine plants of Indian Himalaya shows that nearly 113 taxa are at present threatened and are classified under various categories of threatened plants i.e. endangered (17spp), vulnerable (11spp), rare (79spp) threatened (2spp) and in terminate (4spp) Samant (1994). The following species are listed in the Red Data Book of Indian plants by Nayar and Sastry (1987) *Acer caesium, Allium stracheyi, Aconitum heterophyllum, Arnebia benthamii, Nardostachys grandiflora, Picrorhiza kurrooa, Sassurea costus, Podophyllum hexandrum, Megarcarpae polyandra and Thlaspi andersonii*. In broad outline of their specialization, the medicinal plants in the Himalaya exhibit peculiarities in a number of characteristics, such as morphology, physiology, life form and growth pattern. The State level medicinal plants extraction committee of Uttarakhand has proposed the ban on 11 herb species which are:

Dactylorrhiza hatagiara, Habenaria spp., Swertia chirata, Podophyllum hexandrum, Picrorhiza kurroa, Nardostachys jatamansi, Dioscorea deltoidea, Fritilaria roylei, Lilium polyphyllum, Pamelia spp.

The Himalayas have a great wealth of medicinal plants and its traditional medicinal knowledge. 1748 species are known for its medicinal value in the western Himalayan region including the Uttarakhand (Samant *et al.*, 1998). Himalayan medicinal plants are largely being utilized in two ways i.e. domestic consumption by local inhabited and preparation of pharmaceutical based drug. Medicinal plant is not only major resource for traditional medicine and herbal industry but also provide livelihood and health security to large segment of Indian population. Plants have been used for health care for more than five thousand years. About ten per cent of the plant species on the Earth are considered medicinally important, but hardly one per cent of medicinally plant species have been scientifically studied for their biology, pharmacy, chemistry, conservation etc. Today, ethno-botany plays a crucial role in the study of traditional medicine, as it has an interfacial function linking nature with culture and traditional knowledge with modern technology thus contributing to all understanding of traditional medicinal knowledge (Pei, 2005). The main aim of ethno-botany is to document the knowledge about plants that have come through generations and use the knowledge for the benefit of the society (Chaudhary, 1998).

At present pharmaceutical sectors are using 280 medicinal plant species out of which 175 are from Indian Himalayan Region (Tripathi, 1989). In last few decades, attraction towards herbal medicine has increased, resulting in accelerated rate of trade and research on medicinal plants. In India there exists over one million community based traditional workers and about 600,000 licensed medical practitioners of traditional systems like Ayurveda,

Siddha and Unani, they diagnose and cure different diseases through their own traditional knowledge (Hafeel and Shankar, 1999). At present due to increasing population in India the area under forest is decreasing and demand of medicinal plant is increasing.

Uttarakhand, 27th state of India lies between 28°43′ 31° 27′ N and 77° 34′ 81°02′ E in latitude and longitude, respectively which accounts for nearly 15.5 per cent of the total geographical area of Western Himalayas, bounded by Nepal in East and Himanchal in the west. The state with predominance of mountains and hills is spread over 13 Districts with an area of 53,485 sq.kms., has two regions (Kumaun and Garhwal) which can be divided into main three agro ecological zones, viz. (a) The Alpine Zone; (b) The Temperate zone; and (c) The Sub-Tropical Zone. All these zones have significant physiographic differences in terms of altitude, aspects, hill slope and soils, which have helped, developed riches for a set of specific varieties of herbal and medicinal plants. Maximum species of Medicinal plant have been reported from Uttarakhand, India (Kala, 2004). Due to these great altitudinal variation, wide array of climatic zones are available, which favors the luxuriant growth of diversified and rich vegetation which also has a number of raw drugs described in Ayurvedic texts. Uttarakhand is one such state which from time immemorial has been a rich repository of herb and medicinal plant. Many of these Herb and Medicinal plant are high repute in ayurveda, aromatherapy and other system of natural medicine. The state is declared as "Herbal State" in 2003 by state government.

Plants have traditionally served as man's most important weapon against pathogen. Medicinal plant are widely used by all section of communities whether directly or as folk remedies or medicaments in different indigenous system as well as in modern medicines (Alok, 1991).The traditional system of medicine has led to the discoveries of many important plant based drugs (Uniyal *et al*., 2002., Semwal *et al*., 2010). However, this knowledge orally passed from one generation to the next, thus have vulnerability to wipe out (Kala, 2005). Traditional medicine is defined as sum of knowledge, skills and practices based on theories beliefs and experience (WHO, 2000). The use of alternative medicine is growing because of its moderate cost and increasing faith in herbal medicine. Allopathic medicine can cure wide range of diseases; however its side effect and high prices are causing many people to return to herbal medicine which tend to have fewer side effects (Mukharjee, 2005).

In Himalaya, most of the species considered to be medicinal are long-lived and many show clonal growth reported by many authors (Dhar *et al*., 2000, Lama *et al*., 2001, Ghimire *et al*., 2006). An assessment on Medicinal plants of the Indian Himalaya was done by Samant *et al*. (1998). Different worker at different time gave information on utilization of plant for primary health care which include Negi *et al*. (1985), Samant *et al*. (1993) and Uniyal

(1997). Indigenous use of medicinal plant and conservation of threatened species explain by Kala (2005). Uniyal and Shiva (2005) focus light on medicinal plant in Garhwal Himalaya Uttarakhand. Sharma (2000) gave scientific text in Sanskrit about India Vedas as oldest Vedas in literature. Status of ethno-medicinal plants of Almora district in Kumaun Himalaya, Uttarakhand was studied by Kumari *et al.* (2011). Assessment of species rarity and Uttarakhand as a maximum medicinal plant state is given by Kala (2009). Kandari (2012) studied ethno biological conservation towards medicinal and aromatic plant. Traditional use of medicinal plants was given by Uniyal (1997) in Uttarakhand vanaushadi darshika. Subsequently, with the advancement in the techniques of phyto-chemistry and pharmacology, a number of active principles of medicinal plants were isolated and introduced as valuable drugs in modern system of medicine (Joshi, 2004).

Documentation on ethno-botanical knowledge was done by Maikhuri *et al.* (2000), Nautiyal *et al.* (2001). While a comprehensive review has described a rich diversity and use of medicinal flora within Uttarakhand (Joshi, 2002). Dhar *et al.* (2000) founded that the biological diversity in the Indian Himalayan Region has been a source of medicine for millions in the country and elsewhere.

Medicinal plants can be used to cure almost any medical complications, but due to the luxurious life, one find it more easy to go to the pharmacy whenever such health problems arises, all the medicinal plants have one or more importance, some can treat diarrhea & dysentery while other may work as an antidote against poison of snake or scorpion, even cancer and other cardio-vascular disease can be cured by the help of medicinal plants, just we need is to enhance our knowledge and curiosity towards these plants. Extensive survey of literature was conducted at different medicinal herbs of Uttarakhand along with their indigenous uses. Uttarakhand have exclusive and unique position, as it is a natural habitat for all high altitude plant resources. Kapkoti *et al.* (2014), reported lack of alternate income sources, force people to over-exploits natural resources of the region of Kumaun Himalaya. Ethno-botany has emerged as an important branch of study which focuses on the utility of different plant species and their properties as food, medicine and other uses (Allen *et al.*, 1990; Cotton, 1997).

The day by day rising pressure arise the needs of documentation of some important medicinal herb plants of Himalaya. An extensive review has been collected and mentioned along with their botanical name, altitude, life form and indigenous uses.

1. Enlisted Medicinal Plants After Review

The list contained 101 medicinal herb species according to their attitudinal range, part used in preparation of medicines and uses.

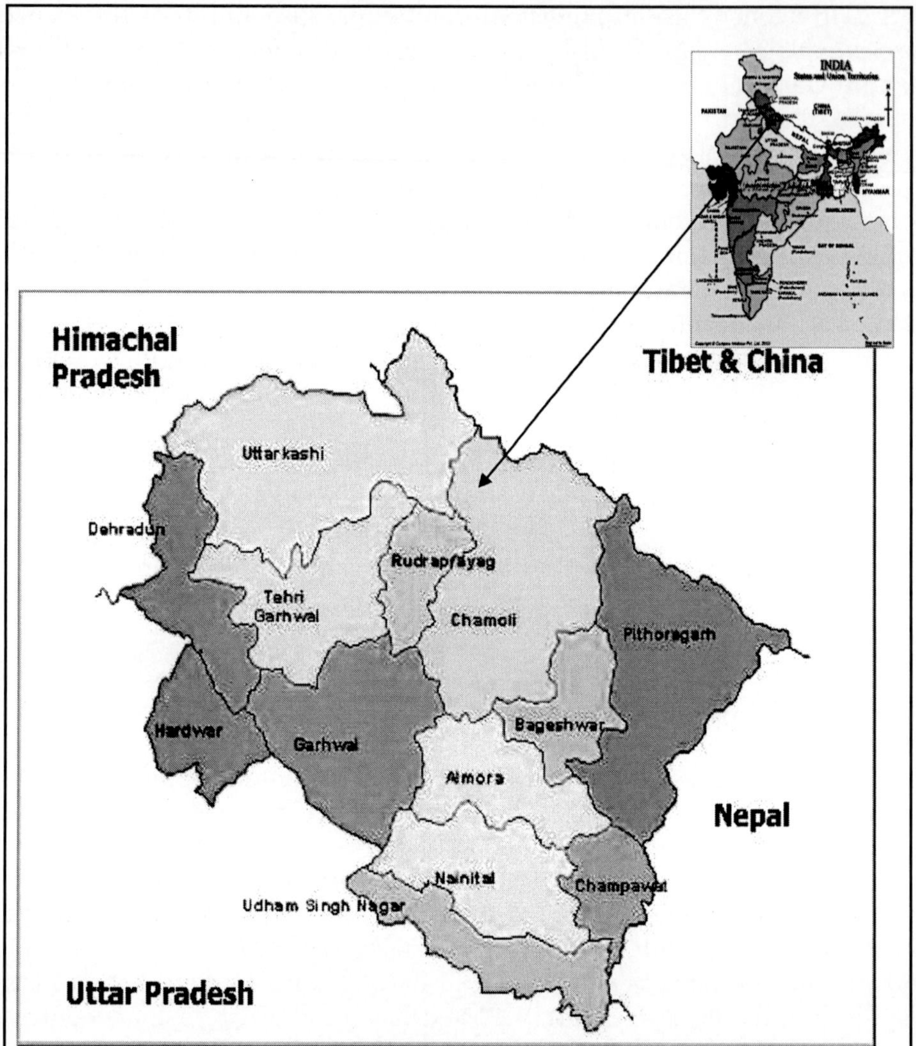

Map of India Showing Uttarakhand State along with Districts

Cordyceps sinensis - Keera Jari

Beside these medicinal herbs Himalayas is well known for a fungal plant known as "Keedajadi" or "Yarsagumba" which has been exported throughout the world for its medicinal properties, often this fungus also named as "Himalayan gold" as the name gold indicates its high price and commercial value.

Table 3.1: Some Enlisted Medicinal Plants of Uttarakhand, Himalaya

Botanical Name	Vernacular Name	Family	Attitude	Life Form	Part Used	Uses
1	2	3	4	5	6	7
Achillea millefolium L.	Momoduru	Asteraceae	1800-3600	Herb	Whole plant	Diaphoretic, astringent, tonic and mild aromatic
Achyranthes aspera L.	Apamarga	Amarantaceae	Above 1800	Herb	Root, leaves	Use to ease the symptoms of malaria, obstetrics
Aconitum balfourii Stapf.	Meetha vish	Ranunculaceae	3200-3800	Herb	Root	Highly effective, analgesic, highly toxic, anti-inflammatory
Aconitum heterophyllum Wall.	Atees	Ranunculaceae	3000-3700	Herb	Root	Anti-periodic, antipyretic, aphrodisiac
*Aconitum ferox*Wall.	Gobriya	Ranunculaceae	2100-3800	Herb	Root	In sciatica, throat & internal inflammation
Acornus calamus L.	Vasa bach	Araceae	1400-2300	Herb	Root	Plant mainly use in Treatment of digestive complain.
Ageratum conyzoides Linn.	Gamlwa	Asteraceae	200-2000	Herb	Leaves	Leaf juice is applied to stop bleeding, recommended in nervous disorder
Aloe barbadensis (L.) Burm. F.	Grahtkumari	Liliaceae	Upto 1800	Herb	Whole plant	Use in skin treatment, the gel of aloe vera has cooling & soothing effect
Allium carolinianum D.C.	Dhungar	Alliaceae	3000-4500	Herb	Bulb &Leaves	Reduces blood cholesterol level, act as a tonic to the digestive system
Allium cepa L.	Pyaz	Alliaceae	Upto 2000	Herb	Bulb	Use to treat respiratory disease & in epilepsy
*Allium stracheyi*Kunth	Jumbo	Alliaceae	3200-4000	Herb	Bulb	Asthma, stomach diseases and jaundice.

(Table Contd…)

1	2	3	4	5	6	7
*Allium sativum*Linn.	Lehsun	Alliaceae	Upto 2400	Herb	Whole plant	Used in the treatment of cholera and dysentery, in heart disorder
Ajuga bracteosa Wall.ex.Benth	Ratpatia	Lamiaceae	Upto 2800	Herb	Leaves, root	Used in gonorrhea and can be applied externally in the wound
Angelica archangelica L.	Anyala	Apiaceae	Above 3000	Herb	Root, fruit	Used in heart disorder, loss of appetite and treating insomnia
Amaranthus polygamus	Doggali koora	Amaranthaceae	Above 1200	Herb	Seeds, root	Used in viral and in cough and cold
Angelica glauca Edgew.	Chora	Apiaceae	2700-3800	Herb	Root	Used in asthma, epilepsy, cold and constipation
Arctium lappa L.	Nakli kuth	Asteraceae	2100-4200	Herb	Root & leaves	Used as diuretic, diaphoretic and a blood purifying agent
Argemone mexicana L.	Satyanash, ganoya	Papaveraceae	200-1500	Herb	Whole plant	Diuretic, purgative destroy worms.
Arisaena costatum	Sanp-kmaki	Araceae	1800-2500	Herb	Root	Wounds are washed with the decoction of root. Paste of root applied in affected part.
Arnebia benthamii (Wall. ex G. Don)	Balchad	Boraginaceae	2800-3800	Herb	Root	Hair tonic, fever, headache, in cuts & wounds
Arnebia euchroma (Royle)	Lal jadi	Boraginaceae	3500-4500	Herb	Whole plant	Used as hair tonic
Asparagus racemosus Willd.	Satavar	Liliaceae	1000-2200	Herb	Shoot, root	Root juice is taken as remedy for stomach pain, colic in cattle
Bergenia ciliata (Haw) Sternb.	Pashan bhed	Saxifragaceae	1600-3200	Herb	Rhizome, leaves	Rhizome powder is given to get relief from roundworm; leaves are used to treat kidney stones.
Boerhavia diffusa L.	Punarnava	Nyctaginaceae	300-1200	Herb	Whole plant	Prevent kidney disorder, in jaundice

(Table Contd…)

1	2	3	4	5	6	7
Cannabis sativa L.	Ganja	Cannabaceae	Upto 3000	Herb	Seed, bark, leaves	The crushed plant of the plant is taken to relieve abdominal pain, plant paste is applied to treat cut and wounds
Carum carvi L.	Jungli jeera	Apiaceae	2000-5100	Herb	Seed	Useful in strengthening the function of stomach.
Cassia absus L.	Chaksu	Caesalpiniaceae	Upto 1000	Herb	Seed, leaves	It acts as a healing agent, it increases the eye sight
Centella asiatica Linn.	Brahmi	Apiaceae	Upto 2100	Herb	Whole plant	Used in enhancing memory, skin diseases & severe headache
Chenopodium album L.	Bathua	Chenopodiaceae	800-4000	Herb	Seed, leaves, root	Anti-helmintic, anti-rheumatic, seeds are chewed in urinary problems
Cicer microphyllum Benth.	Jangali masoor	Fabaceae	3300-4500	Herb	Whole plant	Veterinary medicines
Coriandrum sativum L.	Dhaniya	Apiaceae	Upto 2500	Herb	Seed, leaves	Important in treating disorder like diabetes, blockage in arteries, high blood pressure etc.
Corydalis govaniana Wall.	Balsam jadi	Fumariaceae	2400-4800	Herb	Whole plant	Treatment of fever, pain reliever.
Cuminum cyminum L.	Jeera	Apiaceae	500-1500	Herb	Seed	Treatment of diabetes and various stomach diseases.
Cymbopogon citrates	Lemon grass	Poaceae	600-1200	Herb	Whole plant	Anxiolytic, hypnotic and anticonvulsant, antifungal
Dactylorhiza hatagirea (D. Don)	Hatha jadi	Orchidaceae	2800-4500	Herb	Tubers	Root used as a farinaceous food and nervine tonic, paste of root is applied in cut and wounds.
Datura stramonium L.	Datura	Solanaceae	200-2200	Herb	Root, seeds, leaves	In insanity, fevers, in skin diseases, antispasmodic

(Table Contd…)

1	2	3	4	5	6	7
Daucus carota L.	Gajar	Apiaceae	Upto 2000	Herb	Seed, leaves, tuber	Prevent hyperacidity, myopia, tumor, hemorrhoid and jaundice
Delphinium brunonianum Royle	Kasturi fool	Ranunculaceae	3200-6000	Herb	Root	Destroy ticks on animals
Didymocarpus pedicellata R. Br.	Shilapuspha	Gesneriaceae	–	Herb	Leaves	Help in endocrine and genitourinary disorders
Dioscorea alata L.	Ratalu	Dioscoreaceae	600-1200	Herb	Tuber	Used as a laxative and vermifuge and as a treatment for leprosy, tumors and gonorrhea
Dioscorea bulbifera L.	Genthi	Dioscoreaceae	150-2100	Herb	Root	Used to treat anorexia, conjunctivitis, diarrhea and dysentery
Dracocephalum heterophyllm Benth.	Lutki jhad	Lamiaceae	3400-5500	Herb	Whole plant	Treat disease of heart, blood pressure and migraine.
Eclipta prostrate L.	Bhringraja	Asteraceae	200-1200	Herb	Whole plant	Is considered as a very powerful tonic, effective against liver injury & inflammation
Curcuma longa L.	Haldi	Zingiberaceae	Upto 2500	Herb	Fruit, leaves, rhizome	Lower the level of cholesterol, reducing risk of stroke and heart attack as well as eczema
Euphrasia himalaica Wettst.	–	Scrophulariaceae	3000-4500	Herb	Leaves	Used in eye strain and to relive inflammation by cold cough, sinus infection.
Evolvulus alsinoides L.	Sankhpuspi	Convolulaceae	500-1200	Herb	Whole plant	Used in mental disorders, nervous disturbances and enhance memory
Ferula jaeschkeana Vatke	Jungle hing	Apiaceae	2400-3600	Herb	Root, seed	Used in rheumatic affection and back ache.
Foenculum vulgare Mill	Sanuf	Apiaceae	Upto 2500	Herb	Whole plant	Diuretic, expectorant, increase appetite

(Table Contd...)

1	2	3	4	5	6	7
Fritillaria roylei HK.	Kakoli	Liliaceae	3000-4600	Herb	Bark, root	Anti-asthmatic and anti rheumatic
Fumaria indica (Haussk)	Pit papra	Fumariaceae	2700	Herb	Whole plant	Used in pains, fever, influenza and liver complaints
Gentianella moorcroftiana (Wall. ex G. Don)	Trikta	Gentianaceae	2700-5200	Herb	Whole plant	Used to cure fever & cough cold
*Gloriosa superba*Linn.	Kalihari	Liliaceae	400-2200	Herb	Seed, rhizome	Nausea, vomiting Numbness
Hedychium spicatum Ham. Ex Smith	Ban haldi	Zingiberaceae	1000-2000	Herb	Rhizome	Used in treating vomiting, diarrhoea and as an antidote against snake bite
Hyoscyamus niger L.	Lang tang	Solanaceae	2000-3500	Herb	Whole plant	Sleep and allay pains, ear ache and oil killed lice.
Jurinea dolomiaea Boiss.	Dhup	Asteraceae	3400-4500	Herb	Root	Colic, fever, antioxidant
Lepidium apetalum Willd	Van halim	Brassicaceae	2500-4100	Herb	Whole plant	Paste is applied externally in wound
Leucas caphalotes Spreng.	Guma	Lamiaceae	1800	Herb	Whole plant	Decoction of whole plant is given orally in jaundice & in fever
Linum usitatissimum L.	Alsi	Linaceae	Upto 3500	Herb	Seed	Has an anti-inflammatory and antipyretic activity, wound healing, cures diabetes
Malaxis muscifera Kuntz.	Rishbhak	Orchidaceae	Above 2400	Herb	Stem	Antidysenteric, therapeutic, in insect bite
Malva neglecta Wall.	Sonchala	Malvaceae	3000-3800	Herb	Root	In the treatment of respiratory & gastrointestinal tract
Mentha arvensis L.	Podina	Lamiaceae	1200-2000	Herb	Leaves	In headache, rhinitis & in vomiting
Mentha longifolia (L.) Huds.	Jangali pudina	Lamiaceae	above 1500	Herb	Whole plant	Paste is applied in wound of animals

(Table Contd…)

1	2	3	4	5	6	7
Micromeria biflora (Buch.-Ham.)	Garur-buti	Lamiaceae	900-2200	Herb	Whole plant	Dried powder of the plant is used in eczema
Mimosa pudica L.	Chui mui	Mimosaceae	200-1200	Herb	Leaves, root	Prevent hemorrhoids, leprosy, diarrhea and arthritis and body pain
Morina longifolia Wall. ex DC.	Vish kandara	Dipsacaceae	Above 2000	Herb	Root	Have digestive ethenic and stomachic property
Nardostachys jatamansi DC.	Jatamansi	Valerianaceae	3200-5000	Herb	Whole plant	Memory enhancer & neuro-protective, helps in maintaining the circulation system
Nelumbo nucifera Gaertn	Kamal	Nelumbonaceae	Upto 1600	Herb	Rhizomes, flowers and seeds	Used to treat sunstroke & cardiovascular disorder, sedative & depurative
Nomocharis nana (Klotz.) Wilson	Van pyaz	Liliaceae	3000-4000	Herb	Tuber	Used in stomach pain
Ocimum sanctum L.	Tulsi	Lamiaceae	Above 400	Herb	Whole plant	Expectorant, dropped in to ears as a remedy for ear aches, in malarial fevers
Origanum vulgare L.	Van tulsi	Lamiaceae	600-4000	Herb	Whole plant	Carminative and stomachic disorder.
Oryza sativa L.	Dhan	Poaceae	Upto 2000	Herb	Flower	Used for curing breast cancer, stomach indurations, in filariasis
Oxalis corniculata L.	Khatti buti	Oxalidaceae	300-2900	Herb	Leaves	Leaf extract is taken orally to remove open sores, in pimples and other skin disease
Paris polyphyllum Sm.	Satwa	Liliaceae	1500-2400	Herb	Rhizome	Antihelmintic, vaso-constriction in kidney

(Table Contd...)

1	2	3	4	5	6	7
Picrorhiza kurrooa Royle ex Benth.	Kutki	Scrophulariaceae	3200-4500	Herb	Root	Stomachic used in fever & dyspepsia, in scorpion sting
*Plantago ovate*Forssk.	Isabgol	Plantaginaceae	–	Herb	Seed, husk	Lower the level of cholesterol & diabetes, relieves chronic constipation
Polygonatum cirrhifolium (Wall.) Royle	Medha	Convallariaceae	–	Herb	Rhizome	Cold, cough, in kidney pain
Prunella vulgaris L.	Fulari	Lamiaceae	Upto 3800	Herb	Whole plant	Treat fever, wounds, and sore throat
Phyllanthus armarus Schum &Thonn.	Bhumi amlanki	Euphorbiaceae	Above 700	Herb	Whole plant	Used as diuretic, in urinary disorder, in jaundice
Rumex acetosa L.	Chukil jhad	Polygonaceae	1600-4200	Herb	Whole plant	Paste is applied in cuts & wound
Rumex hastatus D. Don	Kathi meethi	Polygonaceae	1000-2600	Herb	Whole plant	Leaf extract of plant are applied on wounds & cuts, root is anti-rheumatic & can be used in skin disease
Rumex nepalensis Spreng.	Jungli palak	Polygonaceae	1200-4000	Herb	Leaves, root	Used as an antidote
Rheum emodi D. Don	Dholu	Polygonaceae	3000-4200	Herb	Root	Treatment of various sprain and pain.
Roscoea alpina Royle	Kakoli	Zingiberaceae	2000-3800	Herb	Root	Treatment of cough cold and stomach diseases
Satyrium nepalense D. Don	Salam mishri	Orchidaceae	2000-3500	Herb	Whole plant	Chronic diseases
Saussurea gossypiphora D. Don	Kapasi	Asteraceae	4200-5600	Herb	Root, inflorescence	Applied in cut and wounds.
Saussurea obvallata (DC.) Edgew.	Bhrama kamal	Asteraceae	3800-5000	Herb	Whole plant	Used in rheumatism, liver pain and bone ache.
Sida cordifolia L.	Balu	Malvaceae	400-1200	Herb	Leaves, root	Simulates the brain, heart rate and expands bronchia

(Table Contd…)

1	2	3	4	5	6	7
Solanum nigrum L.	Makoi	Solanaceae	800-3000	Herb	Whole plant	Anti-oxidant, diuretic, anti-inflammatory, antipyretic and anti cancer agent
Spinacia oleracea	Palak	Chenopodiaceae	–	Herb	Leaves, fruit	Used against urinary calcui, liver & jaundice
Swertia chirayita Burtt.	Chiraita	Gentianaceae	1500-4500	Herb	Leaves	Help preventing diabetes, as a blood purifier
Tagetes erecta L.	Hajri	Asteraceae	1000-2000	Herb	Leaves	Leaves juice applied in ear ache
Tagetes minuta L.	Jangali genda	Asteraceae	–	Herb	Flowering tops	Useful in colds, inflammations or stomach problems
Tanacetum dolichophyllum (Kitam.)	Guggal	Asteraceae	3000-4400	Herb	Whole plant	In various disorders of heart and liver
Taraxacum officinale Wigg.	Kanful	Asteraceae	1800-4500	Herb	Whole plant	Blood purifier, febrifuge
Thalictrum foliolosum DC.	Kirmuri	Ranunculaceae	1300-3400	Herb	Root	Used in the treatment of ulcers, ingestion, fever, toothache and haemorrhoids
Thymus linearis Benth.	Mirchi gash	Lamiaceae	2000-4500	Herb	Leaves	Used in cuts & wound
Trigonella foenumgraecum L.	Meethi	Fabaceae	Upto 2500	Herb	Fruit, seed	Beneficial for respiratory, poor digestion & gastrointestinal problems
Viola serpens Wall.	Vanfsa	Violaceae	500-3000	Herb	Whole plant	Used in treating asthma & bronchitis
Waldheimia tomentosa (Decne.) Regel	–	Asteraceae	3600-5000	Herb	Whole plant	Heart diseases & in burns
Zingiber officinale Roscoe	Adarak	Zingiberaceae	Upto 2000	Herb	Rhizome	Helps in combating cancer, sore throat and as an antioxidant

PICTURES OF SOME OF THE MEDICINAL HERBS OF UTTARAKHAND, HIMALAYA

Aconitum heterophyllum

Acornus calamus

Ageratum conyzoides

Ajuga bracteosa

Allium cepa

Allium sativum

Aloe vera

Argemone mexicana

Arnebia benthamii

Centella asiatica

Ocimum sanctum

Oxalis corniculata

Phyllanthus amarus

Rumex nepalensis

Rumex emodi

Tagetes erecta

Scientific Classification

Kingdom: Fungi
Division: Ascomycota
Class: Pyrenomycetes
Order: Clavicipitales
Family: Clavicipitaceae
Genus: *Cordyceps*

DESCRIPTION

Is a parasitic fungus which grows in the living body, kills the host and produces a fruiting body which is used as a valuable herbal medicine, with the beginning of new sprout in alpine meadows in summer season, the *Cordyceps* fungal mycelium initiate to form fruiting body that always emerges from the anterior portion of the insect larva. It is grown above 3300m and upto 4000m in the Himalayan region of Nepal, Bhutan, Indian and Tibet.

Collection of "Yarsagumba" as forest based medicinal resources is already a big business in the northern part of Nepal, Tibet, China and South Korea.

Cordyceps sinensis **(Upper part fungus & Lower part Insect)**

USES

Many researches done in the past about this fungus parasite shows a lot of importance regarding to health benefits.

- *Cordyceps sinensis* is used for lung and respiratory infection, pain, sciatica and backache.
- It is the best rejuvenation for the sport person as it increases physical stamina of the body, and also provides vitality.
- It lowers the cholesterol level, improves blood circulation, lower the range of blood pressure.
- It is used as an aphrodisiac and has higher therapeutic properties.

CONCLUSION

The traditional healers are the main source of knowledge on medicinal plants. Some of the medicinal plants have a huge demand regarding to export to other countries: like *Aconitum heterophyllum, Acornus calamus, Aloe, Nardostachys jatamansi*, due to rapid expansion of pharmaceutical industries, the ever-increasing demand of raw materials of better quality and quantity, it is urgently required to preserve and conserve the rare, vulnerable, threatened and likely to be extinct medicinal plants. Thus an urgent attention is also needed to bring domestication and commercial cultivation to meet the present demand of the industries. It will favour to unregulated collection of the medicinal plant which has resulted depletion of our natural resources of several important drug yielding plants. Women of hilly tracts of Uttarakhand perform most of the farming practices along with the household works; drudgery is a very common phenomenon in hills of Uttarakhand. This can be sorted out if the villagers are given field training in cultivation, exploitation and storage of medicinal plants, these hard task-performing women/villagers will be able to conserve medicinal plants in their fields. This will enhance their economy as well as natural resources will be also preserved resulting in reducing the pressure on wild collection.

REFERENCES

Allen, R.P., Allen, C.P. (1990). How Many Plants Feed World. *Conservational Biology*. Vol. 4: 365-374.

Alok, S.K. (1991). Medicinal Plants in India: Exploitation and Conservation. *The Conservation of Medicinal Plant*. Cambridge University Press. pp. 295-303.

Cotton, C.M. (1997). Observations on Ethno-botany of the Tons Valley Region of Uttarkashi District of North-West Himalayas, *Mountain Resource*. Vol. 11: 177-183.

Chaudhary, R.P. (1998). Biodiversity in Nepal (Status and Conservation). India and Tecpress Books, Bangkok, Thailand. pp. 289.

Dhar, U., Airi, S. Rawal, R.S., Purohit, A.N. (2000). Assessment of Availability and Habitat Preference of Jatmas: A Critically Endangered Medicinal Plant of Western Himalaya. *Current Science*. pp. 79-110.

Dhar, U., Manjkhola, S., Joshi, M., Bhatt, A., Bisht, A.K. & Joshi, M. (2000). Current Status and Future Strategy for Development of Medicinal Plant Sector in Uttaranchal, India. *Current Science*. Vol. 83: 956-963.

Ghimire, S.K., Mckey, D & Aumeeruddy-Thomas,Y. (2006). Himalayan Medicinal Plant Diversity: In an Ecologically Complex High Altitude Anthropogenic Landscape, Dolpo, Nepal. *Environmental Conservation*. Vol. 33: 128-140.

Jain, S.K., (1991). Contribution to Ethno-botany of India. Scientific Publishers. Jodhpur, India.

Joshi, B.D. (2002). A Brief Review on the Flora of Medicinal Importance and Prospects of Developing a Sustainable Network of Small Scale Pharmaceutical Industries in Uttaranchal. *Himalayan Journal of Environment and Zoology*. Vol.16(2): 233.

Joshi, S.C. (2004). Uttaranchal: Environment and Development, Gyanodaya Prakashan, Nainital, pp. 1-86.

Kala, C.P. (2004). Assessment of Species Rarity. *Current Science*. Vol. 86(8): 1058-1059.

Kala, C.P. (2005). Indigenous Uses, Population Density and Conservation of Threatened Medicinal Plants in the Protected Areas of the Indian Himalayas. *Conservation Biology*. Vol. 19: 368-378.

Kandari, L.S., Phondani, P.C., Payal, K., Rao, KS., Maikhuri, R.K., (2012). Ethno-biological Study Towards Conservation of Medicines and Aromatic Plant in Upper Catchment of Ganga in Central Himalaya. *Journal Mountain Science* 9: 286-296.

Kumari, P., Joshi, G.C., Tewari, L.M. (2011). Diversity and Status of Ethno-medicinal Plants of Almora District in Uttarakhand, India. *International Journal of Biodiversity and Conservation*, Vol. 3(7). pp. 298-326.

Lama, Y.C., Ghimire, S.K. and Aumeeruddy-Thomas, Y. (2001). *Medicinal Plants of Dolpo: Amchi's Knowledge and Conservation*. WWF Nepal Programme, Kathmandu, Nepal.

Maikhuri, R.K., Nautiyal, S., Rao, K.S., Saxena, K.G. (2000). Indigenous Knowledge of Medicinal Plants and Wild Edibles Among Three Tribal Sub-communities of Central Himalayas, India. *Indigenous Knowledge and Development Monitor*. Vol. 8(2): 7-13.

Mukharjee, P.K. (2005). Chemistry for Green Environment New Delhi; Narosa Publishing House. Exploring Green House for Drug Development Through Ethno-botany; pp. 98.

Mathoo, R.P., Singh, A. (2003). Natural Resource of Indian Foundation. Report on- Pilot Study of Mechanism Sustainable Development and Promotion on Herbal Medicinal Plant in State of Uttaranchal. Vol. 7(3): 15-27.

Nautiyal, S., Rao, K.S., Maikhuri, R.K., Semwal, R.L., Saxena, K.G. (2001). Traditional Knowledge Related to Medicinal and Aromatic Plants in Tribal Societies in a Part of Himalaya. *Journal of Medicinal and Aromatic Plant Sciences*, 22(4A) & 23(1A): 528- 541.

Nayar, M.P. & Sastry, A.R.K, (1987). Red Data Book of Indian Plants. Vol. I-III. *Botanical Survey of India*, Calcutta.

Negi, K.S., Tewari, J.K., Gaurav, R.D. (1985). Economic Importance of Some Common Trees in Garhwal Himalaya– An Ethno-botanical Study. *Indian Journal of Forest*. pp. 276-289.

Pei, S.J. (2005). Ethno-botany and Modernization of Traditional Chinese Medicine: In Himalayan Medicinal and Aromatic Plants, Balancing, Use and Conservation. Ministry of Forest and Soil Conservation, HMG, Nepal.

Samant, S.S., (1993). Diversity Status of Plant in Nanda Devi Biosphere Reserve in Scientific and Ecological Expedition to Nanda Devi Report of Army Headquarters. New Delhi. pp. 54-85.

Samant, S.S., Dhar, U., Palini, L.M.S. (1998). Medicinal Plants of Himalaya: Diversity Distribution and Potential Value. Himvikas, Gyan Prakashan, Nainital. Vol. 13: 163-172.

Semwal, D.P., Saradhi, P.P., Kala, C.P., Sajwan, B.S. (2010). Medicinal Plant Used by Local Vedas in Uknimath Block, Uttarakhand. *Indian Journal of Traditional Knowledge*. Vol. 9: 480-485.

Sharma, K.V. (2000). Scientific Text in Sanskrit. Critical Trees Edition and Study. *Indian Journal of History and Science*.Vol. 8: 14-20.

Triphati, M. (1989). Thesis- Ecophysiology. Lab Department of Botany K.U, Almora.

Uniyal, M.R. (1997). Uttarakhand Vanaushadi Darshika CCRIMH, New-Delhi.

Uniyal, S. (2005). Traditional Knowledge on Medicinal Plants Among Rural Women of the Garhwal Himalaya, Uttaranchal. *Indian Journal of Traditional knowledge*: pp. 259-266.

WHO. (2000). General Guidelines for Methodologies on Research and Evaluation of Traditional Medicines. World Health Organization, Geneva.

Pages: 73-97

MEDICINAL PLANTS: *DISTRIBUTION, UTILIZATION AND SIGNIFICANCE*

Edited by: **Dr. Pankaj Sharma; Dr. Pawan Kumar 'Bharti'** and **Dr. Narayan Singh**

ISBN: 978-93-5056-734-0

Edition: **2015**

Published by: **Discovery Publishing House Pvt. Ltd., New Delhi (India)**

4

Cultivation and Conservation Implications of Some High Value Medicinal Plants of Himachal Pradesh

Usha Devi; Pankaj Sharma and **J.C. Rana**

INTRODUCTION

Mountain regions of world have rich assemblages of species (Fu *et al.* 2006; Nowak *et al.* 2011; Khan *et al.* 2013) and endemic plants (Myers *et al.* 2000; Halloy and Mark 2003; Kazakis *et al.* 2007; Khan 2012). This is mainly attributed to unique topography, diverse habitats, aspects and altitudinal ranges. Himalayan region, which is geo-dynamically consider as young mountain region and have been recognized as one of the globally important biodiversity hotspots (Singh 2006; Khan *et al.* 2013). Himalayas have enormous treasure of medicinal plants which continue to be an important therapeutic aid for alleviating ailments of humankind. These are primarily used in Ayurvedic, Unani, Homeopathic drugs in Indian Sub-continent. The indigenous knowledge about medicinal plants usually passed through words of mouths from one generation to the next or their descendants inherit the medico-spiritual manuscripts (Malik *et al.*, 2011). This is the oldest form of medical therapy that has survived in most countries till date. The part of

National Bureau of Plant Genetic Resources, Regional Station, Phagli, Shimla (HP) - 171 003, India.

Himalayan region occurring in India and popularly called Indian Himalayan Region (IHR) shares 15% of the India's geographical area and 25-30% endemic species (Singh and Hajra 1996; Phani Kumar *et al.* 2011).

The state of Himachal Pradesh occupying western region of IHR has around 3500 species of plants (Chowdhery and Wadhwa 1984; Aswal and Mehrotra 1994; Kaur and Sharma 2004; Singh and Sharma 2006). The forests of Himachal Pradesh in particular are the repositories of a large number of medicinal and aromatic plants due to the presence of varying types of climatic conditions ranging from tropical, subtropical, temperate and alpine, and provide raw materials for various kinds of drugs preparations and formulations. The high species richness and diverse community structure makes Himachal Pradesh one of the most fascinating reservoirs of floral diversity in the Himalaya (Aswal & Mehrotra, 1994).

Owing to its characteristic climate, geology and floristics, Himachal Pradesh becomes a distinct Himalayan territory. Some of the drugs yielding plants occurring in Himachal Pradesh are: *Achyranthes aspera, Aconitum heterophyllum, Acorus calamus, Aesculus indica, Angelica glauca, Berberis lyceum, Bergenia ciliata, Betula utilis, Boerhavia diffusa, Bombax ceiba, Cannabis sativa, Centella asiatica, Cynodon dactylon, Dactylorhiza hatagirea, Dicliptera bupleuroides, Ficus palmata, Ficus religiosa, Girardinia diversifolia, Heracleum candicans, Jasminum officinale, Juglans regia, Juniperus indica, Melia azedarach, Melothria heterophylla, Mentha longifolia, Mentha piperata, Mimosa pudica, Ocimum sanctum, Origanum vulgare, Oxalis corniculata, Papaver somniferum, Picrorhiza kurrooa, Pleurospermum brunonis, Phyllanthus emblica, Podophyllum hexandrum, Rhamnus virgata, Rheum australe, Rhododendron campanulatum, Ricinus communis, Roylea cinerea, Rubia cordifolia, Rubus ellepticus, Rumex nepalensis, Solanum surattense, Tagetes minuta, Taxus wallichiana, Urtica dioica, Valeriana jatamansi, Verbascum Thapsus, Withania somnifera*, etc. (Brandis 1879; Collet 1921; Chandersekar and Srivastva 2003; Chauhan 1999; Chowdhery & Wadhwa 1984; Kachroo *et al.* 1977; Negi 2005; Samant *et al.* 1998; Shabnam 1954; Uniyal 1979).

CONSERVATION IMPLICATIONS

Medicinal plant conservation refers to the management for human use of the biodiversity so that it may yield the greatest sustainable benefit to present generation while maintaining its potential to meet the needs and aspirations of future generations. Considering the threats on medicinal plant species, conservation has been the most important agenda of most *in situ* and *ex situ* programmes. But unfortunately the *in situ* conservation activities have been arrested in most of the protected areas due to unsustained utilization of forest resources.

Due to high rate of deforestation the natural habitats are disappearing rapidly, *ex situ* conservation of rare and endangered species in botanical gardens is gaining greater relevance as they contribute as the safest refuge to the preservation of gene pools of indigenous medicinal flora. Many important species that leads to drug discovery may be lost in the absence of proper documentation, cultivation and conservation initiatives. Therefore documentation of the medicinal plants, their cultivation techniques seems imperative. Keeping in view these needs, the cultivation techniques, harvesting, post harvest techniques etc. of few highly important medicinal species of Himachal Himalaya are mentioned here.

Aconitum heterophyllum Wall.

Family: Ranunculaceae

Local Name/Common name: Atish, Patish (H.P.)

Trade Name: Atis, Bonga, Ativisha. *Part Used:* Dried root & roots etc.

Flowering: May-Aug. *Fruiting:* Aug- Oct. *Status:* Endangered (Indian Himalaya Region)

Cultivation: Aconitum heterophyllum can be cultivated in hilly area ranging height 2000 to 3000 m.

Climate and Soil: This species can be cultivated in sandy loam and acidic soil which is best for seed germination, survival, better growth and yield. It requires cool and temperate climate. Proper water drainage and wet climatic conditions and humus rich soil is most suitable for its cultivation. It thrives best in places which have been used as halting bases for sheep and goats.

Field preparation and manuring: The land is ploughed 2-3 times and compost manure in ample quantity should be mixed in the soil. Approximately 75-80 qt. manure required for initial cultivation in one hectare land.

Nursery raising and planting: It is grown through seeds, tap roots and stem roots. Germination study of seeds of *Aconitum heterophyllum* can be undertaken at lower altitude in polyhouse as well as in open nursery beds. Seeds have to be sown during March-April in open beds above 2200m and inside polyhouse during November and December at lower altitude.

The seeds are sown in raised nursery beds in rows of about 0.9m deep in the soil by keeping 5 cm distance between two rows. In this procedure the seeds requirement per hectare will be 20 kg. The germination takes place after 25 days and completed within 40-45 days of sowing. In open nursery beds seed germination is very low as compare to polyhouse and laboratory condition. After 40-45 days when plants are 3-5 cm in height are to be transplanted in lines. The field should be well prepared and rich with compost manure. The distant should be 10-12cm between two plants and 30cm between two lines. During rainy season, water logging causes bolting of plants and black spot appear on leaves. To avoid this situation, raised beds with slight slope are prepared.

For vegetative propagation top tuber segment having innovation bud is more successful. Topmost segments are transplanted during November-

December in well-spaced rows, early in the following spring the determined bud of each root forms a flowering stem. Vegetative propagation is most successful for multiplication as well as for higher production within short period that cultivation through seedling. About 90,000 plants or 800gms seeds are needed for cultivation in one hectare land.

Manure, fertilizers and pesticides: The medicinal plants have to be grown without fertilizers and use of pesticides. Organic manure like vermicompost, green manure etc. may be used. Bio pesticides such as Neem extract (Kernel, Seeds, leaves) cow's wine, Datura etc. should be prepared to prevent diseases.

Irrigation and weeding: Initially regular watering is necessary to decrease the morality rate of seedlings. During monsoon period, watering is very rarely required. Irrigation requirement also depends on the texture of soil. Frequent watering is required once in 24 hours for 6 months old seedling particularly for plants which are grown at low altitude ranging from 1800-2200 m height. Weeding and hoeing is necessary during growth. During rainy season weeding is required at weekly interval and during winter at 15-25 days interval. During winter irrigation is needed once in a week to retain moisture.

Harvesting: The plant take at least 3 years for maturation when raised through seeds. In third year from plant sowing and after flowering the stem gets dry up and start falling on the ground. Tap roots should be harvested after the completion of reproductive phase and maturation of seeds during the month of October and November. However active content (atisine) and other alkaloids content were found maximum when plants harvested in July-August at the time of onset of flowering period. However, to get the maximum yield and seeds for multiplication, plants must be collected during October-November.

Post harvesting techniques: After harvesting, the roots are washed properly and old and new roots are separated and air dried. Oven and direct sun drying reduces the active contents of the roots. After drying the roots are packed in the gunny bags for marketing and store them securely in day old chambers.

Yield: The estimated yield is 1.22qt/ha. This value depends on mortality rate of plants.

***Angelica glauca* Edgew**

Family: Apiaceae. *Local/Common Name:* Chora, Charaka, Chura.

Trade name: Chora, Gandrayan and Himalayan Angelica. *Part Used:* Dried root & roots etc.

Flowering: June-July. *Fruiting:* Aug- Oct. *Status:* Endangered (Global).

Climate and Soil: The plant can be cultivated in the temperate, alpine and subalpine zone between 1800-3999 m. The plant prefers deep moist fertile soil, rich in organic matter and partial shade.

Propagation and Cultivation: The plant can be propagated through seeds and root cuttings. The land is ploughed till soil become smooth and pliant. Weeds and stones are removed and then vermicompost is mixed in the soil and ploughed to mix the vermicompost to the soil.

Seeds are sown in the raised nursery beds of size 5×10 m^2 in lines during November. After 45-50 germination take place. The seedling rose in nursery bed or polyhouse are transplanted in field during spring. The seeds need pre-chilling & sown before snow fall. Mulching of nursery beds with Pinus needles restore the moisture. The seeds which are sown during spring have low germination power. Vegetative propagation is done through cutting. The rhizome is cut into pieces having at least one or two buds and planted from April to September in well prepared raised beds. Around 9 cutting are required per square meters.

Irrigation and weeding: Regular weeding is required for proper growth and development. During dry season irrigation is done daily and during rainy & summer irrigation is done according to requirement. During winter season irrigation is done once in a week. Weeding and hoeing is done 2-3 times in a month during rainy season and one weeding is sufficient during winter. Water logging condition should be avoided which causes the decay of the roots. Cultivation of this species in high altitudes is generally free from invasion by the pests and insects but at low altitudes the plant is invaded by aphids and other insects and roots are attacked by fungi due to water logging condition. To avoid this condition pesticides are used and a well drainage system should be developed for rainy water.

Harvesting: The fruits mature during September–October and roots are harvested after the senescence of the seeds. The plants propagate through seeds are ready to harvested after 3 years and those propagated through cutting are harvested after two years. Seeds are collected during late September or early October. Seeds are stored in cool and dry condition.

Yield and post harvesting: After harvesting roots are washed and cuts into pieces and dried in partial shade and packed in Jute bags for marketing or store in dry place to avoid fungal attack. Approximately 9-10 quintal yield is obtained per acre (Chauhan 1999; Huxley 1992).

Artemisia maritima L.

Family: Asteraceae. *Local/common name:* Seinski, Nurcha.

Trade name: Santonin Plant. **Part used**: Young flowering top.

Flowering: May-July. **Fruiting:** Aug-Sept.

Soil and climate: The plant is xerophytic and can tolerate drought condition. This species can be cultivated in any type of soil but prefers well drained, slightly alkaline loamy soil of semi-arid climate and sunny position. Plants are more aromatic when they are grown in a poor dry soil.

Propagation and cultivation: The plant can be cultivated through seeds or root cuttings. Seeds are sown in month of March-April either by broadcast or in small drill. The seedlings are transplanted in field during June-July at a distance of 2 feet between plants. Propagation through root cutting is done in spring or autumn.

Irrigation and weeding: The plant require 2-3 weeding during the growth period, Herbicides can be used for weed control. Irrigation is done twice or thrice in a week till the plant is established.

Harvesting: The plant is harvested when bud has fully developed and just for opening. Harvesting is done from mid-summer to early autumn. During this period the plant contains maximum santonin. The crop is cut 30-60 cm above the ground-level tied in bundle and dried in the shade. After drying the leaves and flowers are separated from the stalks and stored in cool and dry place (Chauhan 1999; Huxley 1992).

***Bunium persicum* (Boiss.) Fedt.**

Family: Apiaceae. *Local Name/Common Name:* Kalazira, Umbu, Siahzira.

Trade Name: Kala Zira. *Part Used:* Fruits.

Flowering: May-June. *Fruiting:* June-July.

Climate and Soil: Sandy loam, moist and humus rich, well-drained soil, cold and humid condition is suitable for the cultivation of this species.

Field preparation and manuring: The land is ploughed 2-3 times and manure is mixed in the soil and ploughed again to mix the manure in the soil.

Propagation and Cultivation: Propagation is done with seeds and bulbs. Seeds need pre-chilling and sown during October-November before snowfall by broadcast in lines by keeping 45 cm distance between two rows. After sowing the soils is made plain with Pickaxe. Vegetative propagation is done by bulb during October-November.

Irrigation and Weeding: Irrigation is done regularly to decrease the mortality. During summer and dry day, irrigation is required daily and 2-3 times in a week in other season. 3-4 times weeding is required during May or June.

Harvesting: The plant is ready for harvesting after 3 years. Seeds are collected during September and November.

Post harvesting techniques and yield: The aerial part bearing seeds are harvested during September and November and dried in sun and seeds are separated by threshing and winnowing. The seeds are collected in bags and stored in cool and dry place.

***Carum carvi* L.**

Family: Apiaceae. *Local/Common name:* Shia Zira, Carvay, Shinguzira, Mawo, Dru.

Trade Name: Caraway, Kala Zira. *Part Used:* Seeds.

Flowering: June-July. *Fruiting:* July-August.

Cultivation aspects: Caraway is a well-known herb that has been cultivated for its culinary and medicinal uses since ancient time. It is native of Europe and West Asia. One marked peculiarity about Caraway is that it is indigenous to all parts of Europe, Siberia, Turkey, Persia, India and North Africa and yet it is cultivated only in a few, comparatively restricted areas. Its cultivation is restricted to relatively small areas in England, Holland, Germany, Finland, Russia, Norway and Morocco, where it constitutes one of the chief agricultural industries. In India the plant is now cultivated in Bihar, Orissa, Punjab, Bengal, Andhra Pradesh and in hills of Kumaon, Garhwal, Kashmir. In Himachal Pradesh the plant is cultivated in Pangi, Lahaul and Spiti, Kinnaur, Bharmaur and Bada Bangal in commercial scale (Chauhan 1999; Dhiman 1976; Khare 2007; Pullaiah 2002).

Climate and Soil: It requires dry temperature climate and plant prefers sandy loam, well drained, humus rich and moist soil in full sun or partial shade and tolerates a pH in the range 4.8-7.6. The plant grows in full sun are richer in essential oils and therefore more aromatic (Samant *et. al.*, 2008).

Field preparation and Manuring: For cultivation the land is well ploughed till soil becomes smooth and pliant and then properly mixed with organic matter. Farm yard manure is mixed with soil at the rate of 20 quintal per acre. (Dhiman, 1976; Samant, *et. al.*, 2008).

Propagation and Cultivation: The plant is cultivated through seeds. About 1.5-2 kg seed is required for cultivation in one acre of land. It is best sown *in-situ* as soon as it is ripe in late summer and early autumn (October). Seeds can also sown in March and April. Seeds are sown in row by keeping a distance 45 cm between two rows. Caraway often sown with other traditional crops (Chauhan 1999; Dhiman 976; Samant *et. al.*, 2008).

Irrigation and Weeding: The ground requires an occasional hoeing and weeding to keep it clean and assist the growth of the plants. Normally irrigation is not required. However, for good germination and growth periodic irrigation after 10 days is required.

Harvesting: Harvesting is done in the month of October when seeds are fully ripened. The plant is cut and Caraways are separated by threshing. They can be dried either on trays in the sun or by very gentle heat over a stove, shaking occasionally. The seeds can also be dried in partial shade. The seeds are then collected in bags and stored in cold and dry rooms. Seeds for cultivation are collected every year.

Post harvesting and yield: The dried seeds are stored in cotton bags and air tight containers and kept in cool and dry places. Approximately 5 qt/acre yield of seeds is obtained after one year (Dhiman 1976; Samant *et. al.*, 2008).

***Dactylorhiza hatagirea* (D. Don) Soo**

Family: Orchidaceae. *Local name/Common Name:* Panja, Hathagari, Salep Hathpanja, Aralu. *Trade name:* Salap, Salam panja, Punja. *Part Used:* The roots. *Flowering:* June-July. *Fruiting:* September-October. *Status:* Critically Endangered (Indian Himalayan Region)

Climate and Soil: The plants grow well in acidic and sandy loam soil rich with organic manure and moisture.

Cultivation and Propagation: The plant can be cultivated between 2000-4200 m. It can be propagated through seeds and division of the tuber having stem portions with bud. The seeds are minute and have low viability. Before sowing seeds are mixed with sand. Seeds for germination also require the association of Mycorrhiza. Seeds collected from its natural habitats, germinate best in soil. For vegetative propagation, small slices of tuber containing meristematic tissues are transplanted at a distance 30 cm and depth 5-7 cm. About 1,10,000 cutting are required for cultivation in one hectare land.

Irrigation and weeding: Irrigation is required daily in initial stage. In later stage, watering after 10 days gap is sufficient. Weeding is regularly required after 10 days in rainy seasons and summer. Monthly weeding is sufficient in other seasons.

Harvesting, Post harvesting and Yield: After 2 years tubers are ready to harvest. Tubers can be harvested every year if plant propagated through whole tuber. After harvesting old tubers are separated from young tubers and steeped in hot water for one hour. Outer membranes are removed and tubers are sun dried. Dried tubers are packed in small gunny bags and stored in dry rooms. 3.7 quintal tubers can be collected in one hectare if cultivated nearby villages of the natural habitat.

***Heracleum candicans* Wall**

Family: Apiaceae. *Local/Common Name:* Padara, Patrala. *Trade name:* Patishan roots, Patrali. *Part Used:* Roots. **Flowering**: June-July. *Fruiting:* September-October. *Status:* Endangered (Indian Himalaya Regions).

Climate and Soil: The plant can be cultivated between 2000-3500 m height from temperate to sub alpine climate. The plant prefers sandy loam to clay loam moist soil. It can also be easily cultivated in land having less fertile soil. The plant can also be cultivated in agriculture fields having sandy loam soil and in orchards having clay soil.

Field preparation and manuring: The land is deeply ploughed as it has branched root system, therefore require loose texture of soil for proliferation of roots. Approximately 20 tons per hectare forest humus is mixed in the soil. The plant requires proper drainage system.

Propagation and cultivation: These can be propagated through seeds and rhizome cuttings but vegetative propagation is not preferred due to high mortality rates due to decaying of roots and poor rooting. The seedlings are prepared in nursery beds as direct sowing has low germination. Seeds are sown in polybags or pots filled with soil and vermicompost as ratio 1:1 in the month of October and November. To enhance germination seeds are treated with sodium hypochlorite for 30 minutes before sowing. Germination starts within two weeks and completed in one and half month. The 4 month old seedlings are transplanted in the field. 2-3 kg seeds are required per hectare.

Irrigation and weeding: Initially watering is done daily, as the plant established watering is done 2 or 3 times in a week. Weeding and hoeing is done at least 3-4 times during rainy and summer season. In other season one weeding is sufficient in a month. Plant also requires well drainage system as water logging system damage the root system.

Harvesting: The roots are ready to harvesting after 3 years. The roots are harvested from September to November months. The roots which are collected during late autumn have been preferred as it contain high content of total coumarins.

Yield and Post Harvesting Techniques: After harvesting roots are washed properly under running tap water and cut into small pieces. These are then dried in partial sunlight for a month. After drying roots are kept in gunny bags and stored in dry condition. The yield is double when vermicompost is used as compare to by using Farm Yard Manure and forest humus. Approximately 9 tons per hectare roots are obtained by using vermicompost (Chauhan, 1999, and Samant *et al.*, 2008).

Humulus lupulus L.

Family: Cannabidaceae. *Local/common name:* Hop, Hops. *Status:* Cultivation. *Part used:* Strobiles. *Trade name:* Hop. *Flowering:* June-July. *Fruiting:* August-September.

Climate and Soil: Hops is adapted to a wide range of climatic conditions; ample moisture early followed by warm, dry weather is ideal. Although hops can tolerate quite a wide range of climate but for commercial importance they grow best in areas having mean temperature range 16-19 °C during summer season. Deep, humus rich loam, and well drained soils are ideal for the growth and cultivation of hops. Poorly drained, strongly alkaline or saline soils should be avoided. Hops plants can be grown on soils varying from sandy loam to clay loam in sunny area, though the hops can tolerate light shade. Plants can also succeed in dry shade soil, once established they are also somewhat drought tolerant.

Cultivation prospects: Hops are frequently cultivated, both commercially and on a domestic scale in temperate zones for their seed heads. Hops is one of the cash crops of dry temperate zone particularly Lahaul & Spiti. There are many named varieties. The varieties recommended for commercial cultivation in Himachal Pradesh are Late Cluster, Harmukhand Hybrid-2. Late Cluster has maximum alpha acid content (8 per cent) and is comparable with best varieties of Europe. This variety flowers very profusely.

Field preparation and manuring: The soil should be tilled to create a weed-free field prior to planting. Add full quantity of farm yard manure, phosphorus and potash in the soil at the time of land preparation. Approximately 25-30 tones/ha FYM is required. Apply half quantity of nitrogen in March-April and the rest half in June in circle around plants.

Propagation and cultivation: Hops plants are propagated both from seed as well as through vegetative methods (layering, strap cutting, soft wood cutting, under runners and lateral branches). Vegetative method of propagation is the general practice and seed is used only while breeding new varieties. Vegetative propagation is done from runners that arise from the crown just below the soil surface. The runners are cut into pieces 6 to 8 inches long each bearing at least two sets of buds. Cuttings should be planted immediately or if not, stored in a cool, moist, well ventilated place. Planting is preferably done in autumn before the soil becomes cool. This way, plants develop new roots giving the plants a good start in spring. The plants can also be planted during first fortnight of February; spacing of the plants should be 1 m and row to row 2 m. Thus, 4000-4500 plants are accommodated per hectare.

Training: A climbing plant, supporting itself by twining around the branches of other plants. The hops plants are trained in a number of ways but Worcester system of training is recommended. In this method of training, the hop plants are trained on wire net with the help of poles. The poles are erected in row in front of rows of hop plants. At the top of poles, hooks and screws are fixed. Parallel to each row, two wires are fixed with poles and hop vines are allowed to spread on it.

Pruning: When the vines reach the stringing wires, the lowest 4 ft of foliage and lateral branches are removed to aid in prevention of disease, especially downy mildew, and insect pests, particularly spider mites. The lower leaves are removed and stripping must be done carefully to avoid damaging the stem. Shoots arising from the crown are continually removed early in the season in order to promote the growth of the selected vines.

Weeding and irrigation: In areas where rainfall is lacking and the water table is more than 5 ft deep, irrigation may be required. The plants must be well watered during the entire length of the growing season for maximum growth. However, high rainfall during cone production is harmful. So dry temperature zone is the best suited for this crop. Generally, for beer making, the unfertilized seed heads are preferred and so most male plants are also weeded out. Weed control normally lasts 4 to 6 weeks or more. When weeds appear, weeding is done regularly.

Harvesting: Hops cones are harvested late in the summer or early in the fall when the cones ripen. Hop is in prime condition for picking for only 5 to 10 days. Flower initiation starts in June and by middle of July, the female inflorescence, commonly called burr, is formed. The cones mature from end of August to end of September. Hops cones can be picked by hand or mechanically. Most hop growers who harvest the crop mechanically use stationary picking machines. The vines are cut loose from the hill and the trellis wires about 4 ft from the ground. The cut vines are laced into "combs" mounted on a flatbed truck and transported to the picking machine, which strips the hop and most of the leaves from the vines. For craft uses, harvesting the cones must be done while the hops cones are still light green in color and in a raw state. This is because, ripened cones tend to crumble up and are difficult to preserve for such uses.

Post harvesting and Yield: The cones after harvesting are dried in kilns. Drying is complete at a temperature of 60-65 °C. Hop cones contain 80 per cent moisture. Use a hop kiln to dry, moisture brought down to 8-12 per cent. After well drying, the cones are packed in a plastic bag, in order to minimize exposure to oxygen. As much air as possible must be squeezed out of the bag before it is sealed, while crushing the hops in the process must be avoided. All storage of commercial hops is carried out under cold conditions, a refrigerator can also be used for this purpose, the hops must be protected from excessive exposure to atmospheric oxygen in the air. If you plan to store hops for periods of months, refrigeration is a very good idea. On an average, 3-year old plants yield 12-15 quintals green cones or 3-4 quintals dry cones. The price of female cones depends upon the alpha acid content present in them.

Plant Protection: Hops is also susceptible to attacks from plant eating spider mites and other insects like the flea beetles, the vine borers, and plant juice sucking aphid species. Insecticides and pesticides may need to be sprayed to control the disease and insects whenever necessary. If the infection from some types of fungus and viruses is too severe, the entire batch of plants may need to be destroyed and it may be necessary to start all over again in another location with different batch of plants. Disease problems can be minimized by selection of resistant varieties and removal of diseased plant tissues. Removing lower leaves on the vines at training time will help prevent the spread of disease and insect pests. Pruning should be performed with clean tools. Caution is advised to avoid damaging crowns during pruning and cultivation.

Hyoscyamus niger L.

Family: Solanaceae. *Local/common name:* Dipya, Parasikayavani, Khurasani ajwain, Tukhlang. *Trade name:* Khurasani ajwain, Henbane. *Status:* Endangered (State); Near Threatened (Indian Himalayan Region). *Part used:* Dried leaves and flowering tops, seeds. *Flowering:* April-July. *Fruiting:* Aug-Sept.

Soil and climate: Altitude ranges from 1200-3600 m is suitable for the cultivation of this species. Hyosyamus, being a foliage crop, require a light, moderate rich, well drained, fertile, porous, sandy loamy soil, rich in organic matter, for optimum growth. High temperature and high humidity also detrimental to this crop and also to their content of alkaloid. A soil pH range of 7-8.5 is preferred by the crop. The plant should be grown in bright sunlight for better growth of the plant.

Cultivation aspects: Henbane is in such a demand for medicinal purposes that it is necessary to cultivate, as adequate supply is not obtained from wild plants. In temperate areas they are raised only as summer crop, while in sub-tropical climates they are raised only in winters. It is a foliage crop and for high yield it requires a good soil, certain range of temperature, light and fertilizers besides timely agricultural operations such as weeding, hoeing and irrigation, approximately once in 20 days after weeding.

Field preparation and manuring: The land is ploughed twice to make soil porous and fine textured and FYM or vermicompost is required. About 15-20 tone FYM is required per hectare.

Fertilization application: Mineral fertilizers containing Ca, K, Mg, Na, N, P and S are applied either alone or in various combinations. Potassium lowers while N and P application (especially in combination with Ca and Mg) raise the alkaloid content in *H. niger*. In plants of high alkaloid content receiving N & P. NPK in the dozer of 150, 75 and 112.5 kg/ha have been recommended for increasing the yield.

Propagation: It is propagated through seeds either by sowing the seeds directly in the main field or by raising the seedling in the nursery and transplanting them. For direct sowing seeds around 2 kg/acre are required. The seeds are very small, hence they should be mixed with 10 kg of powdered soil or for better result with neem cake. Seed germination is increased through pre-sowing treatment of concentrated Sulphuric acid for one minute. After treatment, seeds are kept in cold water for a few minutes. The seeds must be sown not deeper than 2 to 2.5 cm below the soil for good germination. Seed germinate within a week. The plants are thinned out till they are about 50 cm apart in the rows. Best time for direct seedling of henbane is early October to February in sub-tropic areas while June and July are ideal in temperate and hilly regions, when rains have stopped.

The best time for raising nursery is September in the plains and April–May in temperate region. Henbane nursery requires well leveled sandy soil. It should be rich in humus and protected from rain or shower. Raised nursery beds exposed to sun shine is best seeds germinate. For nursery purpose about 1 to 1.25 kg seeds are required per acre. Seeds are sown in nursery at a distance of 15×15 cm and 0.5 cm depth. Germination takes place in about 8-10 days. A mulching with grass or dry fine leaves is helpful for proper germination. The soil of nursery should be well mixed with FYM and neem cake. For rapid growth spraying of urea on 20-23 days old sapling is helpful.

Transplanting: Seedlings (6-8 cm high) of henbane become ready for transplantation after about two months of sowing. Transplanting is done at desired spacing in well prepared field by light irrigation. The seedlings are transplanted at a spacing of 30-45 cm in rows and 15 cm from plant to plant in a well-prepared field and followed up with light irrigation. Before transfer of seedling their roots are dipped in 0.25% Bavistin solution for 40-45 minutes. In rainfed areas, plants are transplanted before rainy season. Transplanted seedling takes about a week to establish. Since there is a heavy mortality in the transplanted seedlings it is recommended that this crop should be grown on commercial scale only by direct sowing.

Irrigation: First irrigation should be given immediately after transplanting. Subsequent irrigations may be done at 8-10 days interval, until it is about a month old and, subsequently, the crop is irrigated at intervals of about 15-20 days. While in case of direct sowing first irrigation, as pre-sowing, the second one at an interval of 8 days, next followed by 10-12 days and remaining 3 at an interval of 15-18 days, are required.

Weeding: The crop raised by direct sowing should be thinner after a fortnight of germination and a spacing of 30 cm within the rows should be maintained. During summer and rainy seasons, weeding is done at least thrice in a month. Water logging should be avoided. Roots should not be damaged during transplantation.

Harvesting, Drying and Storage: Much of the efficiency of henbane depends upon the stage and time at which it is gathered. The leaves and flowering tops are collected at the flowering stage of the plant. The first leaf is collected late in summer and the second year at the time of flowering.

Post harvesting techniques and Yield: The herb is sun dried for 2-3 days followed of 6-7 days is shade with constant racking with sticks. 52° C temperature appears to be optimum for drying the leaves which may be raised to 60° C without damage. Drying can be accomplished in 30 hours without any damage to alkaloid contents. The fresh herb loses 80-86% of its weight on drying. Approximately 7-8 quintal leaves are obtained from one hectare and every 100 g of fresh leaves yield 14 g of dry leaves. The dried herb can be stored in gunny bags and kept in a cool dry place for about two months before further processing. The product should not be stored for more than 2 month.

Hyssopus officinalis L.

Family: Lamiaceae. *Local/Common name:* Hyssop, Juffa, Tengu. *Trade name:* Hyssop. *Part used:* Leaves and flowering tops. *Flowering:* June-July. *Fruiting:* Aug-Sept.

Climate and soil: Hyssopus succeeds best in light, loamy soil in a sunny position. This is a very cold hardy plant and during dormancy period can tolerate temperature down to about -20°C. They grow best in a warm aspect and in a light, rather dry soil.

Propagation and cultivation: The plant can be propagated through seeds and through division of stems, which arise from the common rootstock. Seeds are sown in early spring in nursery beds, either in a cold frame or in the open ground. The seed germination is quick and when they are large enough to handle, the seedling are transplanted in well-prepared field in summer. Vegetative propagation can be done by cutting in spring. The seedling developed through seeds, cutting and division, are transplanted in open field at a distance of 6 inch between two plants and 18 inch between rows. The plants grow best in partial shade. The plants should be watered till they are established.

Harvesting, Post harvesting techniques and yield: When the plant grows under optimal weather condition, Hyssop is harvested twice yearly, once at the end of spring and once at the beginning of the fall. The plant is cut along with stalk, and dried in a cool, dry, well ventilated areas, where the materials are mixed various times. Drying directly to sun is avoided as exposure to sun cause discoloration and oxidation. Once dried, the leaves and flowers are removed and chopped finely, and can be stored up to 18 months. The final dried material is 1/3 to the initial weight. Hyssopus yield is 2-3 tons of dry leaves per hectare under optimal weather condition (Biswas 2006; Chauhan 1999).

Inula racemosa **Hook. f.**

Family: Asteraceae. *Local/Common name:* Manu, Poshkar, Poshkarmul, Pushkar mool. *Part Used:* Fresh roots. *Status:* Cultivated. *Flowering:* July-Aug. *Fruiting:* Aug-Sept.

Climate and Soil: Temperate, sub-alpine and alpine climates are suitable for the growth of the plant. The species grows well in the average garden soil, but require sunny location. It prefers moist and pours soil for faster root growth. It can be cultivated in acid, neutral and basic soils.

Field preparation and manuring: For cultivation of manu, soil is deeply ploughed 2-5 times. Usually the fields are ploughed after the rain or after irrigation, stones, weeds are removed and fields are leveled and farm yard manure is mixed in the soil. About 20 quintal FYM is required in one acre of land.

Propagation and Cultivation: The plants are propagated through seeds and through root cuttings. Seeds are sown in spring or autumn in a cold frame. Seeds are very small and often difficult to sow in agricultural fields and also takes a long period to reach maturity. The propagation through root cuttings gives better performance in sprouting and survival percentage.

The root cuttings are planted in late autumn (October-November). During drought, root cuttings are stored in pits and sowing done in May. The root cuttings are sown by keeping distance of 20 to 25 cm between two cuttings and 7-8 cm deep in soil. These roots sprout in about 6 weeks.

Irrigation and Weeding: Moist and well-drained soil is essential for better growth of the plant and requires large quantity of water. In summer 4-5 times irrigation is required in a month. After germination 2-3 times weeding in a month is necessary.

Harvesting: The roots are dug after 3 years in September-October, when the flower heads start drying. However, in September the aerial parts are removed and the crop is left for one month. After harvesting fresh roots are cleaned, cut into small pieces. The roots used for propagation are stored in pits, covered with soil and the remaining roots are sun dried and packed in gunny bags for storage in dry chambers or marketed. Seeds for propagation are collected in September-October. After drying for two weeks in room temperature, seeds are stored at low temperature (Arora *et al.*, 1980; Chauhan, 1999; Samant *et al.*, 2008).

***Jurinea macrocephala* DC.**

Family: Asteraceae. *Local/Common name:* Guggal Dhoop. *Trade name:* Guggal Dhoop. *Part used:* Roots. *Status:* Endangered (Indian Himalaya region). *Flowering:* June-July. *Fruiting:* Aug-Sept.

Climate and soil: The plant can be cultivated between 2500-500 m height. The species prefers alpine and sub-alpine climate. The plant succeeds in sandy and porous soils in a sunny position (Dhiman, 1976; Huxley, 1992; and Samant et al., 2008).

Field preparation and manuring: The field is ploughed 2 or 3 times and raised beds are prepared to preventing water logging condition. Approximately 60-80 quintal manure is required for one acre land.

Propagation and cultivation: The plant is propagated through seeds and rootstock at collar level. The seed are sown at a distance of 30 cm in May and June. At high altitudes seed are sown before snow fall during October and November inside polyhouse and by the end of March, seedlings are transplanted. 33000 plants are transplanted in one acre land. Propagation through division of rootstock can be done in spring.

Irrigation and weeding: During the months of March, April and May, regular irrigation after two days interval is required. Weeding and loosening of soil is frequently required in early stage of plants growth. After the second year of growth, monthly weeding is sufficient.

Harvesting: The roots are ready for harvesting after 3 or 4 years. Harvesting is done during September and October. Seeds are collected during October for propagation. Post harvesting techniques and Yield: After harvesting roots are cut into pieces and dried in shade and packed in cotton bags for marketing. 5-6 quintal roots are obtained per acre after 3 or 4 years (Chauhan 1999; Dhiman 1976; Huxley 1992; Samant *et al.* 2008).

Nardostachys grandiflora DC.

Family: Valerianaceae. *Local/Common name:* Jatamansi, Mansi, Marchhi, Spikenard. *Trade name:* Balchharh. *Part used:* Rhizome. *Status:* Critically endangered (State), Endangered (Indian Himalayan Region). *Flowering:* July-Aug. *Fruiting:* Sept-Oct.

Climate and soil: The plants cultivated between 2000-4200 m. It requires sandy loam, acidic and humus rich soil and partially sunny areas.

Field preparation: The land is ploughed 2 or 3 times to make soil porous and fine and weeds, stone are removed. Above 20-25 tone FYM is mixed in soil per hectare.

Propagation and cultivation: The plant is propagated by cutting, division and seeds. Seeds are sown in November-December in open bed. Seedling are transplanting in well prepared field in June-July. Propagation through root cutting gives better than seeds. Cuttings are planted in May or October at 20×20 cm distance.

Irrigation and Weeding: During dry season, watering is must to decrease the mortality of plants and watering is done regularly in every two days. During rainy season watering is not required. Weeding is done weakly during first year of seedling. Twice in a month in second and third year.

Harvesting: The plant in ready for harvesting within 4 years. Harvesting is done during September-October. Plants which cultivated at low altitude harvested in August-September. Seeds for propagation are collected in late September and October and dried in shade and stored in cool dry place. Seeds are viable for very short period.

Yield, Post-harvesting techniques: After harvesting rhizomes are washed, dried in partial bags and store in dry cold area. About 6-7 quintal rhizome is obtained per hectare (Chauhan 1999; Samant *et. al.* 2008).

Picrorhiza kurrooa Royle ex-Benth.

Family: Scrophulariaceae. *Local/Common Name:* Kutki, Karru, Kadu. *Part Used:* Roots/Stolons. *Trade Name:* Kutki. *Status:* Endangered (Indian Himalaya Region). *Flowering:* May-July *Fruiting:* August-September.

Climate and Soil: The plant can be cultivated between 2200-4200m and prefers sub-alpine and alpine climate. Sandy alluvial soil with a thick layer of humus. Wet and humid climate is suitable for its cultivation.

Cultivation: The plant can be propagated through seeds and stolons. Fields with gentle slopes are suitable for Kutki cultivation. The fields are prepared after 3-4 deep ploughing. Decomposed FYM or forest humus is the roughly mixed with the soil. Manuring is done during the winter or before transplanting. Seeds are minute, therefore mixed with sand before sowing. The seeds are sown in the months of April-May in open beds and in November-December in polyhouse. The seeds are sown in nursery beds in regular row. 250 gms seeds are required per hectare. Seedlings grown in nursery should be transplanted during May or august. Vegetative propagation through stolons is more successful. Rooting can be increased following water dip treatment for 48 hours. About 1,08,000 plants are required for one hectare land.

Irrigation and weeding: Regular irrigation is required every 24 hours in the initial stage. During winter watering should be done every two days. Weeding and loosening of soil is necessary. Weekly weeding is required during the summer and rainy season.

Harvesting: The crop gets matured in the fourth year. The roots are to be up-rooted from the land in the months of September-October. The roots are to be dried at room temperature and then filled them in the hermetic containers or jute bags marketing and for safe storage in dry places.

Yield: 30-38 quintal of roots and 5 kgs of seeds per hectare can be derived from good crop.

***Podophyllum hexandrum* Royle.**

Family: Podophyllaceae. *Local/Common name:* Bankakri, Bankakar, Kandari-mokri, Rikhpat, Papra, Papri. *Trade Name:* Bankari, Indian Podophyllum. *Status:* Endanged (Indian Himalaya Region). *Flowering:* May-June. *Fruiting:* June-July. *Part Used:* The rhizome and the roots.

Cultivation aspects: Bankakri grows wild in temperate and subalpine regions. In India and most of the commercial supplies are met from wild sources. Due to over exploitation, the species has now become rare in its original habitat. It appears that no serious efforts have been made to cultivate this important medicinal crop on large scale anywhere. However, some reports are available wherein cultivation on small scale has been reported. In Himachal Pradesh the plant is cultivated in Dalhousie, Chamba, Kullu, Siraj, Kotgarh, Kinnaur, Rohru (Chauhan 1999).

Climate and Soil: The plant can be cultivated in sub-alpine and alpine climate ranging height between 2100-3000m with cold winter and mild summer. The plant flourish well in soil rich with humus and decayed organic matter in its natural habitat. The plant loves moist and shady localities. It is generally associated with the species of *Rhododendron, Salix* and *Juniper* but it is also found within open alpine meadows where its occurrence is less frequent. The plant prefers medium or light medium loam, fertile, well drained soils for its cultivation.

Field preparation and manuring: The land may be ploughed well two to three times until a fine tilth of the soil obtained. Need, stones and gravels are removed. About 6-10 tons/hectare farm yard manure or forest humus is mixed with the soil. Requirement of manure is less during second and third years.

Propagation and cultivation: It can be cultivated through seeds and vegetatively from rhizome splits. Rhizome cutting are preferred as seed germination is poor.

The seeds have a dormancy period of about one to two years. They may even fail to germinate if sown without the pulp. Before sowing seeds are soaked in hot water or treating with sodium Hypochloride for 30 minutes before sowing. Seeds kept in the solution of cow dung for 48 hours give better result in germination. The seeds may be sown in October inside polyhouse in polybags at a distance of 15cm and 1cm depth. They germinate in 7-10 months and the percentage of germination will be from 42 to 45.5%. The seedlings are transplanted into the field when they are 6-10cm tall. The crop raised from seedling usually takes a number of years to produce four sized at marketable rhizomes.

Propagation through rhizome cutting picks up fast growth and development. Rhizome cutting of 1-3cm in length and bearing leafy buds gives the best result. Before planting rhizome cutting are treated with IBA (10µm) for 24 hours. Transplantation is done during May-June at a distant 15-20 × 30-35cm or 30 × 30 cm. However, their growth was slow and took 4-6 years to produce rhizome suitable for exploitation.

Irrigation and weeding: Regular irrigation is required in the initial stage. During the winter 2-3 times irrigation is required in a week weeding and hoeing may be done as and when necessary. During rainy seasons and summer weeding should be frequent and in winter season once in a month is required.

Harvesting and packing: The rhizome of this plant is very slow growing; usually it takes 5-6 years through seeds and 3-4 years through rhizome cutting. The yield of rhizomes and root is reported to be high if the crop is harvested 5 or 6 years after planting. During winter the underground rhizome remain dormant and produce aerial shoot in April or May. During summer that short bear flowers and fruits and die down in November. Usually the rhizomes having 3-5 aerial shoots are considered suitable for harvesting. The rhizomes and roots are dug up in spring or autumn. The rhizomes harvested in spring (May) have a higher resin content than those obtained in autumn (November). Freshly harvested rhizomes contain large quantities of active principles which are lost on prolonged storage. After harvesting roots and rhizomes are washed with running tap water and then cut into small pieces and kept in the sun. After drying kept in gunny bags and store at cool and dry place or sold in the market. The yield of dried rhizomes and roots is 4 tons per hectare.

Rheum australe D. Don

Family: Polygonaceae. *Local/common name:* Chunkri, Gandhini, Revandcheni, Archha, Rhubarb. *Trade name:* Revandcheni. *Part used:* Root and rhizome. *Status:* Endangered (Global). *Flowering:* June-July. *Fruiting:* Aug-Sept.

Climate and soil: Rheum australe usually grow in sub-alpine and alpine climate. It can be cultivated between 2000-3500m height. The plant is drought resistance. Plant can be grown in quite coarse grass which can be cut annually in the autumn. The plant requires deep fertile, moderately heavy, humus rich, moisture retentive, well-drained soil in sun or semi-shade. The plant can grow well in heavy clay soils.

Field preparation and manuring: The land is ploughed deeply 2-3 times. The rotten manure or forest manure or FYM is mixed in the soil. About 20 quintal FYM is required for one hectare.

Propagation and cultivation: The plant can be propagated through seeds and rhizome cutting. Seeds are sown in autumn during October-November in polyhouse and in spring during April-May in open bed. Direct sowing of seed in field is preferred because the mortality rate of transplantation is high. Seedlings raised in Nursery bed are transplanted in field during April-May. Germination is immediate, and no cold stratification is required. Ariel portions wither during winters and die off and regenerate during spring. 6-7 kg seeds are needed for one hectare land. Vegetative propagation through cutting is done in early spring or autumn. Rhizome top are cut into pieces with a sharp knife making sure that there is at least one growth bud on each division.

Irrigation and weeding: Initially regular watering is necessary for establishment of roots. Irrigation is done 2-3 times in a week, during winter watering is not required. 3-times weeding and loosening of soil is essential during rainy season and summer. One time weeding is sufficient in other seasons.

Harvesting: Harvesting of root and rhizome is done during September. Roots and rhizomes are dug after 3-4 years if propagated through seeds and after 1-2 years when crop is produced through rhizome cutting Rhizome and roots are dug up from 3-10 years old plants.

Post harvesting techniques and Yield: The dugout rhizome and roots are washed with running tap water and cut into pieces of proper size and dried in partial shade. After drying they are kept in gunny bags and stored in cool and dry place. Approximately 9-10 tone roots and rhizome are obtained after 3 years (Chauhan 1999; Huxley 1992; Samant *et. al.*, 2008).

Saussurea costus (Roxb.) Buch.-Ham. ex C.B. Clarke

Family: Asteraceae. *Local/Common name:* Kuth, Kushtha, Pachak, Kooth, Kuste, Costus. *Trade Name:* Kuth. *Part Used:* Roots. *Flowering:* May-July. *Fruiting:* July-Aug. *Status:* Critically Endangered (Global).

Cultivation aspects: Saussurea costus grows commonly on the lower slopes of the Himalaya and in Kashmir Valley. In Himachal Pradesh the plant is cultivated in Lahaul valley in commercial scale. This critically endangered medicinal plant is enlisted in Appendix I of CITES (Convention on International Trade in Endangered Species of Wild Fauna and Flora) and is among the Himalayan endangered medicinal and aromatic herbs (Anonymous 1973; Nayar and Shastry, 1987, 1988, 1990). Due to a resource base bottleneck, the ministry of commerce, government of India, has prohibited export of this plant, either in crude form or in processed products that could be separated (Anonymous 2000). Prior to the 1920s, natural habitats were the exclusive sources of its extraction for pharmaceutical uses. As the commercial requirement increased, some innovative farmers of the Lahaul valley simultaneously started its large scale cultivation.

Climate and Soil: The species requires a cool and humid condition. However, when supported with adequate irrigation, this species also thrives well in areas of cold desert having dry temperate agro climatic condition. The area, where the blast of the monsoon is heavy, should be avoided. Sandy, alluvial, porous, well drained soils with a lot of carbonic materials and good depth are suitable for vigorous development of roots (Chauhan 1999; Samant *et al.* 2008).

Field preparation and manuring: The field is deeply ploughed 2-3 times and farm yard manure is mixed in the soil. About 15 tones FYM is required for one hectare.

Propagation and cultivation: Kuth can be propagated through seeds and root cuttings. Propagation through seed is common. Seed viability decrease after 1 year of storage. Nursery bed of 10□10 ft size are prepared and seeds are sown at a distance of 30 cm in the month of April and October. The requirement of seeds per hectare is 3.5-4 kg or about 50,000 seedling required per hectare. The plants prepared in nursery should be transplanted in the field after 6-9 months growth. The distance between two plants should be 3 and 4 ft between two rows. This species could also be propagated vegetatively, through planting a 2-3cm long root collar zone. However, farmers in the cold desert areas of the Lahaul valley generally propagated through seeds. Vegetative propagation through root cutting gives early yield than seeds.

Irrigation and weeding: Watering is required every day in initial stage and after one year little irrigation is required. Weeding is required 3-4 time in month during summer and rainy season. Generally 2-3 weeding and loosening of soil is necessary for better production.

Harvesting: The crop gets ready in 3 years. Harvesting is done after seed maturation during late September and October. The plant raised through root cuttings becomes mature in 1-2 years. For high yield and quality, roots should be harvested immediately after seed maturation. The fruits are harvested in September or October and sun dried for a week before threshing. Seeds are segregated from the fruits and air dried for 1-2 weeks and stored under low temperature (4° C).

Post harvesting techniques and yield: The roots should be washed with running tap water after removing from the farm. The roots are cut into pieces and dried in partial shade. After drying roots are packed in gunny bags for storage or marketed. The yield derived from a good crop is 30 to 40 quintals of roots and 25 kgs of seeds per hectare.

***Swertia chirayita* (Rox. ex Flem.) Karsten**

Family: Gentianaceae. *Local/Common name:* Chirayata. *Trade name:* Chirayata. *Part used:* Whole plant. **Flowering:** July-Sept. *Fruiting:* Oct-Nov. *Status:* Critically Endangered.

Climate and soil: The plant can be grown above 1600 to 3000 m height. The plant prefer loamy or clay loamy soil, moist, humus rich, with good drainage, and slightly acidic soil. The plant can grow best in areas with cool summer. A partial shade moist atmosphere is ideal for its cultivation. The land is ploughed 2 times to make the soil porous, mixed with 15 quintal Farm Yard Manure and 40 kg neem cake per hectare.

Propagation and cultivation: The crop is cultivated by means of seeds. The crop can be cultivated by direct sowing or through nursery. Approximately 800 gm seed is sufficient for one acre. Seeds are sown in spring or autumn. The seeds are mixed with 12 kg of neem cake or Farm Yard Manure or soil and sown in rows by keeping 40 cm difference between two rows. Seeds are sown in burnt soil for high germination. The seeds germinate in 5-10 days. Seedling are sprayed with urea (2 gm/liter) dissolved in water which boost the growth of seedling. Seedlings are raised during the autumn become ready for harvesting during summer. Seedling can also develop in nursery beds, however seed germination is very poor in nursery beds. The nursery can be prepared in the month of October-November and March-April. Raised bed of 3×1 m size are prepared. Each bed is mixed with 3 kg Farm Yard Manure and 500 gm neem cake. The seeds are sown in line that are 15 cm apart and watering is done daily. After 40-45 days seedling are ready for transplanting. The seedling is transferred in the main field and transplanting in line by keeping a distance 30 cm within lines and 15 cm between two plants.

Irrigation and weeding: The crop needs moist atmosphere and is very sensitive to frost and snowfall thus needs special car when planted during winter. In early stage plant require frequent irrigation to keep the soil moist. During first two months, crop growth is slow, hence 2-3 weeding are necessary.

Harvesting: The plant is harvested after fruits maturation during October-November. The species flower within 6-8 month of sowing. The plants are pulled out along roots and soil attached to roots are cleaned. Some portion of crop is left in the field for seed purpose. Fruits are collected during October-December and dried in shade for 10 days, threshed and seeds are segregated. Seeds are dried and kept in air tight container. Cultivation of this species is very useful as the plant is harvested every year.

Post harvesting techniques and Yield: The stem and roots are dried and divided into small pieces and kept in air tight containers. 4-6 quintal herb obtained in one acre (Chauhan 1999; Samant *et. al.*, 2008).

***Thymus serphyllum* L.**

Family: Lamiaceae nom. alt. Labiatae. *Local name/Common name:* Banajwain, Lepto, Masho, Wild thyme. *Part used:* Whole plant. *Flowering:* April-July. *Fruiting:* Aug-Sept.

Climate and soil: The plant can grow in any soil, but well drained, fertile and calcareous soil in sunny portion is preferred for good growth and for good oil content. The plant succeeds in dry soils. Thyme dislikes wet conditions especially in the winter. On heavy, wet soils the aroma of the leaves will be less and the plant may soon dry up. It can grow best in warm climate. It can grow both in hills and plains.

Field preparation and manuring: The field is ploughed repeatedly until a fine tilth is not obtained and land is divided into plots of convenient size. The field is manure with Farm Yard Manure in autumn or winter and by nitrates in spring.

Cultivation and propagation: Thyme can be propagated by seeds, root cuttings. Seeds are sown in March or April in well prepared nurseries beds or directly in broadcast. Fine soil is preferred for the nursery because the seedlings are very small and remain inconspicuous for several weeks after germination. Seeds can be sown in autumn in polyhouse. When seeds are sown directly, they can be sown in rows about 90 cm apart and after germination the seedling may be thinned out to 30-45 cm apart and 60 cm between rows. Root cutting and nursery plants are planted 60 cm apart and 30-45 cm between rows. 50-60 g seeds are required per hectare.

Irrigation and weeding: Initially watering is necessary for proper growth, but once the plant established it can withstand in drought and frost equally. Weeding is done at regular interval to encourage the good growth of plants.

Harvesting and Yield: The leaves and flowers are harvested five months after sowing and planting. The leaves and flower are dried in the shade and stored in airtight containers to prevent loss of flavour. The dried shoots are powdered and packed. 1100-2200 kg dry herb is obtained per hectare. The oil is distilled from the fresh flowering tops by steams distillation. 21 kg oil is recovered after distillation per hectare (Chauhan 1999; Huxley 1992)

***Valeriana Jatamansi* Jones**

Family: Valerianaceae. *Local/Common name:* Niham, Tagar, Sungandhbala, Mushkbala, Naknihani. *Trade name:* Tagart, Tagargamt, Sameda, Sungadhwala.

Part used: Roots and rhizome. *Flowering:* March-May. *Fruiting:* June-Aug. *Status:* Vulnerable (Indian Himalaya Region).

Climate and soil: The plant is cultivated between 1500-3000 m height. The plant can grow in all types of soils but prefer sandy loam, humus rich soil.

Field preparation and manuring: The land is ploughed for 2 or 3 times. Approximately 30-35 tone FYM is required per hectare.

Propagation and cultivation: The plant can be propagated through seeds and rhizome cutting. Propagation through seeds is done in March-April. Seedling are ready for transplanting in 2-3 months and transplanting is done from June-October by keeping distance 30×30 cm. Vegetative propagation through rhizome cutting is done in October or March-April. Vegetative cultivation is more successful seeds. 800-1000 g seeds are required for one hectare and approximately 1 lakh plants are required per hectare.

Irrigation ad weeding: Irrigation is done according to requirement. Water logging condition should be avoided during seedling germination. During rainy season and summer, weeding is done 3 times/month and in remaining season one weeding in a month is sufficient

Harvesting: The plants are ready for harvesting after 3 year when plant propagated through roots and rhizome and harvested after 3-4 years when plant propagated through seeds. The roots are harvested in month of September-October. Seed for propagation are collected during May-June.

Post harvesting technique and Yield: After harvesting roots and rhizome are washed and dried in shade. After drying roots are packed in gunny bags for marketing or storage. 10-12 quintal roots are obtained per hectare. The roots and rhizome are stored in cool, dry and airy place (Chauhan 1999; Dhiman 1976; Samant *et. al.* 2008).

CULTIVATION ISSUES AND CONCERNS

Cultivation provides only a very small percent of medicinal plants as large proportion of the total consumption of medicinal plants are harvested from the wild. The difficulties experienced in the collection of plants from forest and the problems encountered therein together with heavy demand of medicinal plants necessitates the domestication of medicinal plants. In the present scenario end user industries are dominating the cultivation of medicinal plants at present. They go for cheaper alternatives in order to have a grip in price of medicinal plants. This is perhaps the most important limiting factor for large-scale cultivation of medicinal plants. Increasing interest by multinational pharmaceutical companies and domestic manufacturers of herbal-based medicines is contributing significant economic growth of the global medicinal plants sector. The cultivation is becoming both profitable and environmentally friendly as increasing interest by pharmaceutical companies and domestic manufacturers of herbal-based medicines is contributing significant economic growth of the global medicinal plants sector. But the Governments and Research institutions should prioritize the conservation and domestication of important medicinal plants prior to labeling these as important natural wealth for trade. If it does not happen soon chances are that in near future majority of Medicinal Plants will be lost forever.

REFERENCES

Arora, R.K., Maheshwari, M.L., Chandel, K.P.S. and Gupta, R. 1980. Mano *(Inula racemosa)*: Little Known Aromatic Plant of Lahul Valley, India. *Eco. Bot.* 34(2): 175-180.

Aswal, B.S. and Mehrotra, B.N. 1994. *Flora of Lahaul Spiti* (A Cold Desert in North-West Himalaya). Bishen Singh Mahendra Pal Singh, Dehradun, India. 761 pp.

Bown, D. 1995. *Encyclopaedia of Herbs and Their Uses.* Dorling Kindersley, London. ISBN 0-7513-020-31.

Brandis, D. 1879. *Vegetation and Country from Narkanda to Pangi,* Government Central Branch Press, Simla.

Chandra Sekar, K. & Srivastava, S.K. 2003. Ethnomedicinal Studies in Pin Valley National Park, Lahaul–Spiti, Himachal Pradesh. *Ethnobotany* 15: 44-47.

Chauhan, N.S. 1999. *Medicinal and Aromatic Plants of Himachal Pradesh.* Indus Publishing Co., New Delhi. 632 p.

Chowdhery, H.J. and Wadhwa, B.M. 1984. *Flora of Himachal Pradesh.* 3 Volumes. Flora of India Series 2. Botanical Survey of India, Howrah, Calcutta. 860 pp.

Collett, H. 1902, 1921. *Flora Simlensis,* A Handbook of Flowering Plants of Simla & the Neighbourhood. Thacker, Spink and Co., London, 2nd edition by Thacker, Spink and Co., Calcutta and Simla, 652 pp. (Reprinted Many Times by Bishen Singh, Mahendra Pal Singh, Dehradun, India). Chopra, R.N., Nayar, S. L. and Chopra,I. C., *Glossary of Indian Medicinal Plants,* CSIR, New Delhi, 1986.

Dhiman, D.R. 1976. *Himachal Pradesh Ki Vanoshdhi Sampada.* Imperial Printing Press, K.B. Dharmshala, (H.P.).

Fu, C., Hua X; Li, J., Chang, Z., Pu. Z., & Chen, J. 2006. Elevational Patterns of Frog Species Richness and Endemic Richness in the Hengduan Mountains, China: Geometric Constraints, Area and Climate Effects. *Ecography* 29: 919-927.

Halloy, S.R.P. and A.F. Mark. 2003. Climate-change Effects on Alpine Plant Biodiversity: A NewZealand Perspective on Quantifying the Threat. *Arctic, Antarctic and Alpine Research* 35: 248-254.

Huxley, A. 1992. *The New RHS Dictionary of Gardening.*MacMillan Press 1992 ISBN 0-333-47494-5.

Kachroo, P., Sapru, B.L. & Dhar, U. 1977. *Flora of Ladakh,* Bishen Singh and Mahendra Pal Singh. Dehradun.172 p.

Kaur, H. & Sharma, M.. 2004. *Flora of Sirmaur, Himachal Pradesh.* Dehradun: Bishen Singh Mahinder Pal Singh.

Kazakis, G., Ghosn, D., Vogiatzakis, I.N. & Papanastasis V.P. 2007. Vascular Plant Diversity and Climate Change in the Alpine Zone of the Lefka Ori, Crete. *Biodiversity and Conservation* 16: 1603-1615.

Khan, S.M. 2012. *Plant Communities and Vegetation Ecosystem Services in the Naran Valley, Western Himalaya.* Ph.D. Thesis, University of Leicester.

Khan, S.M., Page, S.E., Ahmad H., & Harper D.M. 2013. Sustainable Utilization and Conservation of Plant Biodiversity in Montane Ecosystems: The Western Himalayas as a Case Study. *Annals of Botany* 112(3): 479-501.

Khare, C.P. 2007. Indian Medicinal Plants – An Illustrated Dictionary. Springer (India), Private Limited. 812 pp.

Malik, A.H., Khuroo, A.A., Dar, G.H., Khan, Z.S. 2011. Ethnomedicinal Uses of some Plants in the Kashmir Himalaya. Ind J Trad Knowl. 10(2): 362-366.

Myers, N., Mittermeler, R.A., Mittermeler, C.G. Da Fonseca, G.A.B., & Kent, J. 2000. Biodiversity Hotspots for Conservation Priorities. *Nature* 403: 853-858.

Negi, V. 2005. *Studies on Diversity of Medicinal and Aromatic Plants of Sangla Valley in Himachal Pradesh*. M.Sc. Thesis, Department of Forest Products, Dr. Y.S. Parmar University of Horticulture and Forestry, Nauni, Solan, H.P. India, 197 p.

Nowak, A., Nowak, S., & Nobis M. 2011. Distribution Patterns, Ecological Characteristic and Conservation Status of Endemic Plants of Tadzhikistan– A Global Hotspot of Diversity. *Journal for Nature Conservation* 19: 296-305.

Phani, K., Gupta, S., Pal M.M. & Singh, S.B. 2009. Ethnobotanical Studies of Nubra Valley - A Cold Arid Zone of Himalaya. *Ethnobotanical Leaflets* 13: 752-65.

Pullaiah, T. 2002. Medicinal Plants in India. Regency Publications, New Delhi. 2 Vols. Ltd. London, 192 pp.

Samant, S.S., Butola, J.S. & Lal, M. 2008. Agrotechniques of the Commercially Viable Medicinal Plants in the Indian Himalayan Region. GBPIHED, Himachal Unit, Mohal-Kullu.

Shabnam, S.R. 1954. Medicinal Plants of Chamba. *Indian Forester* 90: 50-63.

Singh, D.K. & Hajra, P.K. 1996. *Floristic Diversity*; p. 23-38. *In*: Gujral, G.S. and Sharma, V. (eds). *Changing Perspectives of Biodiversity Status in the Himalaya*. New Delhi: British Council.

Singh, H. & Sharma, M. 2006. *Flora of Chamba District (Himachal Pradesh)*. Dehradun: Bishen Singh Mahinder Pal Singh.

Singh, J.S. 2006. Sustainable Development of Indian Himalayan Region: Linking Ecological and Economic Concerns. *Current Science* 90(6): 784-788.

Uniyal, M.R. & Chauhan, N.S. 1979. *A Preliminary Study of the Indigenous Drugs Used at the Tibetan Medical Centre Dharmshala, HP*. Nagarjun 22(8): 190-193.

Pages: 98-112

MEDICINAL PLANTS: *DISTRIBUTION, UTILIZATION AND SIGNIFICANCE*

Edited by: **Dr. Pankaj Sharma; Dr. Pawan Kumar 'Bharti'** and **Dr. Narayan Singh**

ISBN: 978-93-5056-734-0

Edition: **2015**

Published by: **Discovery Publishing House Pvt. Ltd., New Delhi (India)**

5

Diversity, Uses and Prioritization of Medicinal Plants in Kais Wildlife Sanctuary, North Western Himalaya, India

Manohar Lal and **S.S. Samant**

ABSTRACT

Fossil records date, human use of plants as medicines at least to the Middle Paleolithic age some 60,000 years ago. Out of the total 4, 22, 000 flowering plants reported from the world, >50,000 are used for medicinal purposes. The Indian Himalayan Region is one of the most astonishing physical features on the surface of the earth for its diverse landscapes and aesthetic, cultural and biological values. The richness accompanied with uniqueness, sensitivity and use value make the biological resources of the region important from different angles. The resources are used by the inhabitants for various purposes such as fodder, fuel, timber, medicinal, wild edible *etc.* Utilization of plants for medicinal purposes in India has been documented long back in ancient literature. With the increasing human population, demand of the biological resources is also increasing, leading to loss of biodiversity.

G.B. Pant Institute of Himalayan Environment and Development, Himachal Unit, Mohal-Kullu - 175 126, Himachal Pradesh, (India).

The present study was conducted in Kais Wildlife Sanctuary. The Kais Wildlife Sanctuary (31°59.684'-32°03.558'N Lat. & 77°09.092'-77°12.723'E Long.; area: 14.19km^2; altitudinal range 2000-3850m) is one of the notified Wildlife Sanctuaries of Himachal Pradesh. Total of 277 medicinal plants belonging to 187 genera and 80 families have been recorded. Of these, 35 families were monotypic. 142 species were native to Himalayan Region; 98 near-endemic and 5 species endemic to the IHR. Amongst the medicinal plants, 30 species were identified as Critically Endangered, 16 species as Endangered, 7 species as Vulnerable, and 43 species as Near Threatened for the Kais Wildlife Sanctuary.

Population assessment of these species using standard ecological methods and notification of Medicinal Plants Rich Areas as Medicinal Plants Conservation Area's (MPCAs) for the in-situ conservation with the involvement of Forest Department and local inhabitants. In addition, for the ex-situ conservation of these species, mass multiplication using conventional (through vegetative and seeds) and in-vitro methods are urgently required. Establishment and maintenance of Herbal Gardens and Medicinal Plants Nurseries for ensuring the availability of quality planting material for cultivation. Further, education and awareness programme are essentially required for the motivation of different stakeholders for large scale cultivation of medicinal plants.

Key words: Medicinal plants, diversity, native, endemic, rarity, Kais Wildlife Sanctuary.

INTRODUCTION

Fossil records date, human use of plants as medicines at least to the Middle Paleolithic age some 60,000 years ago. However, the value of these systems is much more than a significant anthropologic or archeologic fact. Their value is as a methodology of medicinal agents, which, according to the World Health Organization (WHO), almost 65% of the world's populations have incorporated into their primary modality of health care. Out of the total 4,22,000 flowering plants reported from the world, >50,000 are used for medicinal purposes. The Himalayan Region has been identified as one of the richest habitats for medicinal plants. The loss of biological diversity in the world's forests has experienced a colossal depletion in the recent past. The International Union for Conservation of Nature and Natural Resources (IUCN) has estimated about 10% of the vascular plants totaling to about 20,000-25,000 species are varying degree of threats and nearly 25% of the floral species in the world may become extinct within the next 50 years (Schemske et al., 1994). In India, more than 43% of the total flowering plants are reported to be of medicinal importance. Utilization of plants for medicinal purposes in India has been documented long back in ancient literature. However, organized studies in this direction were initiated in 1956 and off late such studies are gaining recognition and popularity due to loss of traditional knowledge and declining plant population. In the Indian Himalayan Region, 1748 species of medicinal plants have been recorded (Samant *et al.*, 1998). Out of the total 3500 flowering plants reported from the Himachal Pradesh, more than 643 species are used for medicinal purpose (Samant *et al.*, 2007a). With the increasing world demand and renewed global interest in traditional ethnopharmacy coupled with the increasing preference for natural substances in the health care system, the natural stock of medicinal plants of Indian Himalayan Region (IHR) is under tremendous pressure. Overexploitation and habitat degradation of the species have resulted the rapid depletion of the population of most of the commercially viable species.

A large number of studies on medicinal plants have been carried out in the IHR (Jain, 1991; Samant *et al.*, 1998, 2001; Samant and Pal, 2003; Rai *et al.*, 2000). In Himachal Pradesh, such studies are fragmentary and mainly focused on inventory (Bhattacharya and Uniyal, 1982; Chauhan, 1988, 1999; Badola, 2001; Badola and Pal, 2003; Kala, 2003, Kapahi, 1990; Sood *et al.*, 2001; Kala, 2006; etc.) except a few studies which deals with diversity, distribution patterns, nativity, endemism, rarity and conservation prioritization of medicinal plants (Samant *et al.*, 2007a, b). Such integrated study on medicinal plants in The Kais Wildlife Sanctuary is first attempt and it's key to management action plan of the Sanctuary. Therefore, the present attempt has been made to study diversity, distribution patterns, indigenous uses, nativity, endemism, rarity and prioritization of medicinal plants for conservation.

MATERIALS AND METHOD

Study Area

The present study has been carried out in Kais Wildlife Sanctuary of the Himachal Pradesh. The KWLS lies between 31°59.684′ to 32°03.558′ N Latitudes and 77°09.092′ to 77°12.723′ E Longitudes located in Pir-Panjal mountain ranges of Lesser Himalaya of Kullu District in Himachal Pradesh. Notified on February 26, 1954 under the Punjab Birds and Wild Animals Protection Act, 1933 and covers 14.19 km^2 area with an altitudinal range, 2000-3850m, amsl. Geologically area exposes rocks belonging to the Kullu and Rampur Groups. Under lying rocks Carb Phyllites, Platy Limestone, Gneisses, Quartzites and Chloritic Phyllites with minor schist bands (Sharma *et al.*, 1986). The soil is mainly silty loam in texture with light brown to dark brown and slightly acidic in nature. In the Sanctuary, pH of the soil ranged 5.27-7.33, moisture content 13.5-35.04% and Organic content 1.24-7.67%. Along the entire altitudinal range, the Sanctuary supports temperate, sub-alpine and alpine vegetation. Temperature ranged from -5°C-30°C. The mean annual rainfall is 1071mm and mean snowfall 218mm (Anonymous, 2001-2002; Singh et al., 1990). The inhabitants residing in the periphery of the Sanctuary are dependent on the Sanctuary for minor forest products.

SURVEYS, INFORMATION GENERATION, IDENTIFICATION AND DATA ANALYSIS

Six peripheral representative villages namely Tondla, Dhara, Ghout, Sharan, Farmeha and Chaunjal were selected to collect information on the indigenous uses of medicinal plants of the inhabitants. Participatory Rural Appraisal (PRA) technique has been followed for information generation (Samant *et al.*, 2002, 2003). Further, knowledgeable persons including village *Vaidhyas* from each village were interviewed. With the help of village experts, useful plant species were collected from the wild habitats. Information on the local names, altitudinal range, life forms, part (s) used, and use values including indigenous knowledge and practices was gathered. Fresh samples of the useful species were collected and identified with the help of floras (Polunin & Stainton, 1984, 1987; Dhaliwal & Sharma, 1999b; Singh & Rawat, 2000 and Khullar, 1994 & 2000). The information on the indigenous uses of the species is based on the survey as well as secondary information (Jain, 1991; Samant & Pangety, 1995; Samant *et al.*, 2007; Chauhan, 1999; etc.). All the medicinal plants recorded from the Sanctuary are not used by the inhabitants, but in other part of the IHR they are used for the treatment of various diseases. Such species have also been considered under medicinal plants.

IDENTIFICATION OF NATIVITY, ENDEMISM AND RARITY

The nativity of the species was identified following Anonymous (1883-1970) and Samant *et al.* (1998). Endemism of the species was assessed based on Biogeographical distribution. The status of the species has been identified based on the cumulative values of habitat preference, population size, distribution range, use pattern, extraction, nativity and endemism of species (Table 5.1). Each criteria used for calculating the cumulative value were grouped in to three sub categories. In the first category, for each criterion 10 marks have been given, second category 06 marks and third category 02 marks have been given. Cumulative values of the species were calculated and used to categorize the species under different threat categories. Based on the cumulative values species categorize as Critically Endangered (>60%), Endangered (56-60%), Vulnerable (51-55%), Near Threatened (46-50%) and Least concern (<46%). The status of the species in Himachal Pradesh and globe is based on Samant *et al.*, 1998; Dhar et al., 2002; Ved *et al.*, 2003 and Samant & Pal, 2003.

Table 5.1: Criteria Used for Threat Categorization of Floristic Diversity in the Kais Wildlife Sanctuary

Maximum Marks for each Criteria	Habitat	Distribution (m)	Population (Ind)/Location	Use Pattern	Extraction	Native/Endemic
10	Single	<500	<250 Ind/2 localities	4 &>4	Commercial	Native & Endemic
6	2-3	500-1000m	250-1000 Ind/3-5 localities	2-3	Self Use	Native/Endemic
2	>3	>1000	>1000 Ind/>5 localities	Single	No	Non-native

RESULTS

Diversity of Medicinal Plants

Total 277 species (Angiosperm 270; Gymnosperms 3 and Pteridophytes 4) of medicinal plants belonging to 187 genera and 80 families were recorded. Of these, 17 species were trees, 47 shrubs and 213 herbs. Maximum medicinal plants recorded in Asteraceae (23 genera and 28 spp.), followed by Rosaceae (11 genera & 18 spp.), Ranunculaceae (9 genera & 17 spp.), Lamiaceae (12 genera and 16 spp.), Polygonaceae (4 genera & 14 spp.), Apiaceae (7 genera and 12 spp.), Brassicaceae and Fabaceae (6 genera and 7spp., each), Orchidaceae (7 genera and & 7 spp.), Scrophulariaceae (5 genera & 7 spp.) and Ericaceae (4 genera and 7 spp.). In thirty five (35) families only one species, each recorded as medicinal.

DISTRIBUTION PATTERN OF MEDICINAL PLANTS

The maximum number (240 spp.) of medicinal plants were recorded in the altitudinal zone 2000-2800m, followed by 2801-3800m zone (157 spp.) and lowest (*i.e.*, 40 spp.) >3801m altitudinal zone.

UTILIZATION PATTERN OF MEDICINAL PLANTS

The different parts of plants such as leaves (97 spp.), roots (73 spp.), whole plant (67 spp.), fruits (31 spp.), aerial part (30 spp.), seeds (21 spp.), flowers (15 spp.), bark, stem and rhizome (10 spp., each), wood (7 spp.), bulb and tubers (6 spp., each) inflorescence, latex, oil and resin (2 spp., each) and frond (1 sp.) were used by the communities for curing the different aliments.

One hundred one species of Medicinal plants used for curing various diseases/ailments by the different ethnic group. For instance, 42 species were used to cure cough; 40 species, each in Fever and wounds; 34 species in Skin disease; 32 species in stomach problem; 31 species in diarrhoea; 28 species in dysentery; 27 species in cuts; 24 species in cold; 20 species in eye problem; 16 species each in bronchitis and urinary problem; 14 species each, in asthma, boils and tooth problem; 13 species, each in gastric and ulcer problem; 12 species, each in Headache and snake bite; 11 species, each in colic and piles; 10 species, each in sore and ear problem; 8 species in burns; 7 species, each in jaundice, digestive and liver problem and 6 species, each in bodyache, gonorrhoea, insect bite, kidney, leucoderma, malaria, ringworm and vomiting (Table 5.2). To core other diseases less than six species were used.

The most preferred medicinal plants were *Aconitum heterophyllum, Angelica glauca, Allium humile, Betula utilis, Dactylorhiza hatagirea, Dioscorea deltoidea, Podophyllum hexandrum, Picrorhiza kurrooa,* Rheum *australe, Rhododendron anthopogon, Pistacia integerrima, Cortia depressa, Selinum tenuifolium, Jurinella macrocephala, Berberis lycium, Rhododendron arboreum, Juglans regia, Punica granatum, Zanthoxylum armatum, Olea ferruginea,* etc.

Table 5.2: Medicinal Plants Used for Curing Some Common Ailments by the Inhabitants of Surrounding Villages of Kais Wildlife Sanctuary

Common Ailments	Species Used to Cure
Cough	*Dicliptera bupleuroides, Achyranthes bidentata, A.aspera, Pistacia integerrima, Pimpinell diversifolia, Selinum* candollii, *Hedera nepalensis Asparagus filicinus Achillea millefolium, Impatiens racemosa, Cynoglossum lanceolatum, C.zeylanicum, Cannabis sativa, Gypsophila cerastioides, Gaultheria trichophylla, Rhododendron campanulatum, R.anthopogon R.lepidotum, Euphorbia hirta Indigofera heterantha, Trifolium pratense, Leucas lanata, Salvia lanata, S.nubicola, Malva verticillata, Oxalis acetosella, O.corymbosa, O.latifolia, Plantago himalaica, P.ovata, Cymbopogon distans, Podophyllum hex*and*rum, Polygonum amplexicaule, Aconitum heterophyllum, Agrimonia pilosa, Zanthoxylum armatum Verbascum thapsus, Solanum nigrum , Viola biflora, V.canescens, V. odorata* and *Taxus baccata* subsp. *wallichiana*
Fever	*Bupleurum falcatum, Ainsliaea aptera, Echinops cornigerus, Jurinella macrocephala, Saussurea heteromala, Melothria heterophylla, Rhododendron arboreum, R.campanulatum, Halenia elliptica, Swertia angustifolia, S.paniculata, Iris kemaonensis, Ajuga bracteosa, Nepeta leucophylla, Origanum vulgare, Prunella vulgaris, Polygonatum cirrhifolium, Toona serrata, Syringa emodi, Epipactis helleborine, Spiranthes sinensis, Oxalis acetosella, O.corymbosa, O.latifolia, Plantago himalaica, P.ovata, Imperata cylindrical, Podophyllum hex* and *rum, Oxyria digyna, Rheum australe, Aconitum heterophyllum, D.vestitum, Ranunculus arvensis, Zanthoxylum armatum, Bergenia ciliata, B.stracheyi, Picrorhiza kurrooa, Solanum nigrum, Viola biflora* and *Onychium contiguum*
Wounds	*Barleria cristata, Dicliptera bupleuroides, Achyranthes aspera, Anaphalis busua, Anaphalis triplinervis, Gnaphalium hypoleucum, Saussurea heteromala, Solidago virga-aurea, Alnus nitida, Rorippa indica, Thlaspi arvense, T.* andersonii, *Stellaria media, Lyonia ovalifolia, Rhododendron arboreum, Parochetus communis, Geranium nepalense, Leucas lanata, Mentha longifolia, Salvia nubicola, Cardiocrinum giganteum, Polygonatum cirrhifolium, Morina longifolia, Dactylorhiza hatagirea, Podophyllum hex*and*rum, Rheum australe, Delphinium vestitum, Cotoneaster acuminatus, Potentilla atrosaguinea, Prinsepia utilis, Rosa moschata, Spiraea bella, Boenninghausenia albiflora, Bergenia ciliata, B.stracheyi, Smilax aspera, Nicotiana tabacum, Urtica dioica* and *Roscoea alpina*
Skin disease	*Achyranthes aspera, Cyathula tomentosa, Rhus javanica, Arisaema flavum, A. jacquemontii, Berberis jaeschkeana, Cannabis sativa, Chenopodium album, Rosularia rosulata, Rhododendron campanulatum, Corydalis govaniana, Elsholtzia ciliata, Thymus linearis, Jasminum humile, Oxalis acetosella, O. corniculata, O.corymbosa, O.latifolia, Cymbopogon martinii, Podophyllum hex* and *rum, Polygonum hydropiper, P. recumbens, Rheum australe, Clematis barbellata, Rhamnus triqueter, Galium acutum, G.aparine, Lindenbergia indica* and *Viola biflora*

(Table Contd...)

Common Ailments	Species Used to Cure
Stomach problem	*Achyranthes aspera, Angelica glauca, Cortia depressa, Pleurospermum angelicoides, Aralia cachemirica, Ainsliaea aptera, Aster peduncularis, Alnus nitida, Melothria heterophylla, Parochetus communis, Swertia cordata, Geranium nepalense, Elsholtzia ciliata, Leucas lanata, Thymus linearis, Oxalis acetosella, O. corniculata, O.corymbosa, O.latifolia, Rumex acetosa, Iris kumaonensis, Aconitum heterophyllum, A.violaceum, Rubus ellipticus, R.niveus, R.paniculatus, Rubia manjith, Datura stramonium* and *Solanum nigrum*
Diarrhoea	*Amaranthus hybridus, Asparagus filicinus, Siegesbeckia orientalis, Cyanoglosum zeylanicum, Capsella bursa-pastoris, Euphorbia hirta, Indigofera heterantha, Elsholtzia ciliata, Origanum vulgar, Salvia lanata, Oxalis acetosella, O. corniculata, O.corymbosa, O.latifolia, Plantago himalaica, P.ovata, Podophyllum hex* and *rum, Polygonum affine, Aconitum heterophyllum, Delphinium vestitum, Agrimonia pilosa, Cotoneaster acuminatus, Geum elatum, Rosa moschata, Rubus biflorus, R.paniculatus, Bergenia ciliata, Picrorhiza kurrooa, Verbascum thapsus* and *Solanum nigrum*
Dysentery	*Achyranthes aspera, Angelica glauca, Asparagus filicinus, Cirsium wallichii, Dioscorea deltoidea, Euphorbia hirta, Indigofera heterantha, Trillidium govanianum, Toona serrata, Ficus palmata, Oxalis acetosella, O.corymbosa, O.latifolia, Plantago himalaica, P.ovata, Cynodon dactylon, Polygonum amplexicaule, Rheum australe, Punica granatum, Aconitum heterophyllum, Geum elatum, Rubs ellipticus, Boenninghausenia albiflora, Picrorhiza kurrooa* and *Solanum nigrum*
Cuts	*Anaphalis busua, Bidens bipinnata, Gnaphalium hypoleucum, Alnus nitida, Rorippa indica, Thlaspi arvense, T.* and *ersonii, Melothria heterophylla, Cuscuta reflexa, Euphorbia hirta, Parochetus communis, Geranium nepalense, Polygonatum cirrhifolium, Sida cordata, Oxalis acetosella, O.corymbosa, O.latifolia, Podophyllum hex* and *rum, Rheum australe, Delphinium vestitum, Cotoneaster acuminatus, Duchesnea indica, Prinsepia utilis, Boenninghausenia albiflora, Bergenia ciliata, B.strachey* and *Roscoea alpina*
Cold	*Achyranthes aspera, Pistacia integerrima, Pimpinella diversifolia, Hedera nepalensis, Achillea millefolium, Impatiens racemosa, Cynoglossum lanceolatum, Cannabis sativa, Gaultheria trichophylla, Rhododendron campanulatum, R. anthopogon R.lepidotum, Ajuga bracteosa, Prunella vulgaris, Salvia lanata, S.nubicola, Plantago himalaica, P.ovata, Cymbopogon distans, Polygonum affine, Picrorhiza kurrooa, Viola biflora, V.canescens* and *Taxus baccata L.* subsp. *wallichiana*
Antihelminthic	*Pleurospermum angelicoides, Asparagus filicinus, Cannabis sativa, Sawersia.cordata, Thymus linearis, Punica granatum, Aconitum heterophyllum, Delphinium denudatum, Runanculus hirtellus, Nicandra physalodes* and *Cedrus deodara*

(Table Contd...)

Common Ailments	Species Used to Cure
As astringent	*Berberis jaeschkeana, Trifolium repens, Geranium wallichianum Clinopodium umbrosum, Clinopodium vulgare, Dactylorhiza hatagirea, Rheum spiciforme, Cotoneaster microphyllus, Geum elatum, Potentilla fruticosa, Gallium aparine, Rubia manjith, Bergenia stracheyi* and *Urtica dioica*
As Tonic	*Achyranthes aspera, Achillea millefolium, Sonchus oleraceus, Rhododendron campanulatum, Astragalus chlorostachys, Corydalis govaniana, Clinopodium umbrosum, C.vulgare, Origanum vulgare, Polygonatum verticillatum, Dactylorhiza hatagirea, Spiranthes sinensis, Meconopsis aculeata, Imperata cylindrical, Polygonum amplexicaule, Rhamnus triqueter, Zanthoxylum armatum, Bergenia stracheyi, Urtica dioica* and *Roscoea alpina*
Asthma	*Achyranthes aspera, Selinum c* and *ollii, Solidago virga-aurea, Cynoglossum zeylanicum, Silene vulgaris, Saccharum spontaneum, Rheum australe, Sorbaria tomentosa, Bergenia ciliata, Verbascum thapsus, Datura inoxia, Viola canescens, Viola odorata* and *Hedychium spicatum*
Boils	*Achyranthes aspera, Stellaria media, Lyonia ovalifolia, Rhododendron campanulatum, Ajuga bracteosa, Morina longifolia, Rheum spiciforme, Runanculus diffuses, Rhamnus triqueter, Bergenia ciliata, Datura inoxia* and *Solanum nigrum*
Bronchitis	*Barleria cristata, Achyranthes aspera, Cannabis sativa, Silene vulgaris, Rhododendron anthopogon, Rhododendron lepidotum, Euphorbia hirta, Trifolium pratense, Origanum vulgare, Toona serrata, Rheum australe, Galium elegans, Lindenbergia indica, Viola canescens, Viola odorata* and *Hedychium spicatum*
Colic	*Ainsliaea latifolia, Inula cuspidate, Jurinella macrocephala, Saussurea heteromala, Euphorbia hirta, Astragalus himalayanus, Origanum vulgare, Salvia lanata, Meconopsis aculeata, Rumex nepalensis* and *Mazus pumilus*
Ear problems	*Senecio graciliflorus, Parochetus communis, Piptanthus nepalensis, Geranium wallichianum, Clinopodium umbrosum, Clinopodium vulgare, Jasminum humile, Anemone rivularis, Fragaria nubicola* and *Solanum nigrum*
Eye disorder	*Berberis jaeschkeana, B.lycium, Betula utilis, Cannabis sativa, Silene edgeworthii, Euphorbia hirta, Corydalis govaniana, Geranium wallichianum, Phlomis bracteosa, Rheum australe, Punica granatum, Clematis gouriana, Thalictrum foliolosum, Duchesnea indica, Solanum nigrum, Viola canescens* and *V. odorata*
Gastric	*Dicliptera bupleuroides, Rhus javanica, Angelica glauca, Pleurospermum angelicoides, Asparagus filicinus, Arctium lappa, Gerbera gossypina, Corydalis govaniana, Plectranthus rugosus, Prunella vulgaris, Toona serrata, Podophyllum hex* and *rum* and *Aconitum heterophyllum*

(Table Contd...)

Common Ailments	Species Used to Cure
Headache	*Barleria cristata, Dicliptera bupleuroides, Achyranthes aspera, Asparagus filicinus, Inula cappa, Tanacetum dolichophyllum, Gypsophila cerastioides, Rhododendron arboreum, R.campanulatum, Leucas lanata, Prunella vulgaris* and *Cynodon dactylon*
Piles	*Achyranthes aspera, Heracleum c* and *icans, Cannabis sativa, Dioscorea deltoidea, Malva sylvestris, M.verticillata, Cynodon dactylon, Rheum australe, Zanthoxylum armatum, Bergenia ciliata* and *Solanum nigrum*
Rheumatism	*Achyranthes aspera, Cortia depressa, Hedera nepalensis, Asparagus filicinus, Solidago virga-aurea, Impatiens racemosa, Rhododendron campanulatum, Euphorbia stracheyi, Juglans regia, Olea ferruginea, Plantago himalaica, P.ovata, Cymbopogon martinii, Fagopyrum esculentum, Aconitum violaceum, Anemone obtusiloba, Coteneaster bacillaris, Prinsepia utilis, Datura inoxia, D.stramonium, Solanum nigrum, Abies pindrow* and *Cedrus deodara*
Snake bite	*Barleria cristata, Amaranthus viridis, Pistacia integerrima, Vincitoxicum hirudinaria, Galinsoga parviflora, Euphorbia hirta, Sida cordata, Parnassia nubicola, Imperata cylindrical, Delphinium vestitum, Rubia manjith* and *Parnassia nubicola*
Sore	*Achyranthes aspera, Senecio chrysanthemoides, Iris kumaonensis, Juglans regia, Calanthe tricarinata, Apluda mutica, Anemone rivularis, Spiraea bella, Lindenbergia indica* and *Smilax aspera*
Swelling	*Barleria cristata, Achyranthes bidentata, Rorippa indica, Thlaspi* and *ersonii, Oxalis acetosella, O. corniculata, O.corymbosa, O.latifolia, Plantago himalaica, P.ovata, Polygonum nepalensis, Rheum australe, Rumex nepalensis* and *Duchesnea indica*
Tooth problem	*Achyranthes aspera, Achillea millefolium, Sedum ewersii, Euphorbia hirta, Geranium nepalense, G.wallichianum, Juglans regia, Delphinium denudatum, Skimmia laureola, Zanthoxylum armatum, Astilbe rivularis, Lindenbergia indica, Datura stramonium* and *Nicotiana tabacum*
Ulcer	*Geranium nepalense, Malva sylvestris, M.verticillata, Podophyllum hexandrum, Rheum australe, Delphinium denudatum, Duchesnea indica, Rubia manjith, Solanum nigrum, Abies pindrow* and *Cedrus deodara*
Urinary problem	*Ainsliaea aptera, Echinops cornigerus, Inula cappa, Youngia japonica, Indigofera heterantha, Herminium lanceum, Primula denticulata* and *Agrimonia pilosa*

NATIVITY AND ENDEMISM OF MEDICINAL PLANTS

One hundred forty two (142) species were Native to the Himalayan Region. Remaining 135 species were Non-natives representing different biogeographic regions of the world *i.e.*, Asia, America, Indian Oriental, Siberia, Africa, United State Soviet Union, Amphigaea, Australia, Malaysia, New Zealand, Mongolia, Japan, Turkistan, Mediterranean, Russia, Afghanistan, Gerontia, Norway, North Mexico, Korea, Soongarica, Caucasus, etc. 98 species were endemic to the Himalayan Region and 5 species *i.e., Angelica glauca,*

Cortia depressa, Pinpinella acuminate, Pleurospermum candollii and Pleurospermum brunonis were identified as Endemic to the India Himalayan Region.

RARITY CATEGORIZATION AND CONSERVATION PRIORITIZATION OF MEDICINAL PLANTS

The status of medicinal plants particularly within the Sanctuary, thirty (30) species were identified as Critically Endangered, 16 species Endangered, 17 species Vulnerable and 43 species Near Threatened (Table 5.3) by using the criteria for the medicinal plants.

By using current criteria of International Union for Conservation of Nature and Natural Resources (IUCN) (Ved *et al.*, 2003), Twenty three (23) species which were recorded from the Sanctuary, has been placed under different threat categories *i.e.*, Critically Endangered (*Dactylorhiza hatagirea* and *Aconitum heterophyllum*); Endangered (*Taxus baccata* subsp. *wallichiana, Picrorhiza kurrooa, Zanthoxylum armatum, Rheum australe, Podophyllum hexandrum, Meconopsis aculeata, Polygonatum cirrhifolium, Dioscorea deltoidea, Betula utilis, Jurinella macrocephala* and *Angelica glauca*); Vulnerable (*Heracleum candicans, Rhododendron campanulatum, R. anthopogon, R. lepidotum Polygonatum verticillatum, P. multiflorum, Aconitum violaceum, Bergenia stracheyi* and *Valeriana jatamansi*); and one species Near Threatened (*Hippophea salicifolia*) (Ved *et al.*, 2003).

Six medicinal plants recorded from the Sanctuary, have been identified Globally as Critically Endangered (*Aconitum heterophyllum*); Endangered (*Rheum australe, Meconopsis aculeata, Dioscorea deltoidea* and *Angelica glauca*) and Vulnerable (*Aconitum violaceum*) (Ved *et al.*, 2003).

The species identified as Critically Endangered, Endangered and Vulnerable have been prioritized for conservation. A total of 87 species facing problem of habitat degradation, 40 species over-exploitation and 60 species both, habitat degradation and over-exploitation.

The species prioritized for conservation and commercial cultivation in are *Aconitum heterophyllum, Angelica glauca, Dactylorhiza hatagirea, Dioscorea deltoidea, Jurinella macrocephala, Podophyllum hexandrum, Picrorhiza kurrooa, Rheum australe, Taxus baccata* subsp. *wallichiana, Polygonatum cirrhifolium* and *Valeriana jatamansi*.

DISCUSSION

The database on medicinal plants is pre-requisite for the developmental planning of sanctuary. Therefore, the present attempt has been made to investigate the medicinal plants diversity of the sanctuary. Occurrence of 277 species of medicinal plants in the sanctuary indicates that environmental conditions of the area are suitable for the growth and development of medicinal plants. The altitudinal zone, 2000-2800m was identified as potential zone supporting maximum medicinal plants.

Table 5.3: Status of Species Under Threat Categories in Kais Wildlife Sanctuary and Their Comparison to Other Places

Area	Critically- Endangered	Endangered	Vulnerable	Near-Threatened
Kais Wildlife Sanctuary	*Allium humile, Pistacia integerrima, Angelica glauca, Cortia depressa, Heracleum candicans, Pleurospermum angelicoides, P.candollii, Selinum tenuifolium, Echinops cornigerus, Jurinella macrocephala, Berberis jaeschkeana, B.lycium, Hippophea salicifolia, Rhododendron arboreum, Juglans regia, Dactylorhiza hatagirea, Rheum australe, R. speciforme, Punica granatum, Aconitum heterophyllum, A. violaceum, Zanthoxylum armatum, Picrorhiza kurrooa, Olea ferruginea, Celtis australis, Ulmus wallichiana, Valeriana jatamansi* and *Hedychium spicatum*	*Rhus javanica, Impatiens racemosa, Dioscorea deltoidea, Elaeagnus conferta, Cardiocrinum giganteum, Viscum album, Myrsine africana, Meconopsis aculeata, Rubus biflorus, Astilbe rivularis, Syringa emodi, Juniperus indica, Abies pindrow, Cedrus deodara* and *Taxus baccata* L. subsp. *Wallichiana*	*Pleurospermum brunonis, Aralia cachemirica, Alnus nitida, Viburnum cotinifolium, Coriaria nepalensis, Corydalis govaniana, Polygonatum cirrhifolium, Ficus palmate, Epipactis helleborine, Herminium lanceum, Thalictrum foliolosum, Rhamnus triqueter, Cotoneaster bacillaris, Prinsepia utilis, Spiraea bella, Bergenia ciliata* and *Valeriana hardwickii*	*Allium wallichii, Amaranthus viridis, Cythula tomentosa, Selinum candollii, S.vaginatum, Vincitoxicum hirudinaria, Asparagus filicinus, Aster peduncularis, Inula cuspidata, Saussurea heteromalla, Siegesbeckia orientalis, Betula utilis, Rosularia rosulata, Melothria heterophylla, Rhododendron campanulatum, Indigofera heterantha, Lespedeza gerardiana, Salvia lanata, Polygonatum verticillatum, P.multiflorum, Reinwardtia indica, Sida cordata, Goodyera repens, H.edgeworthii, Parnassia nubicola, Podophyllum hexandrum, Fagopyrum dibotrys, Oxyria digyna, Rumex acetosa, Delphinium denudatum, Thalictrum reniforme, Rhamnus virgatus, Cotoneaster acuminatus, Rubus paniculatus, Sorbaria tomentosa, Galium acutum, Leptodermis lanceolata, Skimmia laureola, Datura inoxia, D.stramonium, Wikstroemia canescens* and *Roscoea alpina*
Himachal Pradesh	*Dactylorhiza hatagirea* and *Aconitum heterophyllum*	*Taxus baccata* subsp. *wallichiana, Picrorhiza kurrooa, Zanthoxylum armatum, Rheum australe, Podophyllum hexandrum, Meconopsis aculeata, Polygonatum cirrhifolium, Dioscorea deltoidea, Betula utilis, Jurinella macrocephala* and *Angelica glauca*	*Heracleum candicans, Rhododendron campanulatum, R. anthopogon, R. lepidotum Polygonatum verticillatum, P. multiflorum, Aconitum violaceum, Bergenia stracheyi* and *Valeriana jatamansi*)	*Hippophea salicifolia*
Global	*Aconitum heterophyllum*	*Rheum australe, Meconopsis aculeata, Dioscorea deltoidea* and *Angelica glauca*	*Aconitum violaceum*	

This zone requires regular monitoring to understand the dynamics of the vegetation. Occurrence of 51.26% Natives, 35.38% Near Endemics and 1.80% Endemics showed high conservation value of the area. Habitats degradation and over exploitation of these species may lead their early extinction from the area. Over exploitation of parts such as whole plants, roots, rhizomes, tubers, inflorescence, fruits and seeds of the medicinal plants from the area may lead to poor regeneration and untimely extirpation of the medicinal plants from the area. Occurrence of 30 critically Endangered, 16 Endangered and 17 Vulnerable medicinal plants in the area indicated high anthropogenic pressure on these species. If over exploitation and habitat degradation of these species continue, they may disappear from the area within a few years. Therefore, regular monitoring of these species using standard ecological methods is essentially required. So, that adequate management planning for these species could be done in time. Further, mass multiplication of these species using conventional and in vitro methods is suggested. Establishment and maintenance of these species in nursery and herbal garden and their rehabilitation in in-situ conditions would help in their conservation and management. Establishment of these species under cultivation in the nearby areas of their occurrence may help in conservation and reducing pressure from their natural habitats.

REFERENCES

Anonymous, 1883-1970. Index Kewensis Plantarum Phanerogamarum Vol. 1-2 (1883-1885) and 15 Suppl. (1886-1970). Clarendron Press, Oxford.

Anonymous, 2001-2002. Ecodevelopment Plan, Kais Wildlife Sanctuary, Wildlife Division, Kullu, Himachal Pradesh.

Badola, H.K. 2001. Medicinal Plant Diversity of Himachal Pradesh. In: Samant, S.S., Dhar, U., Palni, L.M.S. (eds.) Himalayan Medicinal Plants: Potential and Prospects, Occasional Publication No. 14, Gyanodaya Prakashan, Nainital. pp. 87 116.

Badola, H.K., Pal, M. 2003. Threatened Medicinal Plants and Their Conservation in Himachal Himalaya. Indian Forester, 129, 55-68.

Bhattacharya, U.C., Uniyal, B.P. 1982. A botanical tour to Pangi and Trilokinath in Upper Chenab. Journal of Bombay Natural History Society India, 79, 57 78.

Chauhan, N.S. 1988. Endangered Ayurvedic Pharmacopoeial Plant Resources of H.P. In: Kaushik, P. (ed.) Indigenous Medicinal Plants. Today and Tomorrows Printers and Publishers, New Delhi. pp. 187-198.

Chauhan, N.S. 1999. Medicinal and Aromatic Plants of Himachal Pradesh. Indus Publishing Company, New Dehli.

Dhaliwal, D.S., Sharma, M. 1999. Flora of Kullu District (Himachal Pradesh). Bishen Singh Mahendra Pal Singh, Dehra Dun.

Dhar, U., Manjkhola, S., Joshi, M., Bhatt, A., Bisht, A.K. & Joshi, M. 2002. Current Status and Future Strategy for Development of Medicinal Plants Sector in Uttaranchal, India. *Current Science*, 83 (8): 956-964.

Jain, S.K. 1991. Dictionary of Indian Folk Medicine and Ethnobotany. Deep Publications, New Delhi.

Kala, C.P. 2003. Medicinal Plants of Indian Trans-Himalaya. Bishen Singh Mahendra Pal Singh, Dehradun.

Kala, C.P. 2006. Medicinal Plants of the High Altitude Cold Desert in India: Diversity, Distribution and Traditional Uses. International Journal of Biodiversity Science and Management, 2(1), 43 56 (14).

Kapahi, B.K. 1990. Ethnobotanical Investigations in Lahaul (Himachal Pradesh). Journal of Economic and Taxonomic Botany, 4(1), 49 55.

Khullar, S.P. 1994 & 2000. *An Illustrated Fern Flora of the West Himalaya* Vol. I & II. International Book Distributors, Dehradun.

Khullar, S.P. 1994 & 2000. *An Illustrated Fern Flora of the West Himalaya* Vol. I & II. International Book Distributors, Dehradun.

Polunin, O. & Stainton, A. 1987. Concise Flower of the Himalaya. Oxford University Press, Delhi.

Polunin, O., Stainton, A. 1984. Flowers of the Himalaya. Oxford University Press, Oxford.

Rai, L.K., Prasad, P., Sharma, E. 2000. Conservation Threats to Some Important Medicinal Plants of the Sikkim Himalaya. Biological Conservation, 93, 27 33.

Samant, S.S., Dhar, U. Palni, L.M.S. 2001. Himalayan Medicinal Plants: Potential and Prospects. Gyanodaya Prakashan, Nainital.

Samant, S.S., Dhar, U., Palni, L.M.S. 1998. Medicinal Plants of Indian Himalaya. Diversity Distribution Potential Values. Gyanodaya Prakashan, Nainital.

Samant, S.S., J.S. Butola, A. Sharma. 2007b. Assessment of Diversity, Distribution, Conservation Status and Preparation of Management Plan for Medicinal Plants in the Catchment Area of Parbati Hydroelectric Project Stage – III in Northwestern Himalaya. Journal of Mountain Science. 4(1), 34 56.

Samant, S.S., Joshi, H.C., Arya, S.C., Pant, S. 2002. Studies on the Structure, Composition and Changes of the Vegetation in Nanda Devi Biosphere Reserve of West Himalaya. Final Technical Report submitted to Ministry of Environment and Forests, New Delhi.

Samant, S.S., Joshi, H.C., Arya, S.C., Pant, S. 2003. Planning for the Conservation and Management of Natural Resources Using Participatory Approach: A Case Study from Pindari Area of Nanda Devi Biosphere Reserve, West Himalaya, India. Van Vigyan, 38 (1-4), 41-54.

Samant, S.S., Pal, M. 2003. Diversity and Conservation Status of Medicinal Plants in Uttaranchal State. Indian Forester, 129(9), 1090 1108.

Samant, S.S., Pant, S., Singh, M., Lal, M., Singh, A., Sharma, A., Bhandari, S. 2007a. Diversity, Distribution Pattern, Indigenous Uses and Conservation Prioritization of Medicinal Plants of Himachal Pradesh, India, International Journal of Biodiversity Science and Management, 3, 234 251.

Schemske, D.W., Brain C. husband, Mary H. Ruckelshaus, Carol Goodwillie, Ingrid M. Parker and John G. Bishop. 1994. Evaluation Approaches to the Conservation of Rare and Endangered Plants. Ecology. 75(3), 584-606.

Sharma, J.C., Sharma, H.C. & Arya, S.R. 1986. Revised Working Plan for Kullu Forest Devision (1979-80 to 1993-94) Part 1 & 2. Working Plan Circle, Government of Himachal Pradesh, Shimla.

Singh, S., Kothari, A. & Pande, P. 1990. Directory of National Parks and Sanctuaries in Himachal Pradesh, Management Status and Profiles. Environmental Studies Division, Indian Institute of Public Administration, New Delhi.

Singh, S.K. & Rawat, G.S., 2000. *Flora of Great Himalayan National Park*, Himachal Pradesh, Bishen Singh, Mahendra Pal Singh, Dehradun.

Sood, S.K., Nath, R., Kalia, D.C. 2001. Ethnobotany of Cold Desert Tribes of Lahoul–Spiti (North West Himalaya). Deep Publications.

Ved, D.K., Kinhal, G.A., Ravikumar, K., Prabhakaran, V., Ghate, U., Vijaya Shankar, R., Indresha, J.H. 2003. Conservation Assessment and Management Prioritization for the Medicinal Plants of Jammu & Kashmir, Himachal Pradesh & Uttaranchal. Foundation for Revitalization of Local Health Traditions, Bangalore, India.

Pages: **113-125**

MEDICINAL PLANTS: *DISTRIBUTION, UTILIZATION AND SIGNIFICANCE*

Edited by: **Dr. Pankaj Sharma; Dr. Pawan Kumar 'Bharti'** and **Dr. Narayan Singh**

ISBN: 978-93-5056-734-0

Edition: **2015**

Published by: **Discovery Publishing House Pvt. Ltd., New Delhi (India)**

6

Common Medicinal Herbs of Shimla City, Himachal Pradesh, India

Anil Kumar Thakur[1] and **Kamal Jit Singh**[2]

INTRODUCTION

Shimla, the capital city of the North Indian state of Himachal Pradesh is located at 31° 6′ 12 degrees North and 77° 10′ 20 degrees East (Fig. 6.1). It was the summer capital of British India. Its name is derived from the goddess Shyamala Devi, an incarnation of the Hindu goddess Kali. It lies on a ridge and spreads on its seven spurs in Himalaya's South-Western ranges. It is a mountainous region with altitude rising up to 2454 meters at Jakhu hill. It has a subtropical highland climate with cool winters and moderately warm summers. The temperature ranges from "4 °C to 30 °C with moderate snow during the winters. The average total annual precipitation is 1,575 millimetres with heavy downpour during July and August (Climate-Data.Org, 2014). Pines, deodars, oaks and rhododendrons form the main forests in and around the city. The varied climatic conditions have made the area home for numerous medicinal and other useful plants. Most of these plants find their use in traditional medicine, folk uses and in modern industry (Singh and Thakur, 2014).

[1] Department of Botany, Govt. P.G. College, Solan - 173 212, Himachal Pradesh, India.

[2] Department of Botany, Panjab University, Chandigarh - 160 014, India.

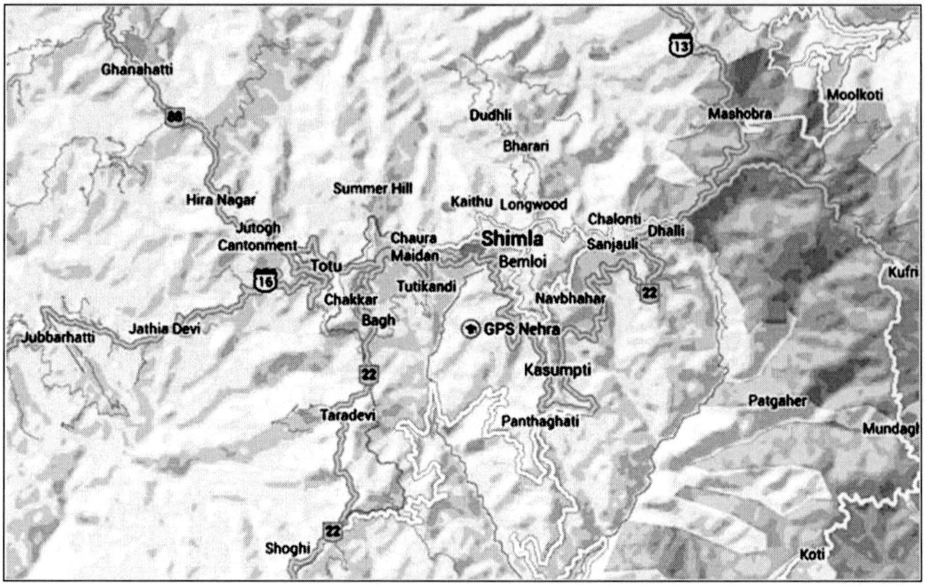

Fig. 6.1: Google Map of Shimla and Adjoining Areas

Shimla has a rich diversity of plants as is evident from the works of Sir Henry Collett (1902) in *Flora Simlensis* and Lady Elisabeth Smith and H. Babington Smith (1899) in *Simla Flowers*. The area is represented by 1326 species of plants belonging to 639 genera. This includes 1003 species of Dicotyledons belonging to 498 genera and 313 species of Monocotyledons grouped in 133 genera. The gymnosperms are represented by only 10 species and 8 genera (Collett, 1903). The state of Himachal Pradesh has approximately 500 species of medicinal and 150 species of aromatic plants (Chauhan, 1999).

A systematic account of the medicinal herbs of Shimla city is given in alphabetical order of their botanical names along with their common names and medicinal uses.

1. *Achyranthes bidentata* Blume

Synonyms: A. aspera var. *fruticosa* (Lam.) Boerl., *A. chinensis* Osbeck, *A. fruticosa* Lam., *A. hispida* Moq., *A. japonica* (Miq.) Nakai

Family: Amaranthaceae

Enlish name: Prickly Chaff Flower, Chaff-Flower, Devil's Horsewhip

Hindi name: Chirchita, Latjira, Apamarg, Puthkanda

Medicinal and Other Uses

The roots, leaves and stems are widely used in Chinese herbal medicine. Plants are anodyne, antirheumatic, bitter, digestive, diuretic, emmenagogue and vasodilator. They are also used in the treatment of aching back and knees and asthenia of the lower limbs. Stem is useful in pyorrhea. The root juice is used in the treatment of toothache, indigestion and asthma. The herb is taken internally to treat hypertension, back pains, urine in the blood, menstrual pain, bleeding (Yeung, 1985; Bown, 1995; Chevallier, 1996; Manandhar, N.P. 2002).

2. *Ajuga integrifolia* Buch.-Ham.

Synonym: Ajuga bracteosa Wall. Ex Benth.

Family: Lamiaceae

Enlish name: Bracted Bugleweed

Hindi name: Neelkanthi

Medicinal and Other Uses

Leaves are used as diuretic, febrifuge and tonic. Herb is also used in gout, rheumatism, palsy and amenorrhoea (Anonymous, 1945-76; Chauhan, 1999; Khare, 2007).

3. *Aloe vera* (L.) Burm. f.

Synonym: Aloe barbadensis (L.) Webb. & Berth

Family: Liliaceae

Enlish name: Aloe, Common Indian Aloe

Hindi name: Ghikumari, Gvarapatha, Kumari

Medicinal and Other Uses

Leaves are cooked and used for discomfort in stomach and jaundice. Gel is applied as an emollient for burning sensation of soles of the feet and also in treatment of burns. Also useful in band-aid for suppuration of boils and healing external injuries (Anonymous, 1945-76; Ambasta, 1986; Chauhan, 1999; Khare, 2007; Sharma and Sood, 2007).

4. *Bergenia ciliate* (Haw.) Sternb.

Family: Saxifragaceae

Enlish name: Frilly bergenia, Hairy bergenia

Hindi name: Pashanbhed, Patharchat

Medicinal and Other Uses

Rhizomes and roots are considered astrin-gent, diuretic and tonic. They are also used in fever and swollen joints. Crushed roots are applied to boils. It is an important drug for dissolving kidney and bladder stones (Anonymous, 1945-76; Ambasta, 1986; Chauhan, 1999).

5. *Boenninghausenia albiflora* (Hook.) Reichb ex. Meissn.

Family: Rutaceae

Enlish name: White Himalayan Rue

Hindi name: Pissumar Booti

Medicinal and Other Uses

Leaves are pounded and applied on cuts and wounds to speed the healing process. The leaves are also applied externally in the treatment of scabies. The leaf juice is dropped into wounds in order to kill germs. The leaf juice is said to relieve headaches when applied externally. Whole plant is placed under the pillow to relieve headaches. A decoction of the root is used in the treatment of malaria. The dried leaves are used as a flea repellent (Natural Medicinal Herbs, 2013).

6. *Cuscuta reflexa* Roxb.

Family: Convulvulaceae

Enlish name: Doddar

Hindi name: Akashbel, Amarbel

Medicinal and Other Uses

A bath in warm decoction of stem is considered good to relieve swelling and rheumatic pains. Poultice of the plant paste is applied to cure red spots due to blood clotting. Massage of mustard oil boiled with powdered climber is good for internal injuries (Anonymous, 1945-76; Ambasta, 1986).

7. *Datura stramonium* Linn.

Family: Solanaceae

Enlish name: Apple of Peru, Devil's Apple, Devil's Trumpet, Mad Apple, Thorn Apple.

Hindi name: Dhatura

Medicinal and Other Uses

Flowers are considered sacred and offered to appease Lord Shiva. Inhalation of smoke of burning leaves is believed to cure asthma. Fruits are intoxicating. Powdered seeds are prescribed with cow's milk for fever (Anonymous, 1945-76; Ambasta, 1986; Khare, 2007).

8. *Fagopyrum acutatum* (Lehm.) Mansf. ex K.Hammer

Family: Polygonaceae

Enlish name: Perennial Buckwheat

Hindi name: Ban ogal, Kanjolya

Medicinal and Other Uses

Leaves are cooked and eaten as vegetable. Grains are used in colic, choleric diarrhea and intestinal obstructions. The whole plant is considered anodyne, anthelmintic, carminative, depurative and febrifuge. It stimulates blood circulation (Anonymous, 1945-76; Ambasta, 1986).

9. *Habenaria intermedia* D.Don

Family: Orchidaceae

Enlish name: Intermediate Habenaria

Hindi name: Vridhi, Ridhi

Medicinal and Other Uses

Tubers are important constituents of many medicines in Indian System of Medicine, health tonic, astverga group (a combination of 8 rejuvenating herbs), and in preparation of Ayurvedic tonic 'Chyawanprash'. Tender leaves as well as tubers are edible and cooked as vegetables (Ahuja, 2003; Khare, 2007).

10. *Hedychium spicatum* Smith

Family: Zingiberaceae

Enlish name: Spiked Ginger Lily

Hindi name: Kapurkachri

Medicinal and Other Uses

The rhizomes are aromatic, anti-arthritic, appetizer, cardiac stimulant, carminative, deodorant, hair tonic and stomachic. Also useful in cough, asthma, diarrhoea, dropsy headache, hair falling, liver complaints, rheumatism and skin diseases. Leaves are woven into mats (Anonymous, 1945-76; Ambasta, 1986; Chauhan, 1999; Khare, 2007).

11. *Malaxis acuminata* D.Don

Family: Orchidaceae

Hindi name: Jeevak

Medicinal and Other Uses

The pseudobulbs are sweet, refrigerant, aphrodisiac, febrifuge and tonic. They are useful in fever, seminal weakness, burning sensations, tuberculosis and general debility (Khare, 2007; Flowers of India, 2013).

12. *Ocimum tenuiflorum L.*

Synonym: Ocimum sanctum L.

Family: Lamiaceae

Enlish name: Holy Basil

Hindi name: Tulsi, Ajaka

Medicinal and Other Uses

Oil from the leaves possess antibacterial and insecticidal properties. Seeds are useful in urinary troubles. Leaves are diaphoretic, stimulating and expectorant. Used in gastric problems, bronchitis and common cold (Anonymous, 1945-76; Ambasta, 1986; Chauhan, 1999; Khare, 2007).

13. *Origanum vulgare* Linn.

Family: Lamiaceae

Enlish name: Origano

Hindi name: Sathra, Ban Tulsi

Medicinal and Other Uses

Used for flavouring foods. Its oil possesses carminative, stomachic, diuretic, diaphoretic and ammenagogue properties. Also given as tonic in diarrhoea. Useful in toothache, bronchitis, cough, rheumatism and earache. Tablet prepared from leaves are given in bone fractures (Chauhan, 1999; Khare, 2007).

14. *Rubia cordifolia* L.

Family: Rubiaceae

Enlish name: Indian Madder

Hindi name: Majit, Manjit, Manjhist

Medicinal and Other Uses

Whole plant is considered antidote to scorpion sting. It has antiseptic, astringent, deobstruent, diuretic and vermifuge properties. It is also useful in amenorrhoea, bone fractures, inflammation, chest complaints, headache, hepatic obstructions, leucoderma, menstrual disorders, rheumatism, sinusitis, stomachache, ulcers, obstructions in the urinary passages and paralysis (Watt, 1972; Ambasta, 1986; Jain, 1991; Chauhan, 1999; Khare, 2007).

15. *Solanum nigrum* Linn.

Family: Solanaceae

Enlish name: Black nightshade, Poisonberry

Hindi name: Makoi, Kakamachi, Bandakh

Medicinal and Other Uses

It has antiseptic, diuretic, laxative and anti-dysenteric properties. Freshly prepared juice of the plant is effective in liver cirrhosis and opium poisoning. Leaves are used for the treatment of psoriasis, eczema, piles, syphilis, gonorrhoea, dropsy and liver and spleen enlargement. Berries are useful in fever, ulcers, eye troubles and diarrhea (Ambasta, 1986; Chauhan, 1999; Khare, 2007).

16. *Swertia paniculata* Wall.

Family: Gentianaceae

Enlish name: Panicled Swertia

Hindi name: Charaita

Medicinal and Other Uses

Decoction of the plant is used as tonic. Plant is also used as substitute for Chirayita in the treatment of malaria and other fever (Khare, 2007; Flowers of India, 2013).

17. *Tagetus minuta* Linn.

Family: Asteraceae

Enlish name: Wild Marrigold

Hindi name: Gaindri, Jangli gainda

Medicinal and Other Uses

Flowers are used as stomachic, aperients, diuretic and diaphoretic. Volatile oil obtained from the plants has anti-inflammatory, hypotensive, spasmolytic and bronchdialatory properties (Anonymous, 1945-76; Chauhan, 1999).

18. *Taraxacum officinale* Wigg.

Family: Asteraceae

Enlish name: Dandelion, Fortune teller

Hindi name: Kanphul, Dhoodhali

Medicinal and Other Uses

Rhizomes and roots constitute the drug taraxacum used as a mild laxative and increases the flow of bile. Also used as diuretic, stomachic, hepatic stimulant and tonic. Rhizomes and roots are used raw as salad. Leaves are consumed as vegetable. Leaves and flower heads are used in the preparation of beer and wine (Anonymous, 1945-76; Ambasta, 1986; Khare, 2007).

19. *Thalictrum foliolosum* DC.

Family: Ranunculaceae

Enlish name: Leafy Meadow Rue

Hindi name: Mamira, Mamiri

Medicinal and Other Uses

Roots are valued for opthalmia. Also used as diuretic, purgative, and bitter tonic during convalescence and dyspepsia (Anonymous, 1945-76; Ambasta, 1986; Chauhan, 1999; Khare, 2007).

20. *Thymus linearis* Benth.

Synonym: Thymus serpyllum Linn.

Family: Lamiaceae

Enlish name: Himalayan Thyme, Wild Thyme, Creeping Thyme

Hindi name: Jangli ajwain

Medicinal and Other Uses

It contains essential oils including thymol having strong antiseptic properties. It is considered to be an excellent expectorant, antispasmodic and carminative. It has been used to treat gastrointestinal problems, respiratory disorders and against hookworm (Anonymous, 1945-76; Ambasta, 1986; Chauhan, 1999; Khare, 2007).

21. *Valeriana jatamansi* Jones

Family: Valerianaceae

Enlish name: Indian valerian, Jatamansi

Hindi name: Mansi, Tagar, Sugandhbala, Mushakbala

Medicinal and Other Uses

It is considered useful in diseases of eye, blood and liver. It is also used as a remedy for hysteria, nervous unrest and emotional stress. Also considered useful in clearing voice and acts as a stimulant in fever and nervous disorder. The paste of its roots is applied on wounds for better healing (Anonymous, 1945-76; Ambasta, 1986; Chauhan, 1999).

22. *Viola canescens* Wall.

Family: Violaceae

Enlish name: Himalayan Violet

Hindi name: Banafshah

Medicinal and Other Uses

Flowers and whole plants are used in cough, cold and asthma. Flowers and leaves are useful in eye diseases and malaria (Rana and Samant, 2011; Verma et al., 2011)

PLATE 1

Achyranthes bidentata

Ajuga integrifolia

Aloe vera

Berginia ciliata

PLATE 2

Boenninghausenia albiflora

Cuscuta reflexa

Datura stramonium

Fagopyrum acutatum

PLATE 3

Habenaria intermedia

Hedychium spicatum

Malaxis acuminata

Origanum vulgare

PLATE 4

Rubia cordifolia

Solanum nigrum

Swertia paniculata

Taraxacum officinale

PLATE 5

Thalictrum foliolosum

Thymus linearis

Valeriana jatamansi

Viola canescens

REFERENCES

Ahuja, P.S. 2003. *Medicinal Plants in India: Report and Directory*. Institute of Economic and Market Research, New Delhi.

Ambasta, S.P. 1986. *The Useful Plants of India*. CSIR, New Delhi.

Anonymous 1945-1976. *Wealth of India, Raw Materials* Vol. 1-11. Publication and Information Directorate, CSIR, New Delhi.

Bown. D. 1995. *Encyclopaedia of Herbs and their Uses*. Dorling Kindersley, London.

Chauhan, N.S. 1999. *Medicinal and Aromatic Plants of Himachal Pradesh*. Indus Publ. Co., New Delhi.

Chevallier, A. 1996. *The Encyclopedia of Medicinal Plants*. Dorling Kindersley, London.

Climate-Data.Org. 2014. Climate: Shimla. http://en.climate-data.org/ location/3891/ Retrieved on 22th Aug., 2014.

Collett, H. 1902. *Flora Simlensis: A Handbook of the Flowering Plants of Simla and the Neighbourhood*. Thacker, Spink and Co. Calcutta and Simla.

Flowers of India. 2013. *Malaxis acuminata*. http://www.flowersofindia.net/catalog/slides/ Jeevak.html Retrieved: 18th Nov., 2013.

Flowers of India. 2013. *Swertia paniculata* http://www.flowersofindia.net/catalog/slides/ Panicled%20Swertia.html. Retrieved: Nov. 20, 2013.

Jain, S.K. 1991. *Dictionary of Indian Folk Medicine and Ethnobotany*. Deep Publications, New Delhi.

Khare, C.P. 2007. Indian Medicinal Plants: An Illustrated Dictionary. Springer Science+Business Media, LLC.

Manandhar, N.P. 2002. *Plants and People of Nepal*. Timber Press, Oregon.

Natural Medicinal Herbs. 2013. *Boenninghausenia albiflora*. http://www. natural medicinalherbs.net/herbs/b/boenninghausenia-albiflora.php Retreived 13 Jan., 2013.

Rana, M.S. and Samant, S.S. 2011. Diversity, Indigenous uses and Conservation Status of Medicinal Plants in Manali Wildlife Sanctuary, North Western Himalaya. *Ind. J. Traditional Knowledge* 10(3): 439-459.

Sharma, K.R. Sood, M. 2007. *Important Medicinal and Aromatic Plants of Himachal Pradesh*. Directorate of Extension Education and Department of Forest Products, Dr. YS Parmar University of Horticulture and Forestry, Nauni, Solan (H.P.).

Singh, K.J. and Thakur, A.K. 2014. Medicinal Plants of the Shimla Hills, Himachal Pradesh: A Survey. *Int. J. Herbal Med*. 2: Accepted for Publication.

Smith, E. and Smith, H.B. 1899. *Shimla Flowers: An Annotated List of Flowers Collected in the Neighbourhood of Simla and Mashobra*. Privately Printed, Simla and Calcutta.

Verma, G., Dua, V.K., Aggarwal, D.D. and Atul, P.K. 2011. Anti-malarial Activity of *Holarrhena antidysenterica* and *Viola canescens*, Plants Traditionally Used Against Malaria in the Garhwal Region of North-west Himalaya. *Malaria Journal* 10: 20.

Watt, G. 1972. *A Dictionary of the Economic Products of India*, Vol. I-VI. Periodical Experts, Delhi, India.

Yeung, H.C. 1985. *Handbook of Chinese Herbs and Formulas*. Institute of Chinese Medicine, Los Angeles.

Pages: 126-161

MEDICINAL PLANTS: *DISTRIBUTION, UTILIZATION AND SIGNIFICANCE*

Edited by: **Dr. Pankaj Sharma; Dr. Pawan Kumar 'Bharti'** and **Dr. Narayan Singh**

ISBN: 978-93-5056-734-0

Edition: **2015**

Published by: **Discovery Publishing House Pvt. Ltd., New Delhi (India)**

7

Ethnobotanical Importance of Medicinal Plants of Barak Valley, Assam, India

Moharana Choudhury

INTRODUCTION

Ethno medicine is a 5000 years old system of medicine considering this concept of use of plants in several other countries of world. "Ethno botany is the branch of science that deals with relationship with plants and ethnic Group i.e. primitive human." Use of plants is important for the human and so that great attention is paid towards the use of plants and also the records of such uses are very ancient in India. Ethno botanical studies were initiated first in India by Dr. E.K.Juaki Ammal in 1954. She studied subsistence food plants of certain tribal of South India. With this initiation, Jain & his associate carried out organized ethno botanical studies first among the tribes of Central India. (Jain 1963, 1965, 1981)

In 1982, the dept. of environment, government of India sponsored on "All India coordinated Research project on Ethnology" at about a dozen institutes & centers. The studies are still continuing in a no. of institutions such as Botanical Research Institute; Central Institute of Medicinal & aromatic plants & many other universities & colleges. Several books on Indian Ethno

Department of Environmental Science (CODL), Tezpur University, Assam, India.

botany have also been published such as a manual of Ethno botany (Jain 1987). Besides this some important booklets are there.

The study for medicinal plants is important for proper classification & identification of plants which is very essential for any scientific research work because a species is a biological unit & each unit or species is chemically separated from other species. Systematic & thorough investigation area of paramount importance to record the occurrence of plant species & their medicinal investigation will enable one to assess the Botanical potentialities for useful exploration project work on economic utilization of living plants are therefore considered most essential. Moreover, the study of plant particularly the medicinal ones have vast biological importance. Plants are properly collected and preserved accurately, identified and described for a system of classification & then it would be possible to assess the medicinal and food wealth of area.

Study site and the inhibiting different tribal community:

About the study area:

An Ethno botanical survey has been conducted in Silchar town of Assam & its surrounding areas which are located in the heart of Silchar town, Assam, India that is the districts headquarter of Cachar district in Assam and its different communities of people including all types of Religions.

The geographical co-ordinates of area is:

92 55E to 93 5 E & 24 40′ to 29 58′N (approx)

A brief about the study area:

Climatic condition:

Air temperature: Maximum–42 C Minimum–6.1C

Relative humidity: Maximum–90% Minimum–55%

Annual rainfall: Maximum–6000mm Minimum–3000mm

Rainfall per area: Seven-Eight months in avg.

Sources: Via Internal and local body information like Agriculture office, Metallurgy Department of Silchar. The area is full of diversity of natural heritage. In its surrounding some villages are there that are about 3-2 km away from town that contain a diversity of vegetation provided with different types of wild & cultivated fauna. There are main road along with some by-roads & by lanes that connect the villages with the main town. In the surrounding of the main town there are lots of people belonging from different community. The following are some of the tribes of the district:

1. *Barman* (*Dimasa*): This tribe mainly prevails in Khaspur, Borkhola, Harinagar, Jaipur, Dharmi khal, Dhalai areas of the district. Their present population is about 15,000. Due to political reason they were driven by Ahom from Maibong area of N.C Hills (Assam, India).

2. *Kabui-Naga*: This tribe mainly prevails in Fatakbazar area of Silchar, Binnakandi, Ghat near Lakhipur, Kachudaram, Kalain, Bantarapur, Ghungurn area of the district. Their population is about 5000. The chief mode of life of Kabui-Naga of Fatakbazar area is urban trade & commerce.
3. *Khasi*: This tribe mainly live in Damcherra, Digarkhal, Alambag,Thaligram khasipunji, Upper Malidohor, Barjalenga forest area of the district. The population is about 3500. The chief mode of people of Khasi tribe is horticulture & Jhum.
4. *Kuki*: This tribe mainly lives in Barjalenga forest area & Nakshatilla areas of the district. Their population is 550.

   They mainly depend on Jhum cultivation.
5. *Hmar*: This tribe mainly prevails in Markulin village near Phulerthal area, Barjalenga forest area including Nakshatilla. Their population is about 1800. They mainly depend on horticulture and Jhum cultivation. They produce larger quantities of pineapples.
6. *Chakma*: This tribe mainly prevails in Cachar Mizoram border.

   They mainly depend on horticulture Jhum cultivation.

Source: Department of Anthropology G.C.College, Silchar (Assam)

METHODOLOGY

In the study of plants, the following methods and techniques are adopted.

1. Selection of community and site.
2. Collection of information through the local such as local vaidya (medical practitioners), residents of area, villagers, old persons (tribal community) etc.
3. Conducting interviews with the informants.
4. Ethno botanical field work consists of following steps:
   (a) Plan of field trip programme for study
   (b) Actual field trip
5. Collection and processing of plant sample.
6. Identification and matching of the specimen.
7. Preparation of herbarium sheets.

The important of the project on ethno medicine are local people of the area of visit; they contributed some very important information.

The language of interview conducted during the field study is generally Bengali but in some case Hindi & English were also necessary specially during interviewing Mizo community of Mission compound, Silchar. Side by side I also recorded the vernacular name of species during the interview. For the field work, a plan was made previously. According to that, actual field trip was made and specimens along with their description were recorded. The specimen were collected along with their fruits and flower as far as possible and then heir color of flower, habit, habitat, their weight, color of flower & fruits, place of collection, dates, local name, ethno botanical notes etc. Then the specimens were dried according to the procedure. In case of big trees when collection of vegetative parts has not been possible some photographs has been taken for them. According to the plan the field study has been done from 15th November to 22nd March 08-09.The field trip was made for several times and guided by my guide Dr. N.C.Malakar Sir. The dried specimens were then poisoned by saturated solution of Hgcl2 in absolute alcohol and then mounted on 42 x 29 sq.cm size herbarium sheets. All specimens are rightly labeled and identified on the herbarium sheets. Identification of the specimen has been done after analytical study consulting with the floras that are available in the B.C.Gupta Memorial Library of G.C.College Silchar, Assam comparing with authentic specimen have been preserved in the BOTANY department herbarium of G.C.College with the consultation with my guide teacher Dr. N.C.Malakar.

Index of families studied as follows:

- MALVACEAE
- CAESALPINIACEAE
- PAPILIONACEAE
- MIMOSACEAE
- MYRTACEAE
- APIACEAE
- CUCURBITACEAE
- PUNICACEAE
- LAURACEAE
- RUTACEAE
- ANACARDIACEAE
- CARICACEAE
- MELIACEAE
- COMBRETACEAE
- ASTERACEAE
- GENTIANACEAE
- ACANTHACEAE
- LAMIACEAE
- AMARANTHACEAE
- POLYGONACEAE

- EUPHORBIACEAE
- MORACEAE
- PIPERACEAE
- MUSACEAE

ENUMERATION

Malvaceae

Hibiscus L

H, rosa-sinensis L. SP. Pl 694, 1753, FBI 1:344; 1874;

Kanjilal etal FA1 (1): 145, 1934

Local name "Joba" (Bengali) "joba Kim" (Dimasa) "Pangparsen" (Mizo), "Palpah"(Kuki)

Shrubs large on small tree, leaves simply, 6-12 cm long, ovate a cuminate, serrate, 3 nerned at the base, stipules 2 tree lateral Flowers rose red shown in upper anils. Epicalyx segments 6-10 sepals united, corolla 10-15 cm across, Petals 5, twisted, united at base with staminal column. Stamens, many, monadelphus, column exerted, anthers 1-called remiform.

Spm example: Kanakpur Road Silchar collected by Moharana Choudhury

Habitat: Terrestrial, cultivated from clones for showy flowers as ornamental plant.

Fls & Frs: Throughout the year, fruit not produced.

Ethno botanical Records (As ornamental)

Parts used: Whole plant.

Process of utilization: The flower is offered to god during Puja occasion.

In garden it also used as ornamental flower.

CHESALPINIACEAE

Cassia L

Key to the species

1. Leaflets 3-4 pairs...C. tora
2. Leaflets 6-12 pairs...C. sophera

Cassia sophera: L, SP, PI397, 1753, HOOK, F, FBI 2:1451878, FA2, 130, 1938 "Kalkshunda"

A erect under shrub, 1-1.6 m high, wood annual, pungent smelling young parts pubescent purplish green, Leaves long, rachis grooved, leaflets 5-12 pairs, acute sub sessile.

Fls & Frs: May-Oct.

Spm exam: Kanakpur road, Silchar collected by Moharana Choudhury

Habitat: common in wet places in road - side

Pathways and similar situation, Wild in nature

(Photo taken by: Moharana Choudhury)

Ethno bacterial Records (As medicinal)

Plant is medicinally important

Part used: Leaves

Process of utilization: The leaves are used externally for ring worm and a decoction of plant is beneficial in acute bronchitis.

Cassia tora: source: (www.cnseed.org)

PAPILIONACEAE

Cajanus DC

C. Cajan (L) Millsp in Field columb . Mus . Bot 2:53. 1900;

Cytisus indicus spring. Syst .3:248 ; 1826 ;FBI 2:217 1876.

Local name: Arhar (Bengali) "Behliaug" (Mizo), Kashew dai (Rongmei Naga)

An erect shrub upto 3 meter height with many sulcate silky branches. Leaves 3 – foliate, gland dotted beneath . Flowers is loose corymbose cymes or in a terminal panicle calyx gland pubescent, tube campanulate, standard petal yellow with red veins Pod 5-7 cm long, seeds yellow or black.

Spm exam: Kanakpur, Silchar, collected by Moharana Choudhury

Fls & Frs: Sept. - Nov.

Habitat: Terrestrial and cultivated in fields, gardens

Ethnobotanical records (As food and medicines)

Parts used: Seeds, leaves

Process of utilization: The seeds are used as dal i.e. Arhar dal a food. The fresh leaves juices are eaten during jaundice by local people.

Cajanus cajan source: (www.tropicalforages.info)

MIMOSACEAE

Stamens usually 8-10 Mimosa

Mimosa pudica L sp PI, 518, 1753. FBI 2:159. 1878

Local name – Chhoitemara/Lajjaboti (Bangali) "Diaw" (khasi), "Hlomar" (Mezo), Nou-hum (Kuki), Samgablaw (Dimasa)

Under shrub deciduous, Leaves resistive, Pinnae, petiole bristly, stipules linear lanceolate. Flowers pink in heads or slender axillaries peduncles covered with spreading bristles stamens 4 extended. Pods jointed

Fls & Frs Jan. - Feb.

Spm exam: College road silchar, collected by Moharana Choudhury

Habitat: common in waste places, wild in nature

Ethnobotanical Records (Medicinal)

Plants is used medicinally

The paste of leaves and roots is used in toothache.

Mimosa pudica- photo taken by: (Moharana Choudhury)

MYTRACEAE

Key to the genera

1. Fruit baccate, not splitting Psidium

1' Fruit dry, loculicidally splitted above Eucalyptus

Evcalyptus L Herit

E. maculate Hook Fc PI t 169, 1844, Kanjlal etal FA 2:286 1938

Local name: Not specific

Tree tail with column like trunk, bark whitish or grayish, leaves alternate, 10+6 x 1.5-3.5 cm linear lanceolate, folcate flowers thick pedicelled, in clusters of 3, calyx tube adnate to the ovary at the base, Fruit globoich urn shaped.

Spm exam: Trunk road Silchar, collected by Moharana Choudhury.

Fls & Frs: Whole the year.

Habitat: Terrestrial cultivated and also wild in nature

Ethno botanical Records (As wood plant and medicinal)

Parts used: Leaf, bark, stem

Process of utilization: The wood is hard and has various uses as valuable timber. From leaf and bark some important oil are extracted as they used as medicinal importance. From it some kinds of perfume and gum also extracted in industrial purposes.

Psidium guajava & Eucalyptus ssp - photo taken by: (Moharana Choudhury)

APIACEAE

Key to the genera

1 Umbels compound leaves compound Coriandrum

1′ Umbels simple leaves simple

2 Mericarps with three ridges, pericapthin Hydrocotyl

2′ Mericarps with 7-9 ridges, pericarp thick Centella

Coriadrum L

C. sativum L SP Pl 256, 1753, CB Clark in Hook of FBI 2:717 1879

Local name: "Dhaniapata" "Borodhania" (Bengali), "Bakharpata" (Naga) Bramha bakhor (Dimasa) "Bakwan"(Rongei Naga)

Annuals slender branched with a foctil smell. Leaves pinately decompounds flowers white or purple, in unequal compound umbels, fruit globose.

Fls & Frs: Jan. - Mar.

Spm exam: College road Silchar collected by Moharana Choudhury

Habitat Herbs cultivated

Ethnobotanical Records (As spice)

Parts used: Leaves and seeds

Process of utilization: The paste of the leaves and the seeds of the plants are used to make delicious curry, chatney pickles etc.

Centella L

C. asiatica (L) Urbon in mart, Fl Bras II (I) 287. t.78 f . 1 . 1879 Hydrocotyl asiatica L . sp Pl 1:234 . 1753; FBI 2: 669. 1879

Local name: "Thankuni" (Bengali), "cocklai" (Naga), "Lambak" (Mizo), "Jamardoh" (Khasi), "Mekarum" (Dimasa),

Herbs with long creeping stems, rooting at the nodes, Leaves reniform crenate or dentate, palmately nerned, umbels simple, at the node with 3 flowers, fruit didymous, mericarps usually broader than long.

Fls & Frs: Winter season

Habitat: Terrestial, wild

Spm exam: Kanakpur Silchar, collected by Moharana Choudhury

CUCURBITACEAE

Key to the genera

1. Corolla rotate Momordica
2. Corolla campanulate Coccinia

Coccinia wt & Arn

C. grandis (L) voigt. Hort . Suburb. Calc 59. 1845

C. indica wt & Arn. Prodr. 347, 1834 Cephalandra indica Naud. FBI 2:621 1879

Coccinia indica

Local name: "Kaualooli" (Bengali local), "Gang"(Naga), "Sohkhie"(Khasi)

Coriandrum sativum & Centella asiatica - Photo taken by: (Moharana Choudhury)

Herbs climbing, profusely branching, tendril simple, rarely fifid, leaves petiobel, palmately lobed or angled, with a few glistening glands or the mid rib towards the base, flowers dioecious rather large, solitary, corolla white campanulate Carpels 3, comate fruit ovoid or elliptic, bright green or white stripes, bright scarlet when ripe.

Fls & Frs exam: Winter months

Spam exam: Kanakpur road Silchar, collected by Moharana Choudhury

Habitat: Terrestrial climber, wild

Ethno botatanical Records (As food and medicinal)

Parts used: Fruits and leaves

Process of utilization: The fruit is used as a very good vegetable, leaves juice is taken in diabetes.

Coccinia indica-source: (en.wikimedia.org), Momordica charantia: Photo taken by: (Moharana Choudhury)

Momordica L

M.Charantia L 1009 1753 FBI 2:616 1879

Local name: "Korola", Ucche (Bengali),"Jinkia" (Naga), "Chankha"(Mizo), "Krela" (Khasi), "Changkha"(Kuki), "Gala"(Dimasa)

Climbers profusely branching, puberulous, leaves large.

Reniform, pubescent flowers monoccious, flowers solitary fruit 8-20cm long oblong, tuberculate, trivalved dehiscing at te apex seeds compressed tridentate at tye ends. Sculptured on the surface.

5 pm exam Kanakpur road Silchar, collected by Moharana Choudhury

Ethno botanical Records (As food & medicine)

Part used: Fruit

Process of utilization: The boil fruit is used to take before breakfast which prevents worm. It is also suitable for diabetic patient. The fruit is used to make different fried item.

PUNICACEAE

Punica L

P. Granatum L. SP. Pl, 472 1753 FBI 2:581 1879

Kanjilar etal FA 2:315 1938

Local name: 'Dalim'(bangali) "Anar" (Hindi), "Kolbu thei" (Kuki), "Jheibuhfai" (Mezo), "Kolbuthei" (Kuki)

Shrubs or small trees branched often spiny tipped leaves simple, opposite lanceolate glabrous, pellucid punctate,Calyx companulate leathery, 5-7 lobed persistant. Stamens many, filaments slender ovary inferior many celled. Fruit 5-8 cm. across, brownish yellow to red.

Spm exam: Vivekananda Road, Silchar, collected by Moharana Choudhury

Habitat: cultivated, terrestrial

F1s: Frs: flower thrice a year and fruit at different stages of development are found on the plant ground.

Ethno botanical Records (As food & Medicinal)

Parts used: leaf, bud, fruit skin, root skin

Process of utilization: The fruits are eaten directly; its juice is very nutritious & helpful for anemia patients. The roots cure germs & are the best medicine to get rid of worms.

Leaves are helpful in jaundice & miscarriage or bleeding during pregnancy. Grind 20 gm of fresh pomegranate leaves juice in 100 gm water, sieve it & drink it daily.

It is also beneficial for piles. The skin of it is used for piles.

Dose: 100 gm root powder & take it twice or thrice daily for curing bleeding piles.

LAVRACEAE

Cinnamomum Blume

C.tamala (F.Ham) Nees & Eberm. Handb. Med. Pharm. Bot Z:426 1831:FBI 5: 128,1886 Kanjilar etal FA 4:56. 1940

Local name: "Taj patta" (Bengali) "Bakhar pata" (Naga),

Trees medium sized evergreen bark dark brown.Leaves simple,elliptic or oblong-lanceolate, acuminate glabnous, 3-nerved at base, flowers in panicles, pale yellow, fruit small black ovoid.

Punica granatum- photo taken by: (Moharana Choudhury)

Fls & Frs: Jan. - March

Spm exam: Kanakpur Road, Silchar, collected by Moharana Choudhury

Habitat- Terrestrial, Cultivated, also wild in nature

Ethnobotanical Records: (As food)

Part used: leaf

Process of utilization: The leaf are used to mixed with other species to make delicious curry.

Cinnamomum tamala- (photo taken by Moharana Choudhury)

RUTACEAE

Key to genera

1 Leaves unifoliate; pericarp leathery Citrus

1' Leaves trifoliate; pericarp woody Aegle

Aegle Correa

A . marmelos (I) correa in Traus . Linn soc. 5:222 .1800

FBI 1:516 1875 Kanjilal etal FA 1:215. 1936

Local name: "Bel" (Bengali), "Balhna" (Mizo) "Naitha" (Rongmei Naga)

Trees, small deciduous, with stout erect auxiliary thrones, leaves alternate, oetiolate trifoliate, leaf lets ovate – lanceolate sessile, Flowers white stamens many fruit, large chambered many chambered with woody rind.

Fls 7 Frs – Feb. - June

Occurrence – commonly cultivated in domestic compounds also wild.

Spm exam– Vivakananda road, Silchar, collected by Moharana Choudhury.

Ethno botanical Records (As food & medicinal)

Parts used: leaf, fruit

Process of utilization: The fruit is eaten directly is very healthy. The fruit is eaten & is very good remedy for dysentery & other stomach troubles. The root & stem bark is used in fever. A yellow dye is obtained from the rind of unripe fruits. The leaves are much used as religious offerings in temples.

Citrus L

C. medica L sp Pl, 782, 1753, FBI 1:514. 1875 Kanjilal etal FA 1(2): 213 1936.

Local Name: "Lebu" (Bengali)," "Nimbu" (Hindi) "Thaisa" (Dimasa) "Ser" (Mizo), "Schkol" (Kuki)

Shrubs with erect thorns, leaflets ovate – elliptic or oblong lanceolate, erenate, obtuse, narrowed at the base. Flowers white, tinged with red, sweet scented, solitary or racemose.

Fruits 7 – 12 x 5 – 7.5 cm, obovoid – oblong, yellow when ripe with thick spongy rind.

Fls & Frs: April - Nov.

Spm exam: Kanakpur road, Silchar, collected by Moharana Choudhury

Habitat: Terrestrial & cultivated from clones & seeds

Ethno botanical Records (Medicine & food)

Part used: The fruit

Process of utilization: The fruit is used to make sarbat, prickles etc., the juice of the fruit is used on head which reduced blood pressure.

Mangifera L

M. indica L sp Pl. 200 1753, FBI 2: 13 1876 Kanjilal etal FA

1 (2): 335 1936

Local name: "Aam" (Bengali), "Theihai" (Mizo), "haithei" (Kuki) "Thaiju" (Dimasa) "Umbaa" (Rongmei Naga).

Trees large evergreen leaves crowded at the end of branches. Oblong lanceolate acciminate, simple with pulvinus (leaf base), glatrous coriaceous, dark gloosy green, pinkish when very young, turning yellow before falling . Flowers is small sessile in panicle Drupe varione with fleshy edible delicious mesocarp.

Fls & Frs: January & May - June

Habitat: Terrestrial and cultivated usually.

Spm exam: Kanakpur road, Silchar collected by Moharana Choudhury

Ethno botanical Records: (As food)

Part used: The fruit & the stem

Process of utilization: The fruit are used to make different type of prickles, chutney etc. The stem of the plant is used to make different type of domestic furniture.

Aegle marmelos: Source (en.wikimedia.org), Citrus medica, Mangifera Indica (photo taken by Moharana Choudhury)

CARICACEAE

Carica L

C papaya L SP Pl 1036, 1753; FBI 2:599 1879

Local name: "Papaya" "Kapal"(Bengali) "Thingfanghma" (Mizo), "Kopol"(Dimasa) "Sohkynphor" (Khasi), "Thingchangmai"(Kuki) "Maopingthai" (Rongmei Naga)

A herbaceous tree, 3-8 cm high with milky latex, sometimes branching above the mid – height. Leaves alternate forming a crown mostly very long hollow petioled, palmately lobed. Flowers dioecious male flowers in axillary panicles; female flowers larger, sub solitary leaf axillary, ovary large, globose, stigmas 5, Fruit a large one celled berry – globose to pyniform.

Spm exam: Public school road, Silchar, collected by Moharana Choudhury

Fls & Frs: Through the year

Habitat: Terrestrial and cultivated; plant cannot thrive in water logged condition & flood water.

Ethno botanical Records: (As food & medicine)

Part used: Fruit

Process of utilization: The fruit is used to eaten raw, the ripe fruit is also eaten which is very useful for preventing constipation. It is also very nutritious as rich in vitamins.

Carica papaya- (photo taken by Moharana Choudhury)

MELIACEAE

Azadirachta A. Juss

A. indica A . Juss in men. Mus. Paris 19. 220 t. 2 1830; Kanjilal et al FA. 1 (2) 227, 1936, Melia azadirachta L SP, Pl 385 1753; FBI, 1 :554 1875.

Local name: "Neem"(Bengali), "Margosa" "Neemhnah"(Mizo),

Trees large, deciduous (almost) leaves pimate, leaflets 9-15 opposite or alternate, lanceolate, obligne acuminate, sessate glabnous . Panicles axillary . Flowers small, white, petals 5, ciliate ovary 3 celled, Fruit seeded.

Spm exam: College road, Silchar, collected by Moharana Choudhury

Habitat: Terrestrial & cultivated for leaves, young stems, planted in road side & garden.

Ethno botanical Records (As medicinal wood plant)

Part used: Leaves, stems, bark, twigs, seeds, flowers

Process of utilization: Leaves are important as the pastes are used in skin disease, stems are used as wood because it is very hard in nature, leaves, and bark has good antiseptic and antihelamintic property. The tender twigs are used to clean teeth and very affective in pyorrhea. The seeds are source of "margosa" oil which is used in skin disease; applied as a linament in rheumatism and possess antihelmintic and insecticidal properties. The oil cake is used as fertilizer. The bark is very bitter and is beneficial in malarial fever. The dry flowers are tonic and stomachic. Leaves are used in wounds to cure it as it is a very good antiseptic in nature.

Dry powder of leaves and bark of stem is very useful in controlling germs and mosquito by burning the powder in house.

Azadirachta indica–(photo taken by Moharana Choudhury)

COMBRETACEAE

Terminalia L

Key to the species

1. Fruit not winged I. chebula

1' Fruit winged I. arjuna

I. arjuna (Roxb) wight & Arn. Prodor 314. 1834 in note.

FBI 2: 447 1878

Local name: "Arjun" (Bengali), "Arjunething" (Mizo)

Tree large with buttressed trunk large crown and drooping branchlets ; bark smooth, grey, leaves obovote to narrowly oblong, obtuse . Flower white sessile in spikes or panicles. Drupe 2.5-3.5 cm long obovoid – oblong, glabnous dark brown with swings striated with numerous curved veins.

Spm exam: Kanakpur road, Silchar, collected by Moharana Choudhury

Habitat: Terrestrial trees often cultivated in the garden avenue tree.

Ethnobotanical Records (As medicinal & wood plant)

Part used: The bark and seed, stem

Process of utilization: The paste of bark along with water used to drink before breakfast or after dinner once in a day which prevents stomach problem as well as some gynecological disorder, bark is also useful in heart disorder. The seed powder are also apply on heal which increase hair growth and prevent hair fall. The bark has good laxatine, stomachic, tonic and alternative properties. Wood is very hard and used as timber. The bark is used for dyeing and tanning.

T. chebula Retz obs . Bot. 5:31, 1789 FBI, 2: 446 1878 Kanjilal etal FA 2:244 1938.

Local name: "Haritaki"(Bengali)

Trees deciduous, bark grey or ash colored, rough and furrouord, outside leaves elliptic or ovate oblong acuminate . Flowers minute bisexual with abnoxious smell. Drupe 2.5 - 5 cm long ellipsoid or obovoid, yellow green when ripe.

Spm exam: Kanakpur road, Silchar, collected by Moharana Choudhury

Habitat: Terrestrial, cultivated for fruit in garden and in avenues.

Ethno botanical Records: (As medicine)

Parts used: fruit, bark, and wood.

Process of utilization: Wood very hard and is used for furniture & house construction, bark is used for tanning. Fruit is useful in medicine as they have good digestive and stomach problem curing property. The fruit is one constituent of "Trifola" of Ayurvedic medicine; the "trifola" juice is very good for digestive system and blood purification property.

Terminalia arjuna source (ajitvadakayil.blogspot.com) & Terminilia chebula Source: (www.evaidyaji.com)

ASTERACEAE

Key to the genera

1. All florets are similar and tubular
2. pappus of 5 owned scales ....Agerantum

2′ pappus of slender hairs..............................Mikania

1′. Florets dissimilar.................................. .cuodelia

Ageratum conyzoides

1 Heads blue, leaves opposite.....................Ageratum

Ageratum conyzoides L SP P 839 1753, FBI 3. 243

Local name: "Uchandi" (Bengali)

Herb erect 30-80 cm, strongly scented, hispid leaves opposite sometimes the upper alternate, ovate, petioslate crenate, heads homogamous In terminal corymbs or panicles with bluish purple flowers. Involucre campanulate bracts 2-3 sessile, sub equal receptacle that cordla all tubular 5, cleft. Anthers appandaged obtuse at lase style arms elongate obtuse.

Fls & Fps: Oct.-March

Sample exam: Kanakpur road, Silchar, collected by Moharana Choudhury

Occurrence: A common weed in open waste places, wild in nature

Ethno botanical Records (Medicinal)

Part used: Leaf

Process of utilization: The paste made from the fresh leaf is used in cut injury.

The leaf juice is used in cut injury of human body or in animals is more effective than detol.

Mikania willd

M.cordata (Burm. f) B.L Robinson in contrib Gray Herb

M. scandens willid FBI 3: 224 1881

Local name: "Refugeelata" (Bengal), "Samkhabli" (Dimasa)

Herbs twinning, gregarious, leaves opposite petiolate, ovate

Cordata. Heads small, homogamous, 4 flowered racemose, involucres oblong bracts 4, corolla campanulate, 5 fid.Anthers appendiculate style with long acute arms. Cypsella truncate, 5 angled, pappus hairs connate at base.

Spm exam: Public school road, Silchar, collected by Moharana

Fls &Frs: Late summer/autumn

Habitat: Terrestrial climber

Ethno botanical Records (Medicinal)

Part used: Leaf

Process of utilization: The juice extracted from the leaf is used in wounds and cuts.

Wadelia N.S Jack

W. chinensis (osb) Merr in Phil. Journ Sci, 12 (Bot): 111: 1917

W. calendulaceae Less Syn. Comp 222 1832; FBI 3: 306:1881

Local name: "Bhringaraj"(Bengali)

Herb with stem creeping and rooting below, erect branches thinly strigose. Leaves 2.5-7.5 cm long, oblong or lanceolate, oblong, pubescent on both surfaces. Heads 2.3-3 cm across, bright yellow at the end of long peduncles from the upper leaf axils, cypsela of ray florets trigentrous truncate at the tip. pappus denticulate forming a cup.

Spm exam: Ashram road, Silchar, collected by Moharana Choudhury

Ethno botanical Records (Medicinal)

Parts used: Leaves

Process of utilization: The juice of leaves is used as hair tonic in the preparation of hair oil.

Ageratum conyzoides, Mikania willd (photo by Moharana Choudhury), Wadelia chinensis (source: en.wikipedia.org)

GENTIANACEAE

Swertia

S. chirata Buch Ham

Local name: "Chirata"(Bangali),

The plant is an erect annual herb stem 6mm in thickness the lower part rounded, pith easily separable; the upper part produces numerous slender, elongated decussate branches from the axils of the opposite leaves, producing flowers and fruits, the leaves ovate or lanceolate, acuminate entire glabrous, opposite sessile. The roots are tapering; 5-10 cm long 12 mm up to in thickness.

Spm exam: Kanakpur, Silchar, collected by Moharana Choudhury

Habitat: Terrestrial, cultivated for stems

Ethno botanical Records (Medicinal)

Parts used: Stem, leaf

Process of utilization: Leaf juice is taken as tonic which is bitter and help in reduce in liver worms. It is also helpful in stomachic and has laxative property which is helpful in constipations

Swertia chirata (photo taken by Moharana Choudhury)

ACANTHACEAE

Adhatoda Nees

A.Zyylanica Medik. Hist. comment. A cad. Elect. Sc. Thood palet 6: 393. 1790 A. vasica Nees in wall, Pl. Asiat Rar 3: 103. 1832; FBI 4: 540 1885; Kanjilal etal FA 3: 455 1939.

Local name: "Basak" (Bengali), "Maisangsa" (Mizo), "Aluboso" (Dimasa)

Shrubs bushy, leaves 10-20 x 47.5 cm, with a focted small elliptic or elliptic lanceolate, acuminate, entire or undulate, lateral nerves 8-12 on each side. Flowers white in dense bracteates spikes, axillary or terminal bracts conspicuous ovate; bracteoles narrower, corolla 2 lipped. Stamens 2 anther cells 2 ovary 2 – celled with 2 – ovules in each. Capsule 2- 2.5 cm long elevate 4 seeded, seeds tubercled.

Fls: Nov. - Feb., fruits Dec. - Aug.

Spm exam:

Occurrence: Planted in domestic compounds

Ethno botanical Records (As medicinal)

Part used: Leaves

Process of utilization: The fresh leaves are grind and extract the juice and take for cough.

Dose: 2-3 times in a day with honey is very useful in cough.

Adhatoda Vasica (source:www.sanjiviniherbals.in)

LAMIACEAE

Key to the genera:

1	Stamens declinate	Ocimum
1′	Stamens straight or descending	Leucas
2′	Stamens sub equal	Mentha

Leucas R . Br

L. aspera spring syst . 2: 743, 1825, FBI 4: 690, 1885

Leucas Plukenetil Benth in wall Pl Asiat Rar 1: 60 :1830

Local name: "Donkalosh" (Bengali) "Shetdrone"

Annual herbs with branch stem. Leaves sub sessile, linear or narrowly oblong lanceolate, entire or dentate crenate obtuse, narrowed at the base. Flower is terminal and axillary, very dense whorls. Calyx tubular, curved, ribbed, mouth oblique, teeth short, corolla white bilabiate . Nut lets smooth, brown.

Spm exam: College road, Silchar collected by Moharana Choudhury

Habitat: Terrestrial herb

Ethno botanical Records (Medicinal)

Parts used: Leaves and seeds

Process of utilization: The paste that made from the leaves is used to cure wound burn etc. The oil extracted from the seed is used to prepare different food items viz. curry pickles etc.

Mentha piperatia

M. piperita

Local name: "Pudina pata" (Bengali),

Spm exam: Public school road, Silchar collected by Moharana Choudhury

Habitat: Terrestrial herb cultivated

Ethno botanical Records (As food & medicine)

Parts used: Whole plant

Process of utilization: The plant is used in different useful medicinal value. The leave juice is taken for vomiting and digestive problem.

Paste of the leaves is often used in chutney.

Ocimum L

O. basilicum L Sp Pl 597, 1753 FBI 4: 608 1885

Kanjilal et al FA 3: 501 1939

Local name: "Babui Tulsi" "Kala Tulsi" (Bangali), "Gisim Tulsi"(Dimasa)

Herbs glabrescent Leaves petiolate, 5-8 cm long ovate lanceolate, acuminate, toother or entire .Flowers in whorls on simple or branched racemes. Calyx in fruit about 6 mm long. Villous with in corolla white 1-1.2 cm long, stamens exerted, filaments toothed at the base. Nutlets spitted.

Spm exam: College road, Silchar, collected by Moharana Choudhury

Habitat: Terrestrial shrubs.

Occurrence: Cultivated

Ethno botanical Records (As medicine)

Parts used: Leaves, stems and seeds.

Process of utilization: It is used as important insecticidal and insect repellant properties. The plant is stomachache, carminative and a very useful stimulant. Some oil are extracted from it is very important medicinal value.

Leucas aspera, Mentha piperatia & Ocimum basilicum (Photo taken by Moharana Choudhury)

AMARANTHACEAE

Achyranthes L

A. aspera L sp. Pl, 204, 1753;FBI 4:730. 1885; Kanjilal et al FA 4:6. 1940

Local name: "Apang" (Bengali)

Perennial stiff herb, branching from the base; stems thickened above the nodes. Leaves opposite petiolate, variable elliptic, oblong or ovate, aroused at the base. Spikes terminal erect, spines, short, often tinged with purple tapals, hardened in fruit.

Occurrence: common in drier areas along the road or waste places.

Fls: July-Sept. Frt: Aug-Feb.

Spm-exam: Kanakpur road Silchar, collected by Moharana Choudhury

Ethno botanical Records (As medicinal)

Part used: Leaf

Process of utilization: The paste made from the leaf of the plants used to apply on hair to reduce dandruff

Dose: The paste is used thrice in a week.

Achyranthes aspera (source:www.sanjiviniherbals.in)

POLYGONACEAE

Polygonum L

Key to the species

1. Nutlets biconvex..P.orientale

1' Nutlets trigonus..P.hydropiper

Polygonum hydropiper L sp. Pl 361, 1753, FBI, 39, 1886 4:21 1940

Local name: "Pani marich"(Bengali), "Sambarao"(Dimasa)

Small annual herb, 30.0-80.0 cm long with decumbent base and ascending branches, roots adventitious, stems woody, cylindrical nodes slightly swollen, simple, internodes elongated, herbs yellowish ailic c 0.4 c, long leaves submersible. Laminate linear- lanceolate, gland dotted.

Fls & Frs: Almost throughout the year

Spm exam:-Public School road Silchar, collected by Moharana Choudhury

Habitat: common in wet places, wild in nature

Ethnobotanical Records (As medicinal)

Part used: The roots

Process of utilization: The roots are used to wrap on forehead which reduce headache.

Dose: It is used for whole day.

Polygonum orientale L. SP. Pl. 343, 1753, FBI, 5:30 1886 FA 4:21, 1940

Local name: "Borha pani marich" (Bengali)

A branching annual with hollow stems, densely hairy all over stems cylindrical green, internodes, with many thin striations nerves many. Leaves long petiolate, laminae ovate, 3-6 flowers, peduncle long, stout, green, flowers white bract one. Tapals (5)connate basally forming a short tube.

Fls & Frs: April-Sept.

Spm exam: College road, Silchar, collected by Moharana Choudhury

Ethno botanical Records: (As ornamental)

Parts used: The whole plant

Sometimes the plant is planted around house or in garden.

Polygonum hydropiper (source: www.wildflower.org), Polygonum orientale (source www.hear.org)

EUPHORBIACEAE

Phyllanthus L

P.emblica L. sp pl 1982, 1753; FBI, 5:289 1887 Emblica officinalis Gaertn Fruct 122t

108, f 2:1790 Kanjilal etal FA 4:159 1940

Local name: "Amlaki" "Eola" (Bengali) "Awla" "Hamlaitai" (Dimasa),

Trees small or middle sized, deciduous, branchlets feathery with distichous leaves, resembling a pinnate leaf, bark greenish leaves linear closest, globnous, flowers yellowish monoecious, male flowers slender, pedicelled, female flower lower sub sessile ovary 3 celled.

Styles 3-each bifid, spreading, fruit a drupe globose 1.2-2cm across

Obscurely 6 lobed.

Fls: Dec-March, Fruits: March-Oct.

Spm exam: College road, collected by Moharana Choudhury

Occurrence: In drier localities and cultivated for fruit.

Ethno botanical Records (As food & medicine)

Part used: Leaves, fruits, bark

Process of utilization: Fruits are eaten in raw. Dried fruits are used in making different kinds of prickles, which are very digestive, good for stomach; fruits are rich source of Vit. C. Dried fruits are used as shampoo, which is very good for hair nourishment. The bark is used as tanning material.

Phyllanthus emblica (Photo taken by Moharana Choudhury)

MORACEAE

1. Flowers crowded around a oblong or globose receptacle...Artocarpous.

1′ Flowers on the inner wall of the enclosed hollow receptacle which is fleshy in fruit............Ficus

Artocarpus J.R.et. G.Forst

Heterophyllus Lamk. Encycle, Meth 3:210. 1789; A integrifolia mult auct non L T FBI 5:541: 1888

Local name: "Kathal"(Bengali), "Lamkhuang"(Mizo), "Thaiflung" (Dimasa), "Puijwang" (Rongmei Naga)

Trees with milky latex, leaves alternate, coriaceous entire, penninerved, 15-30 x 8-20 cm, obovate-oblong fruit a oblong syncarp, tubercled, large, fleshy, seeds ellipsoid, 2.5 cm long.

Fls: Jan.-March, Fruit: April-Sept.

Spm exam: Kanakpur road, Silchar, collected by Moharana Choudhury

Occurrence: very common, cultivated & wild.

Ethno botanical Records (Food)

Part used: Fruit, seeds, wood & stem

Process of utilization- The fruit is eaten raw i.e. in form of a vegetable & ripe fruit is very delicious & nutrient fruit, seeds are also eaten in form of food, wood is moderately hard is used as a timber & firewood. Leaves are relished by goats at grass scarcity during flood.

Ficus L

F.benghalensis L.sp.pl. 1059. 1753 FBI 5:499: 1888

Kanjilal etal FA 4:240:1940

Local name: "Bat"(Bengali) "Phraphang" (Dimasa)

Trees large, evergreen aerial roots from the branches forming prop roots bark smooth grey leaves 10-20 x 5-13 cm, elliptic to broadly ovate, acuminate, petiole 1.2-5 cm long. Hypanthodium (Receptacles) in axillary pairs, about 1.2 cm in diameter, red when ripe (syconus)

Fls & fruits - July

Occurrence- scattered

Spm exam: College road, Silchar, collected by Moharana Choudhury

Ethno botanical Records: (As medicinal)

Part used: Leaves, bark of stem, latex of leaf, fruit

Artocarpus heterophyllus (photo taken by Moharana Choudhury), & Ficus benghalensis (source: commons.wikimedia.org)

Process of utilization: paste of leaves juice is useful in stomach problem, bark of stem is useful in skin diseases, latex of leaf is very healthy paste of leaf is useful headache & reduces some gynecological problems. Fruit of it is useful in bronchitis & general cough.

RESULTS AND DISCUSSIONS

During the present day investigation, altogether 40 species belonging to 24 families of Angiospermic plants which are the part of the collection. All these plants are found to be of great ethno botanical records in some way or the other. Of all these, 30 plants were found to be of medicinal importance, 19 plants were used 1 plant as narcotics 2 plant insecticides, 1 plant for religious purpose & 3 plants use for construction purpose, 2 plant used as timber wood (table 7.1, 7.3) One plant has also been recorded to be of medicinal value for cattle.

The range of plants used as food by the local people of all communities is vast. There are 19 plants found to be used as food-food addition (table 7.2).These includes root, tubers, stem, leaves, bark, flowers, fruits, seeds and sometimes even the young items. They eat them either ripe or unripe cooked or raw.

These people (including some tribal people) specially are used to consumption of narcotics, irrespective of age and sex, use of various plants for these purposes. On the other hand, they even have antinarcotics drug which reduce the action of these intoxicants such a plant has been recorded amongst the chakma people. Out of these species, 20 are cultivated, 16 are wild state rest may be cultivated or wild. They are cultivated for several purposes like food, medicinal value, ornamental etc. The process of utilization of particular part of plants a specific purpose. The same plant may be used in different ways by different types of people. The same community of people also make use of same plant for several purpose in various ways. Sometimes the fresh juice is extracted from the plant while in others may be used as paste. Besides fresh fruit, roots inflorescence, bark, sometimes the entire plant might be used. In investigation it is also observed that to cure a disease they are used as a combination of several plants. Out of the 35 species identified taxonomically, 26 species are used for medicinal purpose. Of these 2 species are used for gynecological problems.2 species as anti helminthic, 3 species as anti hemorrhagic, 6 species for stomach troubles, 3 species for dysentery, 2 species for jaundice, 1 species for malaria, 2 species as multipurpose, 1 species has been recorded as cattle food where there is scarcity of grass. Among the food plants, 12 species are cooked as vegetable, 6 species of plants are eaten raw, 9 species provide fruit, 1 species is used as cattle food, 2 species are consumed directly & 1 species is used as ingredients for preparation of intoxicant. 3 species are used as timber & manufacture of furniture & house constructions.2 species are used as mosquito repellent and 2 are used as spices.

A systematic list of all these plants is given the following table below:

Table 7.1: Medicinal Plants

Disease	No. of Plants	Specific Name of the Plants	Part Used	Preparation
Ring worm		*Cassia sophera*	Leaves	Juice
Jaundice		*Cajanus cajan*	Leaves	Paste
Toothache		*Mimosa pudica*	Leaves	Paste
Blood pressure		*Centella asiatica*	Leaves	Paste
Liver tonic diuretic		*Hydrocotyl javanica*	Whole plant	Paste
Diabetes		*Coccinia indica*	Fruit	Paste
Liverworm		*Momordica charantia*	Fruit	Boil
Anaemia & piles		*Punica grantum*	Fruit, skin	Raw, paste
Stomach problems		*Aegle marmelos*	Leaf, fruit	Raw
Blood pressure		*Citrus medica*	Fruit	Juice
Constipation		*Carica papaya*	Fruit	Raw
Skin disease		*Azadirechta indica*	Leaves	Paste
Heart disorder		*Terminalia arjuna*	Burks seed	Paste
Hair tonic		*Wedelica calendulae*	Leaves	Paste
Cough		*Adhatoda vasica*	Leaves	Paste

Table 7.2: Food Plants

Scientific Name of the Plants	Parts Used	Preparation
1. *Aegle marmelos*	Fruit	Raw
2. *Atrocarpus heterophyllus*	Fruit, seed	Raw, cooked
3. *Cajanus cajan*	Seeds, leaves	Cooked, Raw
4. *Carica papaya*	Fruit	Raw,cooked
5. *Centella asiatica*	Leaves	Paste
6. *Cinnamomum tamala*	Leaves	Cooked
7. *Citrus medica*	Fruit	Raw
8. *Coccinia indica*	Fruit	Cooked
9. *Coriandrum sativum*	Leaves	Cooked
10. *Embilica officinales*	Fruit	Raw
11. *Mangifera indica*	Fruit	Raw
12. *Mentha piperatia*	Leaves	Paste, Cooked
13. *Momordica charantia*	Fruit	Cooked
14. *Psidum guajava*	Fruit	Raw
15. *Punica grantum*	Fruit	Raw
16. *Musa paradisica*	Fruit	Raw

Table 7.3: Other Useful Plants

Purpose of Utilization	Scientific Name of the Plant	Part Used	Process of Utilization
Ornamental	*Hibiscus rosa-sinensis*	Whole plant	Decorate garden, offered to God during puja
Ornamental	*Polygonum orientale*	Whole plant	
Spice	*Coriandrum sativum*	Leaves, seeds	Decorate house
Wood plant & alternative	*Terminalia arjuna*	Stem	Paste, cooked
food for cattle, goats, cows	*Artocarpus heterophyllus*	Stem, leaves	As timber
Wood plant	*Azadirachta indica*	Stem	As timber, food for animal during scarcity of grass.
Wood plant	*Eucalyptus sp.*	Stem	Construction of house As timber

CONCLUSION

The present ethno botanical survey on town Silchar of district of CACHAR (Assam) clearly indicates their ethno botanical potential in spite of all kinds of modern development. The common people including different communities are living on their own way of life style. Very close to the nature, using various kinds of people makes the use of numerous plants in their day to day life. They have found a better and herbal solution to the various kinds of difficulties and necessities of everyday life is in the field of food, medicine, amusement, religious activities etc. Of all these the medicine and food plants deserve special mention. Especially the use of medicinal plants is better than the use of modern systematic medicine.

For this, the *in-situ* and *ex-situ* conservation along with judicious exploitation of this ethno botanical resource is the need of the day. The conservation of the wild as well as partially cultivated species of resource needs designing of suitable conservation strategies to care the ecological sustainability of the local ethnic groups. It is therefore imperative that further work in this field should be undertaken.

REFERENCES

1. Traditional Medicine, Science Reporter CSIR, New Delhi 37 9-15.
2. Bharti, P.K. and Chauhan, Avnish (2013): Ethnobotany and Medicinal Plants, *Ancient Publishing House*, Delhi, pp: 176 (ISBN: 978-93-8138-597-5).
3. Barthakur, S.K (1979): Less Known Medicinal Uses of Plants Among the Tribes of Karbi Aglong (Mikir Hills) Bull . Bot . Ind 18, 166-171.
4. Barthakur, S.K (1966): Post Natal Care of Women in Traditional System in Assam.Ethnobotany 8: 51-55.
5. Bhattacharjee, S Tiwari, K.C Mazumder, Rand Patowari, B (1977); Assam vis – a vis Plants of Ayurvedic Value. Indian Drug & Pharmaceutical Industry Botany, 89 July-August; 1977 and Vol. XII, No. 6.

6. Baruah, P and Sharma. G.C (1987): Studies on the Medicinal Uses of the Plants by the Boro Tribals of Assam II J.E Con. Tax. Bot. 5 No. 3.
7. Baishya. C.L R Mazumder, (1980) Some Flokore Claims from the Brahmaputra Valley (Assam) Ethnomedicine VI 1-4 139-145.
8. Divya Yog Mandir (Trust), Haridwar YOG, SANDESH December 2006.
9. Hajra, P.K & Baishya S.K (1981) Ethnobotanical Notes on the Meris (Misings) of Assam Plains, *Ibid* 161-169, New Delhi.
10. Jain, S.K (1963), Observation on Ethnobotany of the Tribals of Madhya Pradesh Vanyajati 11: 177-183.
11. Baruah, P & Sharma, G.C (1987): Studies on the Medicinal Uses of the Plants by the North East Tribes – III.
12. Biswas, S & Ahmed A (1987): Ethnobotanical Studies on the Plants of Burnihat Valley Assam/Meghalaya India for 113: 634-639.(Sl).
13. Carter, H.G, *et al*, (1921): Useful Plants for Lakhimpur, Assam Ree, Bot . Surv . Ind 6 (9): 353-420.
14. Hooker J.D (1972-79): Flora of British India I-VI.
15. Jain, S.K (1963): Wild Plants Food of the Tribals of Baster (M.P) India Proc. Nat Inst sci. India – 30 B: 56-80.
16. Jain, S.K (1964a) The Role of Botanist in Flok – lore 5: 145-150.
17. Maheshwari, J.K. K.K Singh & S Saha (1986). The Ethnobotany of Tribals of Mirjapur District U.P. Nat. Bot. Res Ins Lucknow.
18. Yog Sandesh (2005) July.
19. Rao, R.R and N.S Jamir (1982): Ethnobotanical Studies in Nagaland I, Medicinal Plants Econ . Bot 36 (176 – 81–(9).
20. Sen, S (1987): Tribes of Nagaland: Mittal Publication Delhi, India.
21. Saha, S.C (1986): Ethnobotanical Study of Manipur Ph.D. Thesis, Manipur University, Manipur (8).
22. Saklani & Jain (1994): Cross Cultural Ethnobotany of North-east India. Deep Publication, New Delhi.

***Pages:* 162-173**

MEDICINAL PLANTS: *DISTRIBUTION, UTILIZATION AND SIGNIFICANCE*

***Edited by:* Dr. Pankaj Sharma; Dr. Pawan Kumar 'Bharti' and Dr. Narayan Singh**

ISBN: 978-93-5056-734-0

***Edition:* 2015**

***Published by:* Discovery Publishing House Pvt. Ltd., New Delhi (India)**

8

Vegetation Analysis and Impact of Disturbances in Oak Dominated Forest of Kumaun Himalaya

Anita Joshi

INTRODUCTION

The Himalayan vegetation ranges from tropical dry deciduous forests in the foothill to alpine meadow above tree line (Singh and Singh 1992 and Ram *et al.* 2004). Species compositions of major forests types of Central Himalaya have been described by Ralhen *et al.*, (1982), Saxena and Singh (1982), Saxena *et al.*, (1984), Singh and Singh (1987), Tewari and Singh (1981) and Upreti *et al.*, (1985). Singh and Singh (1992) have summarized the information on the structure and functioning of the Himalayan forest ecosystem. Himalayan forest ecosystem has a major contribution to the mega-biodiversity of India; it is one of the 'hot spots' of biodiversity. The usually wide altitudinal range (over 3000m), rapid change in altitude and high endemism (Singh & Singh, 1992; Zobal & Singh, 1997), make it interesting area for studies on biodiversity.

Biodiversity is the totality of genes, species and ecosystem in the region. Various aspect of biodiversity of these forests has been studied by

Department of Forestry and Environmental Science, D S B Campus, Kumaun University Nainital, Uttarakhand, India.

(Dhar *et at.* 1997, Silori 2001, Kumar 2000 and Khera *et al.* 2001). Increasing anthropogenic pressure on forest over the few decades has led to vast exploitation of natural flora in Uttrakhand Himalaya. Anthropogenic disturbances play an important role in change, loss or maintenance of plant biodiversity and more recent phenomenon of climate change will also be responsible for the change in species composition and other ecosystem activities (Ram *et al.* 2005).

Several authors have studied the effect of disturbance on Himalayan forests. The effect of anthropogenic disturbance on plant diversity and community structure in the forest of north eastern Himalaya, India was studied by Khan *et al.* (1987); Misra *et al.* (2004) and Rao *et al.* (1990). Plant diversity in two forest types along a disturbance gradient in Dewalgarh watershed, Garhwal Himalaya was studied by Uniyal *et al.* (2010), in six forest types in Uttarakhand by Ram *et al.* (2004), and tree diversity and population structure in undisturbed and human-impacted stands of tropical wet ever-green forest in Arunanchal Pradesh were studied by Bhuyan *et al.* (2003).

All of the above studies reported that increased degree of disturbance caused loss of plant diversity and brought about a change in community characteristics. Banj oak(*Quercus leucotrichophora*) and Tilonj oak (*Quercus floribunda*) are the two dominant forest forming species of Central Himalayan occurring between 1800-2300m elevations, both are evergreen species. These are multipurpose trees. In the recent years various human generated disturbances occurred in the forest of Uttarakhand Himalaya and Oak happens to be the most effected species, this disturbances includes deforestation; grazing, surface burning, looping and litter removal these disturbances are not only changing the structure of ecosystem but also affecting the biodiversity of the forest as a result many of living species are shifting towards endangered and threatened. It is clearly indicated from various study that banj-oak (*Quercus leucotrichophora*) are failing to regenerate adequately over large areas on the other hand Chir-pine (*Pinus roxburghii*) is regenerating copiously (Saxena and Singh 1984, Singh & Singh, 1985, Rao and Singh, 1986). However depletion of oak forest has contributed to expansion of *Pinus roxburghii*.

Therefore, the conservation and scientific management of this species for socioeconomic development, betterment of soil, live-stock and human assumes a great significance. In this study, an attempt has been made to assess the impact of disturbance on forest vegetation in Kumaun Himalaya, Uttarakhand.

MATERIAL AND METHODS

The study area is located between 29°22′ and 29°23′ N latitude and 79° 26′ and 79° 28′E longitude between 1800-2300m elevations in Uttarakhand Himalaya. The forest were thoroughly surveyed and identified as

Q. leucotrichophora (Banj-oak) dominated forest and mixed (*Q.leucotrichophora and Q.floribunda*) oak forest. The present study was conducted in four different sites each site is further divided into disturbed and undisturbed sites, located between 1800 -2300m elevation in Nainital catchment to assess impact of disturbances in plant community on eight different aspects. The climate of Nainital is monsoonal. The study was conducted during 2012. The minimum temperature in year 2012 ranged from 0.-1.5°C in February to 18.70°C in June, while maximum temperature from 12.5°C in January to 28.4°C in June. the maximum rainfall occurred in July (833.8mm) and lowest in May and October (1mm).

Vegetation analysis was made for all the three layers of forest, i.e. trees, shrubs and hurbs, for identification Osmaston (1926) 'Forest Flora of Kumaun' was used the phytosociological analysis was done by sampling 20 10x10m quadrates on each site The size and number of samples were determined following Saxena and Singh (1982).The vegetational data were calculated for abundance density and frequency (Curtis and McIntosh, 1950). Importance Value Index (IVI) for the tree was determined as the sum of relative density, relative frequency and relative dominance (Curtis, 1959). Tree considered to be individuals > 30cm cbh (circumference at brest hight), saplings 10-30 cm cbh and seedlings <10cm circumference (Saxena and Singh, 1984; Upreti, 1982).

The shrub layer were analyzed by sampling quadrates of 5x5m and the herbs layer by placing quadrates of 1x1 m randomly on each site. The diversity index for all the three layers at each study site was calculated by using Shannon-Wiener (1963) and Concentration of dominance by using Simpson's (1949) Index.

DISTURBANCE REGIME AND ANTHROPOGENIC PRESSURE ON FOREST VEGETATION

Methods

Four dependence communities were identified. The disturbed forest sites were chosen on the basis of their proximity 1-4 km to the village settlements and urban populatio, where people have early access to resources. A questionnaire was used to collect basic village information on the communities residing, dependence on the forest for livestock grazing, fuel wood, timber and non -timber forest products. Households were surveyed in these sample villages for natural resources extraction/use pattern. A random sampling for households with 60% converge was envisaged and actually designed. Primary data were generated using focus group interviews and questionnaires wherever necessary regarding relevant information. Forest natural resources, such as fuel-wood load, fodder bundles, timber extraction, dry leaves, and their quantities were estimated through interview techniques followed by direct weighing (fresh weight= 3.5x dry weight). Data were gathered in three seasons, rainy, summer and winter.

Information on fuel resources extraction and usage practices were generated by weighing each head-load during field visits. Information on fodder usage and forest litter was also generated by weighing head-load at the time of extraction.

All enumerated resources have been found extracted in each community. The main sources of the resources extraction were Quercus forest, adjoining pine forest. Among the settlements, Kailakhan (talla Gathiya-Malla Gathiya), South facing, Nirmala (north facing), government house(north facing) and Tiffin top(north facing). The availability of the resources for the community was concerned, status to medium to high for all the settlements. The availability distance to resource was recorded highest (4km approx.) for talla-gathiya (kailakhan), and government house, (1-2km approx.) for Nirmala and Tiffin top. Natural resource extraction and utilization patterns were examined following Sharma (1992) and Metz (1997).

Table 8.1(a) Forest Resources Use Their Sources and Availability Status in Different Forest Settlements

Settlements		Resource Type	Source	As	D (km)
Stand	Aspect				
S1	(S)	Fuelwood, fodder, leaflitter	QL, PF	H	4
S2	(N-E)	Fuelwood, fodder, leaflitter	QL, QF,	M	3
S3	(N-W)	Fuelwood, fodder, leaflitter	QL, QF	M	3
S4	(E)	Fuelwood, fodder, leaflitter	QF	L	4

QF=Quercus forest, **QL**=Quercus leucotrichophora, **PF**=Pine forest, **AS**=Availibility status, **D**= Distance

RESULTS

Fuel wood is used for cooking food and heating space, boiling water. the mean amount of fuel consumption in south aspect of S1 site was (18.32kg/hh^{-1}/d^{-1}) and yearly it was (6686.8kg/hh^{-1}/yr^{-1}) and at moderately disturbed forest of S2 and S3 it was (15.24kg/hh^{-1}/day^{-1}), (5562.6kg/hh^{-1}/yr^{-1}) and (15.85kg/hh^{-1}/d^{-1}), (5785.25kg/hh/yr^{-1} respectively. At less disturbed site it was (14.42kg/hh^{-1}/d^{-1}) and (5263.3kg/hh^{-1}/yr^{-1}). Fodder was traditionally extracted by chopping tree branches and grasses were collected by harvesting with the use of sickles. Mostly women and children involved in fodder collection during morning and day hours, 1to 2 times/day. Fodder collection was high at highly disturbed site (15.12kg/hh^{-1}/d^{-1}), while yearly it was (5518.8kg/hh^{-1}/yr^{-1}). At moderately disturbed forests it was (13.20kg/hh^{-1}/d^{-1} and 11.0kg/hh^{-1}/d^{-1}) respectively while it was (4818 kg/hh^{-1}/yr^{-1} and 4015kg/hh^{-1}/yr^{-1}) yearly.

Table 8.1(b): Forest Resources Use and Source in Different Forest Settlements

S Aspect		N-E Aspect			N-W Aspect			N-E Aspect		
MC (Kg)	MC(Kg)	MC(Kg)		MC(Kg)	MC(Kg)		MC(Kg)	MC(Kg)		MC(Kg)
Resource	**Extraction**	**Frequency**	**hh^{-1}/day^{-1})**	**hh^{-1}/yr^{-1}**	**$C/hh^{-1}/d^{-1}$**	**$C/hh^{-1}/yr^{-1}$**	**$C/hh^{-1}/day^{-1}$**	**$C/hh^{-1}/day^{-1}$**	**$C/hh^{-1}/day^{-1}$**	**$C/hh^{-1}/yr^{-1}$**
Type	Process									
Fuelwood	Felling, lopping	M/1-2times	18.32	6686.8	15.24	5562.6	15.85	5785.25	14.42	5191.2
	Collecting	A day								
Fodder	Chopping	M/1-2times	15.12	5518.8	13.20	4818	11.0	4015	9.56	3489.4
	Mowing									
Litter	Collecting	1-2 times a week	1.8	657	1.4	511	1.3	474	1.2	438

C-consumption, Hh-House- hold

FOREST FLOOR LITTER

Forest floor litter was found to be used for livestock bedding, mulching and composting, etc. this accumulation. The forest floor litter was found to be usually collected during morning / day times. litter collection was collected 2 days in once a week and it was (1.8kg/hh^{-1}/d^{-1}) at highly disturbed S1 site while (1.4kg/hh^{-1}/d^{-1}) and 1.3kg/hh^{-1}/d^{-1} for both moderate disturbed sites and 1.2kg/hh^{-1}/d^{-1} for less disturbed forest.

DENSITY AND TOTAL BASAL AREA

The undisturbed stands had higher density 825-1170Ind./ha compared to moderately, less and highly disturbed stands where the density was 740Ind./ha, 765Ind./ha and 720Ind./ha respectively in terms of trees. Tree density decreased with increasing level of disturbance in the disturbed forests. Maximum shrub density was recorded in the highly disturbed stand it was 3840Ind/ha at undisturbed stand it was ranged between 2000-3740Ind./ha. Herb density was ranged between 796000-1290000Ind./ha at undisturbed sand it was found to be more 1262000-135000Ind./ha at moderately disturbed stand while it was 754000Ind./ha at less disturbed and 1159000Ind./ha at highly disturbed stand. Total basal area for tree was high (97.5m^2/ha) for undisturbed N-W aspect and low (35.449m2/ha) for disturbed S aspect. Total shrub cover was high 10.3% at highly disturbed site and 27.93% for moderately disturbed N-W aspect. (Table 8.2).

Table 8.2(a): Species Richness, Diversity and Important Vegetational Parameters for Trees in Different Forest

Undisturbed Site	Density (Ind./ha)	T.B.A (m^2/ha)	Diversity	Richness
S1	1170	97.5	2.602	11
S2	825	65.075	2.578	10
S3	990	94.82	2.129	10
S4	985	56.958	1.139	5
Disturbed Site				
S1(HD)	715	35.449	1.976	8
S2(MD)	740	50.8	2.306	6
S3(MD)	765	79.749	2.032	7
S4(LD)	720	38.55	1.096	5

Table 8.2(b): Species Richness, Diversity and Important Vegetational Parameters for Saplings in Different Forest

Undisturbed Site	Density (Ind./ha)	T.B.A (m^2/ha)	Diversity	Richness
S1	280	0.502	2.807	9
S2	220	0.447	2.764	8
S3	410	0.808	2.718	9
S4	250	0.502	2.100	5
Disturbed Site				
S1(HD)	710	1.556	1.365	6
S2(MD)	115	0.273	2.707	7
S3(MD)	155	0.190	2.423	6
S4(LD)	130	0.230	2.181	5

Table 8.2(c): Species Richness, Diversity and Important Vegetational Parameters for Seedlings in Different Forest

S1	1300	0.514	2.609	8
S2	1020	0.369	2.681	8
S3	1300	0.530	2.230	7
S4	1240	0.483	2.262	6
Disturbed Site				
S1(HD)	2760	1.75	0.430	5
S2(MD)	580	0.261	2.611	7
S3(MD)	560	0.29	2.031	6
S4(LD)	420	0.108	2.128	5

Table 8.3(a): Species Richness, Diversity and Important Vegetational Parameters for Shrubs in Different Forest

Undisturbed Site	Density (Ind/ha)	T.B.C%	Diversity	Richness
S1	3740	7.8	2.697	17
S2	2880	6.9	2.287	15
S3	2740	7.0	2.438	15
S4	2000	6.6	2.100	13
Disturbed Site				
S1(HD)	3840	10.3	3.475	17
S2(MD)	3000	7.5	2.323	15
S3(MD)	3280	7.7	2.456	15
S4(LD)	1940	6.9	2.431	13

Table 8.3(b): Species Richness, Diversity and Important Vegetational Parameters for Herbs in Different Forest

Undisturbed Site	Density (Ind/ha)	T.B.C%	Diversity	Richness
S1	1290000	27.58	4.348	31
S2	1252000	27.29	4.293	30
S3	1215000	24.92	4.331	30
S4	796000	19.00	4.049	28
Disturbed Site				
S1(HD)	1159000	26.4	3.985	31
S2(MD)	1262000	27.61	4.561	30
S3(MD)	1350000	27.93	4.462	30
S4(LD)	754000	19.3	4.078	28

DISCUSSION

The anthropogenic disturbances are the major causes of forest destruction in the Uttarakhand Himalaya (Tucker 1983). Even today broadleaf evergreen species like *Quercus* are extensively lopped for fodder, fuel wood and for making agricultural implements by the local people. At higher altitudes, lopping of tree leaves is done for animal bedding especially during winter, which is then used for compost. High concentration of grazing animals is another major cause of forest destruction in the region (Negi & Todaria 1993).

Regular human interventions for collection of fuel wood and minor forest product and grazing and trampling by animal are also common in *Q.leucotrichophora* forest. However, due to disturbances In these forests, the canopy cover was less and the soil became poorer in moisture and fertility compared to undisturbed forests. The tree specis richness were higher at moderately disturbed site and less at highly disturbed site. In *Q. leucotrichophora* forest, tree species richness, declined with increasing level of disturbance. In the present study the tree density varied from (715-1170Ind./ha) which were comparatively lower than the value reported by Singh *et.al.* (1994) they have reported tree density values ranging from (250-2070Ind./ha) for different central Himalayan forests.

This decline may be due to a gradual and consistent increase in the extraction of fuel wood and fodder as Q. leucotrichophora and Q.floribunda are the dominant species in these forests which are extensively used as fuelwood and fodder. On the basis of total basal area of these forest the disturbed forest had basal area generally between (35.449-79.7491m^2/ha) and undisturbed forests had basal area generally between (56.958-97.5m^2/ha) Upreti (1982) have reported total basal area for disturbed area generally below (38.7m^2/ha) and relatively higher basal area (33.71-74.17m^2/ha) for undisturbed forests. Here total basal area also declined with disturbance level that agreed with earlier findings (Bhuyan *et al.* 2001; Bhuyan *et al.* 2003; Ramirez et al. 2001), that showed decreasing density and total basal area with increasing disturbance Intensity. Total basal area has also been correlated with the rate of disturbance (Ramirez *et al.* 2001).

The seedlings and saplings are less in numbers and the density of trees for disturbed forest were less compared to undisturbed forest. Total sapling density varied from (220-410Ind./ha) for undisturbed forest and (115-600Ind./ha) for disturbed forest. Seedlings density at undisturbed site ranged between (1020-1900Ind./ha) while it was (320-2760Ind/ha) for disturbed forest. Total basal area for saplings and seedlings were high at highly disturbed site (1.556m^2/ha) and (1.75m^2/ha) respectively and less at undisturbed S aspect (0.808m^2/ha) and (0.530m^2/ha) respectively.

It's due to more density of pine species. In general the sapling and seedlings density of dominant tree species was much lower in disturbed forest this could be the attributed to the heavy extraction of dominant tree species for use as fuel and fodder and timber decreased number of sapling and seedling at disturbed forest is another consequence of anthropogenic pressure number of saplings and seedlings of dominant species was lower than the number at undisturbed site in the present study, which might be due to the inability of all seedlings to graduate into saplings and saplings into trees the saplings could be cut down for fuel by men and grazed as a fodder by animals and the seedlings could possibly trampled out either by men or by the grazing animals at the disturbed forest further the highly disturbed forest had poor regeneration of dominant tree species due to higher disturbances the soil of the aspect became poorer in moisture and fertility so the moisture observing capacity of the soil become less which led to the other lesser altitudinal forest species i.e. *P.roxburghii* to grow, that can grow in very poorer soil and barren areas (Tewari, 1982,Saxena *et.al.* 1985) in the present study at highly disturbed (S) aspect the pine sapling and seedlings increasing in numbers which indicates the impact of disturbances this shows the depletion of oak forest gradually and expansion of pine and other forest species on the other hand. Banj-oak are failing to regenerate adequately over large areas on the other hand chir pine is regenerating copiously and increasing in numbers (Saxena and Singh, 1984, Singh & Singh, 1985, Rao and Singh 1986).

Similar pattern were observed in the present study. Absence of saplings and seedlings in site 1 and also the conversion of seedlings into saplings of dominant species were low for all the disturbed sites indicate that it may have a significant bearing on the forest structure in coming years. Severe disturbances may reduce vegetation structure by destroying vegetation structure or moving it off site. While mild and moderate severety disturbances may enhance structure complexity by increasing the density of structure type (Franklin, 1992). In the present study shrub density was found more at highly disturbed site whereas herb density was observed less at highly disturbed site but found more at moderately disturbed sites. (Garkoti 1992) reported the herb diversity in the range of (4.09-4.22) for certain high altitude forests of central Himalaya. In the present study the value of herb diversity was in the range of (3.985-4.561) for disturbed forest and (4.049-4.348) for undisturbed forest in certain forests of Kumaun Himalaya.

The diversity and species richness for tree, saplings seedlings, shrubs and herb were decreasing altitudinal. High shrub diversity was observed at highly disturbed forest because high disturbance promotes bushy species to grow, while higher herb diversity was found at mid elevation disturbed forest while less herb diversity was found at highly disturbed forest. Species diversity at highly disturbed forest was low while moderately disturbed forest had high species richness. This indicates that moderate disturbances maintains high number of herbs by opening the canopy disturbance at moderate level providing favorable conditions for undergrowth to grow, where forest canopy was moderately opened as compared to high and less disturbed forest.

This may provide opportunity for invasion of more shrub and herb in the area. According to intermediate disturbance hypothesis (Connell 1978; Huston 1979),with no or little disturbance, only the competitive dominants can survive, while at sufficient high level of disturbance only fugitive species can survive, therefore, the diversity is maximum at the intermediate level of disturbance (Abugov 1982). The mild disturbance provides greater opportunity for species turnover, colonization and persistence of high species richness (Whittaker 1975). From the present study it is evident that increasing intensity of anthropogenic pressure on oak- forests leads to destruction of the saplings and seedlings of oak- species which is very important species for the whole region and if the present trend continues these forests of oak will be replaced by other less important species in the next coming year.

REFERENCES

Abugov, R. 1982. Species Diversity and Phasing of Disturbance. *Ecology* 63: 289-293.

Bhuyan, P., M.L. Khan & R.S. Tripathi. 2001. Tree Diversity and Population Structure in Undisturbed and Human Impacted Tropical Wet Evergreen Forests of Arunachal Pradesh, North East India. pp. 114-115. *In*: K. N. Ganeshaiah, R. Uma Shanker & K. S. Bawa (eds.) *Tropical Ecosystems: Structure, Diversity and Human Welfare.* Proceedings of International Conference on Tropical Ecosystems. Oxford & IBH,New Delhi, India.

Bhuyan, P., M.L. Khan & R.S. Tripathi. 2003. Tree Diversity and Population Structure in Undisturbed and Human Impacted Stands of Tropical Wet Evergreen Forest in Arunachal Pradesh, Eastern Himalayas, India. *Biodiversity and Conservation* 12: 1753-1773.

Connell, J.H. 1978. Diversity in Tropical Rain Forests and Coral Reefs. *Science* 199: 1302-1310.

Curtis, J.T. & R.P. Mc Intosh. 1950. The Interrelations of Certain Analytic and Synthetic Phytosociological Characters. *Ecology* 31: 434-455.

Curtis, J.T. 1959. *The Vegetation of Wisconsin. An Ordination of Plant Communities.* University Wisconsin Press, Madison, Wisconsin.

Garkoti, S.C. 1992. High Altitude Forest of Central Himalaya: Productivity and Nutrient Cycling. Ph.D. Thesis, Kumaun University, Nainital.

Huston, M.A. 1979. A General Hypothesis of Species Diversity. *The American Naturalist* 113: 81-101.

Khan, M.L., J.P.N. Rai & R.S. Tripathi 1987. Population Structure of Some Tree Species in Disturbed and Protected Sub-tropical Forests of North-east India. *Acta Oceologia Oceology Aplicata (France)* 8: 247-255.

Kumar, A. & Jeet Ram. 2005. Anthropogenic Disturbances and Plant Biodiversity in Forests of Uttaranchal, Central Himalaya. *Biodiversity and Conservation* 14: 309-331.

Misra, B.P., O.P. Tripathi, R.S. Tripathi & H.N. Pandey. 2004. Effects of Anthropogenic Disturbance on Plant Diversity and Community Structure of a Sacred Grove in Meghalaya, Northeast India. *Biodiversity and Conservation* 13: 421-436.

Singh, J.S. and Singh, S.P. Forest of Himalaya.Structure and Functioning and Impact of Man. Gynodya Prakashan, Nainital, India; 1992.

Osmaston, A.E. 1926. *A Forest Flora for Kumaun.* International Book Distributors, Dehradun, India.

Ralhan, P.K., A.K. Saxena & J.S. Singh. 1982. Analysis of Forest Vegetation at and Around Nainital in Kumaun Himalaya. *Proceedings of Indian National Science Academy* 48B: 122-138.

Ram Jeet, A. Kumar & J. Bhatt. 2004. Plant Diversity in Six Forest Types of Uttaranchal, Central Himalaya, India. *Current Science* 86: 975-978.

Ramirez - Marcial, N., M. Gonzalez- Espinosa & G. Williams - Linera. 2001. Anthropogenic Disturbance and Tree Diversity in Montane Rain Forests in Chiapas, Mexico. *Forest Ecology and Management* 154: 311-326.

Rao, P., S.K. Barik, H.N. Pandey & R.S. Tripathi. 1990. Community Composition and Tree Population Structure in a Sub-tropical Broad Leaved Forest Along a Disturbance Gradient. *Vegetatio* 88: 151-162.

Saxena, A.K & J.S. Singh. 1982. A Phyto-sociological Analysis of Woody Species in Forest Communities of a Part of Kumaun Himalaya. *Vegetatio* 50: 3-22.

Shankar. U.A Case of High Tree Diversity in a Sal (*Shorea robusta*)-dominated Lowland Forest of Eastern Himalaya: Floristic Composition, Regeneration and Conservation. *Research Article Current Science,* Vol. 81, No. 7, 10 October 2001.

Saxena, A.K., S.P. Singh & J.S. Singh. 1984. Population Structure of Forests of Kumaun Himalaya. Implications for Management. *Journal of Environmental Management* 19: 307-324.

Simpsons, G. 1964. Species Diversity of North American Recent Mammals. *Syst. Zoo.,13:* 57-73. Sexena, A.K, Singh.

S.P. and Singh, J.S. 1985 Population Structure of Kumaun Himalayan Forest Implications for Management. *Journal. Environ. Manage.* 19: 307-324.

Shannon, C.E. & W. Weaver. 1963. *The Mathematical Theory of Communication*. University of Illinois Press, Urbana.

Singh, J.S. & S.P. Singh. 1987. Forest Vegetation of the Himalaya. *Botanical Review* 52: 80-192.

Singh, J.S. & S.P. Singh. 1992. *Forests of Himalaya; Structure, Functioning and Impact of Man*. Gyanodaya Prakashan, Nainital, India.

Singh, S.P. & J.S. Singh. 1991. Analytical and Conceptual Plan to Reforest Central Himalaya for Sustainable Development. *Environmental Management* 15: 369-379.

Singh, S.P., B.S. Adhikari & D.B. Zobel. 1994. Biomass Productivity, Leaf Longevity and Forest Structure in the Central Himalaya. *Ecological Monograph* 64: 401-421.

Singh, S.P. 1998. Chronic Disturbance, a Principal Cause of Environmental Degradation in Developing Countries (Editorial). *Environmental Conservation* 25: 1-2.

Tewari, J.C. & S.P. Singh. 1981. Vegetation Analysis of a Forest Lying in Y Transitional Zone Between Lower and Upper Himalayan Moist Temperate Forests. pp. 104-119. *In*: G.S. Paliwal (ed.). *The Vegetational Wealth of Himalaya*. Puja Publishers, New Delhi.

Tilman, D. 1988. *Plant Strategies and the Dynamics and Structure of Plant Communities*. Princeton University Press, Princeton, New Jersey.

Turner, M.G., W.H. Romme, R.H. Gardener, R.V. O'Neill & T.K. Kratz. 1993. A Revised Concept of Landscape Equilibrium: Disturbance and Stability on Scaled Landscapes. *Landscape Ecology* 8: 213-227.

Uniyal, P., P. Pokhriyal, S. Dasgupta, D. Bhatt & N. P. Todaria. 2010. Plant Diversity in Two Forest Types Along the Disturbance Gradient in Dewalgarh Watershed, Garhwal Himalaya. *Current Science* 98: 938-943.

Upreti, N., J.C. Tewari & S.P. Singh. 1985. The Oak Forests of the Kumaon Himalaya (India): Composition, Diversity and Regeneration. *Mountain Research and Development* 5: 163-174.

Upreti, N. 1982. A Study on Phytosociology and State of Regeneration of Oak Forest at Nainital. Ph.D. Thesis, Kumaun University Nainital, India.

Shankar. U. Research Article, A Case of High Tree Diversity in a Sal (*Shorea robusta*)-dominated Lowland Forest of Eastern Himalaya: Floristic Composition, Regeneration and Conservation. Research Article Current Science, Vol. 81, No. 7, 10 october 2001.

Whittaker, R.H. 1975. *Communities and Ecosystems*. 2nd Edition, Macmillan Publishing Co., New York.

Pages: **174-197**

MEDICINAL PLANTS: ***DISTRIBUTION, UTILIZATION AND SIGNIFICANCE***

Edited by: **Dr. Pankaj Sharma; Dr. Pawan Kumar 'Bharti'** and **Dr. Narayan Singh**

ISBN: 978-93-5056-734-0

Edition: **2015**

Published by: **Discovery Publishing House Pvt. Ltd., New Delhi (India)**

9

Ashwagandha *A Miracle Medicinal Crop*

Archana Rani* and **Sanjeev Kumar[1]**

INTRODUCTION

Among the innumerable gifts of nature the fascinating varieties of natural products have been inseparable parts of mankind's history, since they fulfils many of our most basic requirements. Plants are important source of natural products. Thus, from the very beginning, man has familiarized himself with plants and used them in a variety of ways throughout the ages. In search of food and to cope successfully with human suffering, primitive man began to distinguish those plants suitable for nutritional purposes from others with definitive pharmacological action. Therefore, some plants came to be widely used as a food while others were used for therapeutic purpose and for treatment of diseases. The growth of knowledge to cure disease continued at an accelerating pace and the number of new plants-derived drugs increased like-wise. Since the dawn of civilization upto the twenty-first century, plants have been the most important sources of drugs for the mankind. Herbal

Department of Agricultural Biotechnology and Molecular Biology, (FBS & H), Rajendra Agricultural University, Pusa - 848 125, Bihar (India)

1 Department of Plant Pathology, College of Agriculture, Jawaharlal Nehru Krishi Vishwa Vidyalaya, Jabalpur - 482 004, Madhya Pradesh (India).

medicine is the most ancient form of health care known to humanity. Medicinal plants have been widely used for treatment of various human ailments in all cultures throughout history. Extensive scientific documentation now exists concerning their use in number of health condition.

Consumption of herbal medicines is widespread and increasing. Harvesting from the wild, the main source of raw material, is causing loss of genetic diversity and habitat destruction. Domestic cultivation is a viable alternative and offers the opportunity to overcome the problems that are inherent in herbal extracts: misidentification, genetic and phenotypic variability, extract variability and instability, toxic components and contaminants. As a consequence of unregulated use of these plants, their populations are heading towards alarming depletion, coupled with fragmentation of their natural habitats. Human interference, distraction of medicinal plants during harvesting, trade in high quantities and harvesting for other uses as timber and firewood is accelerating the pace of disappearance of many valuable plant species (Ved *et al.*, 1998). Using the current global rates of species extinction at around 10 to 12% of the plants i.e., around 800-1000 species are likely to be threatened (Verma and Coworkers, 2004). A survey report of International Union for conservation of nature and natural resources (IUCN) informed that India ranked 5th position in case of threatened plant species (Maiti, 2006).

The use of controlled environments can overcome cultivation difficulties and could be a means to manipulate phenotypic variation in bioactive compounds and toxins. Conventional plant-breeding methods can improve both agronomic and medicinal traits, and molecular marker assisted selection will be used gradually more. There has been significant evolution in the use of tissue culture and genetic transformation to alter pathways for the biosynthesis of target metabolites. Obstacles to bringing medicinal plants into successful commercial cultivation include the difficulty of predicting which extracts will remain marketable and the likely market preference for what is seen as naturally sourced extracts.

In view of the tremendously growing world population, increasing anthropogenic activities, rapidly eroding natural ecosystem, etc., the natural habitat for a great number of herbs and trees are dwindling. Many of them are facing extinction. The use of herbal medicines in developed countries is also growing and 25% of the UK population takes herbal medicines regularly. Approximately two thirds of the 50000 different medicinal plant species in use are collected from the wild and, in Europe, only 10% of medicinal species used commercially are cultivated. There is growing concern about diminishing populations, loss of genetic diversity, local extinctions and habitat degradation.

Medicinal plants as a group comprise approximately 8000 species and account for about 50% of all the higher flowering plant species of India.

Millions of rural mass use medicinal plants. In recent years the growing demand for herbal products has led to a quantum jump in volume of plant material traded within and outside the country. Very small proportions of the medicinal plants are lichens, ferns, algae etc; the majority of the medicinal plants are higher plants. Though India has rich biodiversity and one among the twelve centers, the growing demand is putting a heavy strain on the existing resources causing a number of species to be either threatened or endangered category. About 90% of medicinal plants used by industries are collected from the wild.

While over 800 species are used in production by industry, less than 20 species of plants are under commercial cultivation. Over 70% of the plant collections involve destructive harvesting because of the use of parts like roots, bark, wood, stem and the whole plant in case of herbs. This poses a definite threat to the genetic stocks and to the diversity of medicinal plants. Although adequate protection of some species can be achieved through increased regulation and the introduction of sustainable wild harvesting methods, a more viable long-term alternative is to increase domestic cultivation of medicinal plants. Cultivation also opens up the possibility of using biotechnology to solve problems that are inherent in the production of herbal medicines. These include species misidentification, genetic and phenotypic variability, variability and instability of extracts, toxic components and contaminants.

Cultivation offers the opportunity to optimize yield and achieve a uniform, high quality product. The prospective cultivator of medicinal plants must, however, make the difficult decision of which particular species to grow in what is a rapidly shifting, and fashion-prone, market .The high selling species with a large market share, such as *Ginkgo biloba* or *Hypericum perforatum* (St Johns Wort), are those most likely to be under cultivation already by the large European and American herbal companies and are those least threatened by wild harvesting. The future market for less well-known species is highly unpredictable and because many are perennials requiring several years to establish and become harvestable, investment in them could represent a considerable commercial risk.

The family Solanaceae, also called as the 'nightingale' family, is divided into 84 genera and 3000 species widely distributed in tropical and temperate regions. *Withania somnifera* Dunal, a member of Solanaceae is commonly known as 'Ashwagandha'(2n=48) or 'Indian Ginseng' and it is ancient Ayurvedic drug (Rajeswara Rao *et al.*, 2012).The Sanskrit name "ashva" meaning horse and "gandha" meaning smelling was given to this plant due to the smell of the roots resembling a sweating horse. Ashwagandha, is a 50-150 cm tall, erect evergreen tomentose self-pollinating shrub, which has consistent demand in pharmaceutical industries due to its unique medicinal properties (Anonymous, 1976). It is indigenous to India (Indian Ginsang) is one of the most extensively used medicinal plants in Ayurvedic and Unani medicines (Rani and Grover, 1999). *Withania somnifera*(L.) Dun is a much-valued medicinal plant with immense therapeutic applications including anti-stress, anti-depressant, adaptogenic, rejuvenative, aphrodisiac, anticancerous and antioxidant body building herb with great promises (Shanmugaratnam *et al.*, 2013). Ashwagandha has high demand (500 tonnes, during 1999) in pharmaceutical industries, 50% of which is met through harvesting of wild population (NRIF, 2004). Its current domestic sales are approximately Rs. 100-120 million (Rawat and Garg, 2005; Sharada *et al.*,). Extensive cultivation of this species is being done in many tropical regions of India. Report is also available revealing its successful cultivation in a temperate climate zone (Butola and Badola, 2007; Rajeswara Rao *et al.*,2012).

Conventional propagation is achieved through seeds but the seed viability is limited to one year(Waman *et al.*,2011.) and success rate of vegetative propagation in *Withania Somnifera* is very low (Kulkarni *et al.*, 2000 ;Vadawale *et al.*, 2004). The herb has been identified by National Medicinal Plant Board of India as one of the thirty-two selected priority medicinal plants, which are in great demand in the domestic and international markets (Prajapati *et al.*, 2003). Hence, the main purpose of writing this chapter is to depict the properties ,cultivation and conservation techniques, various developments, present and future trends and its application in various fields of *Withania somnifera* Dunal, (Ashwagandha).

COMMON NAMES

Ashwagandha is known by several names as mentioned below:

Language	Name
English	Winter Cherry, Indian ginseng
Sanskrit	Ashvagandha (Horse smelling)
Hindi	Asgandh
Urdu	Asganda nagori
Punjabi	Aksan, Asgand
Haryanavi	Aksin
Gujarati	Ghodaakun, Asuth
Rajasthani	Sarvgandha
Marathi	Askandha, Kanchuki
Konkani	Fatarfoda
Bengali	Ashvaganda
Oriya	Asugandha
Assamese	Asgandhisrol
Kannada	Amangura, Sogadeberu
Malayalam	Amukkiram, Pevetti
Tamil	Amkulan-kalang, Achuvagandhi
Telugu	Penneru gaddalu

BOTANICAL DESCRIPTION

Taxonomic Classification

Division	Spermatophyta
Subdivision	Angiospermae
Class	Dicotyledonae
Subclass	Gamopetalae
Order	Polemoniales
Family	Solanaceae
Genus	*Withania*
Species	*Somnifera*

Characteristic Features

Height	: 0.3-1.5 meter
Stem and Branches	: The stem is green and erect, covered with minute star shaped hair.Branche terete, usually clothed with stellate hoary tomentum
Leaves	: Simple, short petioled, alternate, or in sub opposite pairs at a node,extipulate,broadly ovate,obovate or oblong entire,subacute or obtuse, grey pubescent,5 to 10 cm, long, little less-2.5 to 7 cm .in breadth, the base often attenuated into the petiole and with about six pairs of stout and conspicuous main nerves
Petiole	: 0.6 to about 1.2 cm long
Flowers	: Small, greenish or lurid yellow, sessile or shortly pedicel led
The Pedicels	: Less than or about 5mm in length-axillary solitary or in crowded fascicles of 2-5
Calyx	: Gamosepalous, campanulate, 5mm, long in flower, five or six lobed, the segments linear acute from a broad base or subulate. It is accrescent increasing up to 18mm. becoming inflated and nearly globose and encloses the fruit: ultimately the entire calyx gets memberanous and withers
Corolla	: Small, but longer than the calyx, 0.6 to 1.2 cm, gamopetalous, campanulate, greenish-yellow, three to six lobed to more than half way down lobes short, lanceolate acute and valvate.
Stamen	: Five, included,inserted on the tube of the corolla near its base.

Filaments Linear, or subulate after dilated at the base and together forming a ring around the pistil

Anther : Yellow, broadly elliptic oblong (in level with the stigma) and dehiscing longitudinally

Pistil : Bicarpellary, syncarpous

Ovary : Ovate-glabose, glabrous, surrounded at the base by a thin glandular annular disc, bilocular or falsely four chambered, many ovuled with linear filiform or subulate style and a bifid or shortly two-lobed stigma

Fruit : A small smooth globose, thin walled two chambered berry the size of pea (0.6-0.8 cms in diameter), green when unripe while brick reddish when ripe and enclosed within the enlarged calyx.

Seeds : Small about 2 to 2.5 mm. in diameter, discoid or reniform with smooth or pitted testa and a peripheric embryo.

Roots : The root system consists of a stout main root 20 to 30 cm. long with a few (2 to 3) lateral roots of slightly smaller size.The roots are some what tuberous and attain a diameter of 1 to 2 or 2.5 cm. They are occasionally branched. There distal ends are taperaing and slightly woody.

Chromosome : Variable chromosome numbers are:

(i) 2n = 12, 18, 24, 36, 48, 72 (Iqbal and Datta, 2007)
(ii) $2n$=24 (Ram Mohan and Kamini, 1964)
(iii) $2n$=48 (Gottschalk1954)
(iv) $2n$=72 (Bir and Neelam 1980).

DISTRIBUTION

Withania somnifera the perennial plant belongs to family Solanaceae, is widely distributed in India, Pakistan, Sri Lanka, Mediterranean regions, Canaries, S. Africa, Iraq, Iran, Syria and Turkey (Jafri *et al.*, 1966 and Nasir *et al.*, 1972). *Withania somnifera* cosmopolition and grows throughout the drier parts and sub-tropical India. It is widely distributed in North-Western India, Bombay, Gujarat, Rajasthan, Madhya Pradesh, and Uttar Pradesh, Panjab plains extending to the mountain regions of Punjab, Himachal Pradesh and Jammu. The wild growth of this species has also been reported from Pakistan, Afganistan, Palestine, Egypt, Jordan, Morocco, Spain, Canary Island, Eastern Africa, Congo, Madagascar and South Africa. *Withania somnifera* has a very wide geographical range. In India its range extends from 230 N to 330 N and extending from 180m to 1500m *alt* (Akhatar, 1997). In India it grows well in the drier parts of tropical and sub tropical regions of Punjab, Hariyana,

Uttar Pradesh, Uttarakhand, Bihar, Jharkhand, Rajasthan, Madhya Pradesh, Maharastra and some parts of Himachal Pradesh, Jammu and Kashmir ascending upto 1,650 m in the Himalayas (Kapoor,2005 and Bandhopadhyay and Jha, 2003).

PHARMACOLOGICAL ACTIVITIES AND USES

Different plant parts possess the following activities: anti-inflammatary, antitumour, antistress, anti-arthritic, anti oxidant, immunomodulatory, homeopathic and its dry root power is used extensively as rejuvenating as well as tonic for general debility, having little or no associated toxicity (Andallu and Radhika, 2000; Vadawale *et al.*, 2004; Shanmugaratnam *et al.*, 2013). It is an abortifacient, amoebicide, anodyne, bactericide, contraceptive, diuretic, emmenagogue, fungicide, narcotic, pediculicide, sedative, spasmolitic, adaptogenic and tonic. In folk medicine preparations from this plant were used to treat arthritis, asthma, adenopathy, anthrax, bronchitis, cancer, candida, cold, cough, cystitis, debility, diarrhea, dropsy, dyspepsia, fever, gynecopathy, hiccup, lumbago, nausea, piles, psoriasis, ring-worm, scabies, senility, small pox, sores, syphilis, tuberculosis, typhoid, uterosis. In traditional systems drugs made from Ashwagandha are used to treat general/ sexual/nervine debility, stress, bone weakness, anxiety, constipation, antiageing, muscular weakness, insomnia and as an every day health supplement to cope with modern day stress. Leaves are used for curing fever, lesions, swelling, sore eyes and syphilitic sores. Green berries are used for treating ringworm infection, animal sores and horse's girth galls (Rajeswara Rao *et al.*, 2012).

Precautions

- Caution is advised for patients with diabetes, alcohol dependence or liver disease.
- Consulting doctor or pharmacist about the safe use of Ashwagandha is advocated.
- Ashwagandha is not recommended for use during pregnancy.
- Because of potential risk to the infant, breast-feeding while using Ashwagandha is not suggested.

BIOCHEMICAL CONSTITUENTS

Different parts of the plant contain a number of chemical com-pounds. Some of them are listed below:

- **Alkaloids**

Ashwagandhine, anahygrine, anaferine, cuscohygrine, tropine, isopelletierine, pseudotropine, [3]-tigloyloxtropine, 3- tropyltigloate, dlisopelletierine, hygrine, mesoanaferine, choline, somniferine, withanine, withananine, hentriacontane, visamine, withasomnine etc.

- **Steroidal compounds**

  Ergostane
- **Steroidal lactones**

  withaferin A, withanolides A-Y, withasomniferin-A, withasomidienone, withasomniferols A-C, withanone etc.
- **Saponins** containing an additional acyl group: sitoindoside VII and VIII
- **Withanolides** with a glucose at carbon 27: sitoindoside IX and X
- **Withanolide glycosides**

  withanosides I, II, III,IV, V, VI and VII
- **Pyrazole derivatives**

  pseudowithanine and ashwagandhine

Apart from these contents plant also contains chemical constitu-ents like withaniol, acylsteryl glucosides, starch, reducing sugar, hantreacotane, ducitol, a variety of amino acids including aspartic acid, proline, tyrosine, alanine, glycine, glutamic acid, cystine, tryptophan, and high amount of iron (Rajeswara Rao *et al.*, 2012).

CULTIVATION

Soil

Ashwagandha grows well in sandy loam or light red soil, having pH 7.5-8.0 with good drainage. It can be cultivated between 600-1200 m altitude.

Climate

The semi-tropical areas receiving 500-750 mm rainfall are conducive for cultivation of this rained crop. The crop requires dry season during its growing period. Temperature between 20°C to 35°C is most suitable for cultivation. Late winter rains are conducive for the proper development of the plant roots.

Land Preparation

Ashwagandha is usually grown in fields which are not well covered by the irrigation systems. The field on which food crops cannot be taken profitably for the above reason may be used for Ashwangandha cultivation. The soil of the field selected for Ashwagandha cultivation is well pulverized by ploughing, disking and/or harrowing. The field may be then levelled by the application pata.

Nursery Raising

The crop can be sown either by broad casting or in lines. Line to line method is preferred as it increases root production and also helps in performing intercultural practices properly. The seeds are usually sown about 1-3 cm deep in June-July in nursery. A light shower after shower after sowing ensures good germination. About 500-750 gm seeds are sufficient for 1 ha.

field. Seeds can be treated, with Thiram or Indofil or Dithane medicinal plants - 45 (@ 3 gm/kg seed), before sowing to protect seedlings from seed borne diseases.

Transplanting

The seedling after 25-35 days after sowing can be transplanted in the field marinating 60 × 60 cm. Spacing between the plants & the rows. It may be noted that since 'Asagnadh' is a rainy season Kharif crop, the time of sowing is decided by date of arrival of monsoon in that area.

Thinning

The seeds sown by broadcasting or in the line in furrows should be thinned out by hand at 25-30 days after sowing to maintain a plant population of about 30-60 plants per square meter (about 3.5 to 6 lakh plants/hectare).

Weeding

One hand weeding at an early stage is sufficient to enable the Ashwagandha plants to take over the growth of weed, which get suppressed by its smothering effect.

Manures and Fertilizers

The medicinal plants have to be grown without chemical fertilizers. Organic manures like, Farm Yard Manure (FYM), Vermi-Compost, Green Manure etc. may be used as per requirement of the species.

Plant Protection Measures

The medicinal plants have to be grown without use of pesticides. To prevent diseases, bio-pesticides could be prepared (either single or mixture) from Neem (kernel, seeds & leaves), Chitrakmool, Dhatura, Cow's urine etc.

Irrigation

Excessive rainfall/water is harmful to the crop. There is no need of irrigation if rainfall is at regular intervals. Light shower after transplantation ensures establishment of seedlings. Life saving irrigations may be applied, if required.

Harvesting

The crop is ready for harvest in January-March at 150 to 180 days after sowing. The plants start flowering and bearing fruits from December onwards. The maturity of crop is judged by drying out of leaves and yellow red berries. The entire plant is up rooted for roots which are separated from aerial parts by cutting the stem 1-2 cm above the crown.

Post Harvesting

The roots are then either cut transversely into small pieces (7 to 10 cm) or dried as it is in the sun. About 650-800 kg roots can be obtained from 1 ha on drying it comes to 350-435 kg. Berries are hand plucked separately. They are dried and crushed to take out the seeds. The dried roots, entire or transversely cut into smaller pieces, have to be further cleaned, trimmed and graded. The roots are beaten with a club which removes adhering soil and breaks off the thin, brittle lateral rootlets. Lateral branches, root crown and stem remains on roots are carefully trimmed with the help of knife.

Grading

Root pieces are then sorted out into following grades.

1. A grade

Root pieces up to 6-7 cm in length, 1-1.5 cm in diameter, solid cylindrical with smooth external surface and pure white from inside.

2. B grade

Root pieces up to 5 cm in length, 1 cm or less in diameter, solid, brittle and white from inside.

3. C grade

Solid root pieces up to 3-4 cm in length, 1 cm or less in diameter.

4. D grade

Small root pieces, semisolid or hollow, very thin, yellowish inside and < 1 cm in diameter of late farmers are grading the roots into 7 or more grades.

Yield

On an average yield from one hectare, land under commercial cultivation is approx 3-5 quintals of dried roots and 55-75 kg seeds.

Economics

Expenditure per ha. Rs. 5,600/-

Return per ha. Rs. 30,000/

Net income Rs. 24,000/- Approx

Value addition

- Value added products from Ashwagandha include root powder, capsules, root extract, herbal beer etc. in addition to the traditional drugs made from this plant.
- Health drinks, herbal tea, functional foods, nutraceuticals and cosmeceuticals are some of the value added products on which enterprises can be set up.

APPLICATION OF BIOTECHNOLOGY

Plant Biotechnology is a process to produce a genetically modified plant by removing genetic information from an organism, manipulating it in the laboratory and then transferring it into a plant to change certain of its characteristics . In Nutshell it's the manipulation of plants for the benefit of mankind.

The plants are mainly manipulated for two major objectives:

A. Crop improvement

- Herbicide tolerance (in use)
- Pest resistance (in use)
- Drought tolerance
- Nitrogen fixing ability
- Acidity and Salinity tolerance

B. Nutritional value of crops

- Improving food quality and safety
- Healthier cooking oils by decreasing the conc. of saturated fatty acids in vegetable oils
- Functional foods: foods containing significant levels of biologically active components that impart health benefits

Various technologies applied in plant biotechnology includes:

- Tissue culture
- Genetic engineering/recombinant DNA technology

Traditional plant breeding involves cross-breeding of similar plants to produce new varieties with different traits. But it takes many generations to achieve desired result. By using various biotechnological tools, crop improvement can be achieved faster and it even facilitates to transfer genes from unrelated species.

Fig. 9.1: Callus Mediated Shoot Differentiation from Leaf Explant

Tissue Culture

Tissue culture manipulates cells, anthers, pollen grains, or other tissues; so they live for extended periods under laboratory conditions or become whole, living, growing organisms; genetically engineered cells may be converted into genetically engineered organisms through tissue culture.

Secondary metabolites are obtained by direct extraction from plants grown in natural habitat; several factors can alter their yield. The commercial cultivation of *Withania* spp. is associated with two major problems namely, the plant to plant variation in alkaloid and withanolide yield and quality as well as the long gestation period (4-6 years) between planting and harvesting. Agronomically plants are propagated through seeds since the plants are not available for vegetative propagation and the variability generated by sexual recombination is very high. The natural wild populations of *Withania somnifera* contain a tongue-paralyzing constituent in their roots and hence cannot be used for Ayurvedic treatments. However the improved, cultivated varieties do not have such an active ingredient. The improved, cultivated varieties however do not have such an ingredient.

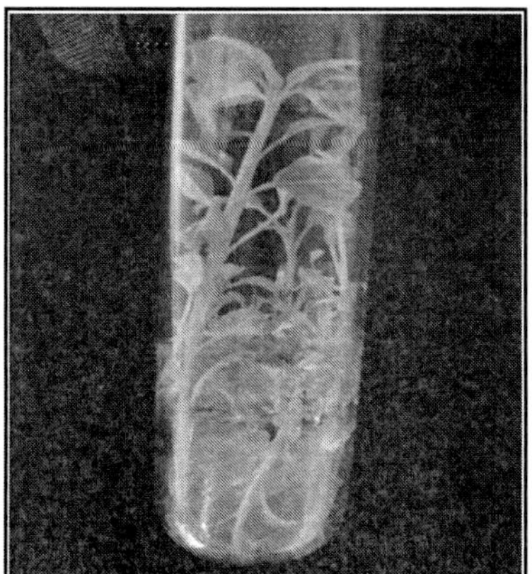

Fig. 9.2: Shoot Differentiation from Shoot Apex Explant in *W.somnifera*

Fig. 9.3

The wild and cultivated plants contain the same alkaloids but exhibit different morphologies and therapeutic actions. Field-grown plants may be subject to seasonal and somatic variations, infestations of bacteria, fungi and insects as well as environmental pollution that can affect the medicinal value of the harvested tissues. To improve the commercial outlook for the production of the secondary metabolites of *W. somnifera,* biological advances must be made that should either increase the yield or reduce the time gap and assure quality (Banerjee *et al.,* 1994). The use of plant cell and tissue cultures has overcome several inconveniences for the production of the secondary metabolites which is an alternative approach to traditional agriculture in the industrial production of these biomolecules . The protocols are designed to provide most optimistic levels of carbohydrates, organic compounds (vitamins), mineral nutrients, environmental factors (e.g. light, gaseous environment, temperature, and humidity) and growth regulators required to obtain high regeneration rates of many plant species *in vitro.*

Efforts of various workers to establish *in vitro* regeneration of *W. somnifera* have been reported and listed in table 9.1. Vishnoi *et al.,* (1979) succeeded in raising embryoids from anther induced callus cultures. Sen and Sharma (1991) were the first to describe *in vitro* shoot multiplication followed by rhizogenesis from aseptically germinated seedlings cultured on BAP enriched MS medium. Multiple shoots were obtained via morphogenesis from axillary bud derived callus (Roja *et al.,* 1991). Baburaj and Gunasekaran (1995) first reported differentiation of shoots from leaf callus cultures. Das *et al.,* (2011) got organogenic totipotency through *in vitro* culture of two elite genotypes (Poshita and Jawahar 22) of *Withania* and quantify their bioactive compounds. Abhyankar and Chinchanikar (1996) have described *in vitro* regeneration of *Withania somnifera* from leaf explant cultured on MS medium supplemented with IAA and BAP without an intervening callus phase. In another study Kulkarni *et al.,* (1999, 2000) reported in vitro propagation through organogenesis using various explants. Kanungo and Sahoo (2011) have described the direct organogenesis of *Withania somnifera* L. from apical bud. Multiple shoot differentiation was achieved on MS medium containing BAP (Kulkarni *et al.,* 1999, 2000). Direct organogenesis of *Withania somnifera* L. was achieved on MS and RT basal medium containing NAA 2,4-D from apical bud explants (Kanungo and Sahoo, 2011). Udayakumar *et al.,* (2013) developed direct and indirect regeneration protocols for multiple shoots development from epicotyls explants of 50 to 60 days old seedlings. Rani *et al.,* (2014a,b) was reported shoot apex and leaf explants. of *Withania somnifera* cultured on MS medium supplemented with NAA,IBA,IAA and BAP and got callus induction, shoot proliferation, root induction and finally regenerated plantlets transfer into the field from.

Table 9.1: *In vitro* **regeneration in** *Withania somnifera*

Initial Explant	Basal medium + PGR	Regeneration Pathway	Reference
Anthers	MS + BAP	Embryoid differentiation *via* androgenesis	Vishnoi *et al.*, 1979
Germinating	MS + BA, IBA, 2,4-D	Multiple shoots, plant regeneration, greenhouse establishment	**Sen & Sharma,1991**
Leaf segments	MS + NAA, Kn	Callus induction, multiple shoot differentiation	**Baburaj &** Gunasekaran,1995
Leaf segments	MS + IAA, BAP, Kn	Callus, multiple shoots, plant regeneration	Abhyankar & Chinchinakar,1996
Germinating seeds	MS + IAA, BAP, TDZ	Regeneration *via de novo* organogenesis	Kulkarni *et al.*,1999, 2000
Leaves, Shoot tips	MS + IAA, Kn, BAP	Callus induction, shoots, rhizogenesis, plantlet regeneration	**Teli** *et al.*,1999
Stem segments	MS + BAP	Plant regeneration *via* callus	Manickam *et al.*, 2000
Leaves, Shoot tips	MS + IAA, NAA, BAP, Kin	Plant regeneration *via* adventitious shoot Differentiation	Pawar *et al.*, 2001
Nodal segments, seedlings	MS + BAP, NAA	Multiple shoot differentiation, rooting	Ghosh & Gupta, 2001
Leaf segments	MS + 2,4-D, KN, BAP, IBA, IAA	Callus induction, shoots, rhizogenesis, plantlets regeneration	Ray & Jha, 2001, 2002
Hypocotyls, axillary, shoots, intermodal	MS + TIBA, BAP, KnIAA, IBA	Callus induction, plantlet regeneration, somatic embryogenesis and cotyledonary leaf segments, reproductive shoots	Rani *et al.*, 2003a, b; 2004
Nodal segments	MS + BA, IBA, 2,4-D	Multiple shoots, plant regeneration	Govindaraju *et al.*, 2003

(Table Contd...)

Initial Explant	**Basal medium + PGR**	**Regeneration Pathway**	**Reference**
Seedling, shoot tips; cotyledon , internodes, root segments	MS + IAA, IBA, NAA, B5 + IAA, IBA, NAA, Kn BAP, 2,4-D	Callus induction, regeneration *via de novo* organogenasis, multiple shoot differentiation, rhizogenesis, root regeneration, plantlet regeneration, establishment, field transfer up to plant maturity	Sharada, 2004
Nodal segments	MS + BA, IBA, 2,4-D	Multiple shoots, plant regeneration	Siddique *et al*., 2004
Leaf disc	MS + BA,IAA,	Multiple shoots, plant regeneration	Logesh *et al*., 2010
Apical bud	MS and RT+ 2,4-D, NAA	Callus induction, regeneration *via de novo* organogenes is, root regeneration, transfer and established into experimental field	Kanungo & Sahoo, 2011
Epicotyl explant	MS + BA, IBA, 2,4-D, GA_3, IBA	Direct and callus mediated plant regeneration, transfer and established into experimental field.	Udayakumar *et al*., 2013
Leaf	MS + BAP, NAA	Callus induction and shoot regeneration	Rani *et al.,* (2014b)
Shoot apex and leaf	MS + NAA, IBA, IAA, BAP	Callus induction, shoot proliferation, root induction and finally regenerated plantlets transfer into the field	Rani *et al.,* (2014,a)

PRODUCTION OF BIOACTIVE METABOLITES *in Vitro*

Production Through Tissue Culture

Cell and tissue culture technique provides a novel approach in the field of production of bioactive substances of medicinal plants. This techniques have been employed in many medicinal plants to produce therapeutically important compounds. *In vitro* culture of plant tissues offers an experimental method to learn production, regulation and enhancement of secondary metabolites under completely controlled conditions (Dorenberg and Knorr, 1997; Charlwood and Pletsch, 2002). In several cases, the cultures have been exploited for commercial production (Rao and Ravishankar, 2002).Although a huge variety of metabolites have been isolated from different parts of *Withania somnifera* and their biological activities confirmed, there are only few reports with respect to production of withanolides and other metabolites *in vitro*. Stoller *et al.*, (1974) raised callus and suspension cultures from germinating seeds of *W. somnifera* and analyzed them for steroid derivatives, withanolides, alkaloids and fatty acid contents. According to these investigators, callus cultures vary in metabolite contents from that in the donor tissues. According to Heble (1985) total withanolide (withanone, withanolide G, withanolide I, withanolide E.) contents in *W. somnifera* shoot cultures, represented 0.32% of dry weight of the biomass. Incidentally, the withanolide profile in the shoot cultures was different from that of the foliar tissues. Withaferin A, the major withanolide component reported from the leaves of naturally growing plants could not be detected in shoot cultures. In another study, Roja *et al.* (1991) compared withanolide synthesizing potential of PGR induced callus, cell suspension and multiple shoot cultures. The callus failed to synthesize withanolides whereas multiple shoots synthesized withanolides along with trace amounts of withanolide D. Furmanova *et al.*, (2001) compared withanolide contents in leaves of *in vitro* and greenhouse-grown tissue cultured plants and highlighted the importance of prolonged incubation environmental conditions on withaferin A production. Recently Ray and Jha (2002) have reported the presence of withaferin A in the shoots and withanolide D in the roots of tissue culture regenerated plants.The synthesis and concomitant release of withanolides in the medium was detected and compared with the controls, which lacked withanolides. Vitali *et al.*, (1996) attempted to develop hairy roots in Italian Chemotype failed to produce any withanolides or withaferin A whereas shoot cultures showed low contents of withanolides.

Production Through Genetic Engineering

Manipulation of genes is called genetic engineering or recombinant DNA technology. It removes gene(s) from one organism and either:

- Transfers them to another
- Puts them back in the original with a different combination

- Various gene transfer techniques used in genetic engineering includes
- Agrobacterium mediated gene transfer: Desired trait is isolated from DNA of original organism, inserted into *Agrobacterium*, target plant is infected. Cells that accept the DNA are grown into plants with the new trait.
- Gene gun: DNA that codes for the desired trait is coated onto tiny particles of tungsten and fired into a group of plant cells. Cells that accept the DNA are grown into plants with the desired trait.

Complementing biotechnology, attempts have been made in the recent years to induce Ri and Ti based genetic transformations in W. somnifera (Table 9.2). Banerjee *et al.,* (1994) proposed withaferin A production at different stages of growth in "hairy root" cultures obtained following infection with *Agrobacterium rhizogenes*. Pawar and Maheshwari (2004) have described a method for hairy root induction from various explants with a 10-fold increase in growth rate. Withanolide synthesis in transformed root cultures of Ashwagandha (Ray and co-workers,1996, 2001). Among the several withanolides synthesized, withanolide D was isolated and identified as a major withanolide when compared with untransformed root cultures. These investigators failed to identify withaferin A in both the types of root cultures. Furmanova *et al.* (1998) described withanolide production in untransformed and transformed "hairy roots" *in vitro* and identified withaferin A and withanolide D. Most recently studies carried out by Kumar *et al.* (2005) have demonstrated the presence of withanolides through high performance liquid chromatography analysis by "hairy roots" induced by infecting leaf segments of *W. somnifera*. The integration of T DNA in the genome was confirmed by polymerase chain reaction for rol A gene and Southern blot test.

The susceptibility of ashwagandha towards wild type nopaline strain of *Agrobacterium tumefaciens* infection and potential of transformed gall for withanolide synthesis have been investigated by Ray and Jha (1999) and recently by Jha *et al.* (2001) using two genotypes of Ashwagandha. According to these studies, the oncogenic strains had different levels of virulence on the genotypes studied, which showed a difference in the nature of galls formed and their subsequent morphological competence. Transformed gall cultures analyzed for the presence of withanolides showed withaferin A and withanolide D production in gall-derived callus. A classification of the biovars representing collections from different biogeographical regions, of this important medicinal plant developed using AFLP molecular markers (Negi *et al.*, 2000) is expected to be helpful in segregating chemotypes and ensuing identification and quality control besides IPR protection of specific types.

Table 9.2: ***Agrobacterium*** **Mediated Ti/Ri Based Genetic Transformation in** ***Withania somnifera*** **and withanolide Production in the Transformed Lines**

Withanolide Production in Transformed Lines	Genetic Transformations			Authors
	Strain Used	Methodology	Physical Manifestation	
Withaferin A, Withacnistine, iochromolide, Withanone, Withanolide E	A4, LBA 9402, LBA 9360	Micro-injection	Hairy roots	Banerjee *et al.*, 1994
Withanolide J, withanolide E, 17- isowithanolide E, 5-ethylwithanolide S, Withanolide S	Agropine type LBA	Micro - injection & Hybridization with Eco R1	Hairy roots	Vitali *et al.*, 1996
Withanolide D present and Withaferin A absent in both root cultures	Agropine-Mannopine type LBA 9402	Micro - injection	Hairy roots	Ray *et al.*, 1996
Withanolide D (0.085-0.025%), Withaferin A (0.07-0.10)	Nopaline C58, N2/73, T37, Succinamopine teratomas A281, Octopine Ach5 disarmed LBA 4404	Co-cultivation	Shooty teratomas	Ray & Jha, 1999
Withanolide D, Withaferin A	–	Co-cultivation	Hairy roots	Furmanova *et al.*, 1998

(Table Contd…)

Withanolide Production in Transformed Lines	**Genetic Transformations**			**Authors**
	Strain Used	**Methodology**	**Physical Manifestation**	
Withanolide D, Withaferin A	Nopaline C58, N2/73, T37, Succinamopine teratomas A281, Octopine Ach5 disarmed LBA 4404	Co-cultivation	Shooty teratomas	Ray & Jha, 2001
Could not be tested	LBA 4404	Co-cultivation	Putative galls	Sharada, 2004
–	*A. rhizogenes*	Micro-injection	Hairy roots	Pawar & Maheshwari, 2004
Withanolides present	*A. rhizogenes*	Micro-injection	Hairy roots	Kumar *et al.*, 2005

NEW INITIATIVES AND FUTURE PROSPECTS

Withania somnifera a commercially important medicinal plant which contains attractive range of secondary metabolites has received good deal of attention on *in vitro* studies. Despite impressive account of tissue culture and biotechnological studies, the following studies are still needed:

The improvement of Ashwagndha is vulnerable by its highly heterozygous character and recalitrancy towards conventional hybridization. Tissue culture strategies offer the solutions to some of these problems. Micropropagation can lead to production of huge number of plants in relatively short time and space from a single mother plant. They are normally disease free, genetically uniform and show more vigour and higher yield. Tissue cultured medicinal plants have been reported to exhibit higher medicinal value. Micropropagation would also help in ensuring the production of uniform plants, thereby restricting the variation in commercial population and quality of roots, which at present, is a major problem encountered with seed and vegetative propagating material. Thus, Plant tissue culture techniques are extensively used for mass production of elite plants as well as to study the basic aspects of primary and secondary metabolism (Chaturvedi, 2007). Medicinal plants are valuable due to therapeutic value of their biochemical constituents. So extensive cytological studies, which is a prerequisite for biochemical properties and genetic improvement in plant species should be done. The *in vitro* production of haploids is extremely valuable in plant breeding genetics, as with haploids, homozygosity can be achieved in a single step by doubling of the chromosomes. Whereas many years are needed to obtain inbreeds by conventional breeding methods. Instead of repeated self pollination, a rapid way to reach 100% homozygosity is through microspore embryogenesis followed by chromosomes doubling to produce doubled haploid plants. Haplo-Tech provides a rapid way to generate F1 varieties. The mechanism of signal recognition by plant cells, and the regulation of differential expression of genes and enzymes are attractive fields in studies of the biosynthesis of natural products, and cell cultures of ashwagandha would be a very suitable model system for these studies. It is important to know the decisive biosynthetic enzymes of withanolide biosynthesis to influence its expression or its regulation. The exploitation of variant cell strains for such studies will improve the chances of using Ashwagandha cell suspension cultures for bioproduction of withanolides by bioreactor cultivation, immobilization and biotransformation, which needs further attention. Further, there is a need for the development of efficient genetic transformation protocols, which could be utilized for recovery of plants with transgenes encoding the enzyme(s) for rate limiting step(s) of withanolide biosynthetic pathway. This may lead to the increased activity of enzyme(s) and higher bioproduction of withanolides in vivo. The potential for gene manipulation of *Withania somnifera* present novel possibilities for enhancing the production of bioactive metabolites and of engineering whole biosynthesis and develop designer plants. Alternative strategies that include the manipulation of genes encoding branch point enzymes such that medicinally important withanolides and glycowithanolides could be produced at much higher concentrations than those seen normally. The work on the possibilities of genetic and molecular approach towards developing genetic engineered plants in *W.somnifera* with desired characteristics being pursued in integrated approach under various national programmes will provide a basis and opportunity to develop reliable biotechnology for practical purpose and developing designer Ashwagandha plants in the near future.

REFERENCES

Abhyankar G.A. and Chinchanikar G.S.1996. Response of *Withania somnifera* Dunal Leaf Explants *in vitro*. *Phytomorphology*. 46 (3): 249-252.

Akhatar.1997. Isolation and Structural Studies on the Chemical Constituents of *Withania somnifera*, Fumaria Flabellata and X-ray Differaction Studies. *Ph.D.Thesis* (*International centre for chemical Science, H.E.J. Research Institute of Chemistry, University of Karachi*) 5-6.

Andallu, B and Radhika, B. 2000. Hypoglycemic, Diuretic and Hypocholesterolemic Effect of Winter Cherry (*Withania somnifera*, Dunal) Root. *Indian Journal of Experimental Biology*. 38: 607-609.

Anonymous (1976). The Wealth of India: A Dictionary of Indian Raw Materials and Industrial Products. Vol. X: sP-W. NISC, CSIR,New Delhi, pp. 580-585.

Baburaj S and Gunasekaran K (1995) *In vitro* Differentiation of Shoots from Leaf Callus Cultures of *Withania somnifera* (L.) Dunal. *J. Ind. Bot. Soc*. 74: 323-324.

Bandyopadhyay, M; Jha, S. 2003. Withania Species - A Review. *Journal of Tropical Medicinal Plants*. 4 (2): 273-284.

Banerjee S, Naqvi AA, Mandal S and Ahuja PS (1994) Transformation of *Withania somnifera* (L.) Dunal by *Agrobacterium rhizogenes*: Infectivity and Phytochemical Studies. Phytother. Res. 8: 452-55.

Banerjee S, Naqvi AA, Mandal S and Ahuja PS (1994) Transformation of *Withania somnifera* (L.) Dunal by *Agrobacterium rhizogenes*: Infectivity and Phytochemical Studies. Phytother. Res. 8: 452-55.

Bir, S.S. and Neelam 1980. In: Chromosome Number Reports LXIX. *Taxon 29*: 703-730.

Butola, J.S. and Badola, H.K. (2007). Use of Sodium Hypochlorite to Enhance Seedling Emergence, Vigour and Survival of *Angelica glauca* and *Aconitum heterophyllum*. *Journal of Herbs, Spices and Medicinal Plants*, 13(4): 1-10.

Charlwood BV and Pletsch M (1990) Manipulation of Natural Product Accumulation in Plants Through Genetic Engineering. *J. Herbs, Spices and Med. Plants* 9: 139-151.

Chaturvedi,HC; Jain Madhu and Kidwai NR. 2007. Cloning of Medicinal Plants Through Tissue Culture: A Review. *Indian Journnal of Experimental Biology*. 45: 937-948.

Das Ananya; Datta Animesh Kumar and Banerjee Devottam. 2011. Organogenic Totipotency *in vitro* Culture of Two Elite Genotypes (Poshita and Jawahar 22) of *Withania somnifera*(L.) Dunal and Quantification of Bioactive Compounds. *International Journal of Ayurveda and Pharmacy*. 2(4): 1175-1179.

Dorenburg H and Knorr D (1997) Challenges and Opportunities for Metabolite Production from Plant Cell and Tissue Cultures. *Food Technology* 51: 47-52.

Furmanova M, Gajdzis-Kuls D, Ruszkowska J, Czarnocki Z, Obidoska G, Sadowska A, Rani R, Upadhyay SN (2001) *In vitro* Propagation of *Withania somnifera* and Isolation of Withanolides with Immunosuppessive Activity. *Planta Med.* 67: 146-149.

Furmanova M, Gajdzis-Kuls D, Starosciak B, Stefanska J (1998) Antibacterial Activity of *Withania somnifera* (L.) Dun. Organs Cultivated *in vitro*. *Herba Polonica* 44: 265-69.

Ghosh S, Gupta K (2001) Responses of Nodal Explants of *Withania somnifera* Grown in Axenic Culture and in Half MS Towards Plant Growth Retardants. *Journal of Medicinal and Aromatic Plant Sciences.* 22: 461-463.

Gottschalk, W(1954) Die Chromosomen Struktur der Solanaceen unter Berucksichtigung Phylogeneticscher Fragestellungen. *Chromosoma.* 6: 539-626.

Govindaraju B, Rao SR, Venugopal RB, Kiran SG, Kaviraj CP, Srinath R (2003) High Frequency Plant Regeneration in Ashwagandha [*Withania somnifera* (L.) Dunal] - An Important Medicinal Plant. *Plant Cell Biotechnology and Molecular Biology* 4: 49-56.

Heble MR (1985) Multiple Shoot Cultures: A Viable Alternative *in vitro* System for the Production of Known and New Biologically Active Plant Constituents. In: (eds) Neumann KH, Barz W, Reinhard E Primary and Secondary Metabolism of Plant Cell Cultures. Springer-Verlag, Berlin Heidelberg, Germany. 281-289.

Iqbal, Mohnisa and Datta, AK 2007. Cytogenetic Studies in *Withania somnifera* (L) Dun. (Solanaceae). *Cytologia,* 72 (1): 43-47.

Jafri, SMH. 1966. *The Flora of Karachi.* 293-298.

Kanungo Satyajit and Sahoo Santi Lata.2011. Direct Organogenesis of *Withania somnifera* L. from apical bud. *International Research Journal of Biotechnology* Vol. 2(3) 058-061.

Kanungo Satyajit and Sahoo Santi Lata.2011. Direct organogenesis of *Withania somnifera* L. from apical bud. *International Research Journal of Biotechnology.* 2(3): 058-061.

Kapoor, LD. 2005. *Handbook of Ayurvedic Medicinal Plants. Boca Ratan.* 416.

Kulkarni, A A. 2000. Micropropagation and Secondary Metabolite Studies in Taxus spp. and *Withania somnifera*(L.) Dunal.Ph.D.Thesis,University of Pune.

Kulkarni, AA; Thengane, SR and Krishnamurthy, KV. 2000. Direct Shoot Regeneration from Node, Internode, Hypocotyls and Embryo Explants of *Withania somnifera. Plant Cell, Tissue and Organ Culture.* 62: 203-209.

Kulkarni, AA; Thengane,SR and Krishnamurthy,KV.1999. De novo Regeneration of Various Explants of Withania somnifera (L.) Dun. *Plant Tissue Culture and Biotechnology: Emerging Trends Proceedings of a Symposium held at Hyderabad, India, 29 31 January 1997. 1999;* 180-186.

Kulkarni,AA; Thengane, SR and Krishnamurthy, KV.2000. Direct Shoot Regeneration from Node, Internode, Hypocotyl and Embryo Explants of *Withania somnifera. Plant Cell, Tissue and Organ Culture.* 62(3): 203-209.

Kumar V, Murthy KNC, Bhamidi S, Sudha CG and Ravishankar GA (2005) Genetically Modified Hairy Roots of *Withania somnifera* Dunal: A Potent Source of Rejuvenating Principles. *Rejuvenation Research* 8: 37-45.

Logesh, Ap. Settu, K. Thangavel and A.Ganapathi. 2010. Direct *in vitro* Regeneration of *Withania somnifera* (L.) Dunal. Through Leaf Disc Culture. *International Journal of Biological Technology* (2010) 1(3): 1-4.

Maiti S. 2006. Inventary and Documentation of Medicinal Plants in India. *Medicinal Plants Research in Asia.* 1: 50-52.

Manickam VS, Mathavan RE and Antonisamy R (2000) Regeneration of Indian Ginseng Plantlets from Stem Callus. *Plant Cell Tissue Organ Cult*. 62: 181-185.

Nasir, E and Ali,SI. 1972. *Flora of West Pakistan*. 628.

Negi MS, Singh A and Lakshmikumaran M (2000) Genetic Variation and Relationship Among and within *Withania* species as revealed by AFLP markers. *Genome* 43: 975-980.

NRIF (2004). Pliot study on "Mechanism for Sustainable Development and Promotion of Herbal and Medicinal Plants (H & MP) in the State of Uttaranchal (India). *Report Forwarded to SER Division, Planning Commission, India by Natural Resources India Foundation*, New Delhi, 205.

Pawar PK and Maheshwari VL (2004) *Agrobacterium rhizogenes* Mediated Hairy Root Induction in Two Medicinally Important Members of Family Solanaceae. Ind. J. Biotechnol. 3: 414-417.

Pawar PK, Teli NP, Bhalsing SR and Maheshwari VL (2001) Micropropagation and Organogenetic Studies in *Withania somnifera* (L.) Dunal. *Journal of Plant Biology* 28: 217-221.

Rajeswara Rao BR., Rajput DK., Nagaraju G. and Adinarayana G. 2012.Opportunities and Challenges in the Cultivation of Ashwagandha {*Withania somnifera* (l.) Dunal} *Journal of Pharmacognosy*. 3(2):88-91.

Ram, Mohan; HY and Kamini, I. 1964. Embryology and Fruit Development in *Withania somnifera* Dunal. *Phytomorphology* 14: 574-587.

Rani Archana, Kumar M. and Kumar Sanjeev.2014a. *In vitro* Propagation of *Withania somnifera* (L.) Dunal. from shoot apex Explants. *Journal of Applied and Natural Science*. 6 (1): 159-163.

Rani Archana, Kumar M. and Kumar Sanjeev. 2014b. *In vitro* Callus Induction and Shoot Regeneration from Leaf Explants of *Withania somnifera*. *Advances of Applied Research*. 6(1): 62-65.

Rani G, Arora S and Nagpal A (2003a) Direct Rhizogenesis from *in vitro* Leaves of *Withania somnifera* (L.) Dunal. *J. Herbs, Spices and Med. Plants* 10: 47-54.

Rani G, Virk GS and Nagpal A (2003b) Callus Induction and Plantlet Regeneration in *Withania somnifera* (L.) Dunal. *In Vitro Cell. Dev. Biol. Plant* 39: 468-474

Rani G, Virk GS and Nagpal A (2004) Somatic Embryogenesis in *Withania somnifera* (L.) Dunal. *J. Plant Biotechnology*. 6: 113-118.

Rani, G; Grover, IS.1999. *In vitro* Callus Induction and Regeneration Studies in *Withania somnifera*. *Plant Cell, Tissue and Organ Culture*. 57(1): 23-27.

Rao SR and Ravishanker GA (2002) Plant Cell Cultures: Chemical Factories of Secondary Metabolites. *Biotechnol. Adv*. 20: 101-153.

Rawat, R.B.S. and Garg, G.P. (2005). Medicinal Plants: Trade and Commerce Opportunities with India. *Indian Forester*, 131(3): 275-287.

Ray S and Jha S (2001) Production of Withaferin A in Shoot Cultures of *Withania somnifera*. *Planta Medica*. 67: 432-436.

Ray S and Jha S (2002) Regeneration of *Withania somnifera* Plants. *Journal of Tropical Medicinal Plants*. 3: 89-95.

Ray S, Ghosh B, Sen and Jha S (1996) Withanolide Production by Root Cultures of *Withania somnifera* Transformed with *Agrobacterium rhizogenes*. *Planta Medica*. 62: 571-573.

Roja G, Heble MR and Sipahimalini AT (1991) Tissue Cultures of *Withania somnifera*: Morphogenesis and withanolide Synthesis. *Physiotherapy Research*. 5: 185-87.

Sen J and Sharma AK (1991) Micropropagation of *Withania somnifera* from Germinated Seeds and Shoot Tip. *Plant Cell Tissue Organ Cult*. 26: 71-73.

Shanmugaratnam Suvanthini, Mikunthan Gunasingham and Thurairatnam Shyama. 2013.Potential of *Withania somnifera* Dunal Cultivation as a Medicinal Crop in Jaffna District. *American-Eurasian J. Agric. & Environ. Sci.*13 (3): 357-361.

Sharada M, Ahuja A, Suri KA, Vij SP, Khajuria RK, Verma V and Kumar A (2007) Withanolide Production by *in vitro* Cultures of *Withania somnifera* (L) Dunal and its Association with Differentiation. *Biol. Plant.* 51: 161-164.

Sharada Mallubhotla, Ahuja and Vij Suraj Prakash. Application of Biotechnology in Indian Ginseng (Ashwagandha): Progress and Prospects. *Recent advances in Plant Biotechnology and its Applications*. 560-582.

Siddique NA, Bari MA, Shahnewaz S, Rahman MH, Hasan MR, Khan MSI and Islam MS (2004) Plant Regeneration of *Withania somnifera* (L.) Dunal (Ashwagandha) from Nodal Segments Derived Callus an Endangered Medicinal Plantin Bangladesh. *J. Biol. Sci.* 4: 219-223.

Stoller EW, Stohs SJ, El-Olemy MM, Yu PC and Tarng CS (1974) Fatty Acid Composition of Lipids of *Corchorus, Yucca, Dioscorea, Withania* and *Rivea* Tissue Cultures. *Lloydia* 37: 309-312.

Teli NP, Patil NM, Pathak HM, Bhalsing SR and Maheshwari VL (1999) *Withania somnifera* (Ashwagandha): Regeneration Through Meristem Culture. *J. Plant Biochem. Biotechnol.* 8: 109-111.

Udayakumar R; Choi C W; Kim K T; Kim SC; Kasthurirengan S; Mariashibu TS; Sahaya Rayan JJ and Ganapathi A.2013. *In vitro* Plant Regeneration from Epicotyl Explant of *Withania somnifera* (L.) Dunal *Journal of Medicinal Plants Research*. 7(1): 43-52.

Udayakumar R; Choi C W; Kim K T; Kim SC; Kasthurirengan S; Mariashibu TS; Sahaya Rayan JJ and Ganapathi A.2013. *In vitro* Plant Regeneration from Epicotyl Explant of *Withania somnifera* (L.) Dunal*Journal of Medicinal Plants Research*. 7(1): 43-52.

Vadawale, AV; Bhatt PA and Dave, AM. 2004. Rapid Propagation of Ashwagandha (*Withania somnifera*) Through Axillary Bud Multiplication and Indirect Organogenesis. *Phytomorphology*. 54(1&2): 59-64.

Ved, DK; Barve,V; Begam, SN and Latha, R.1998. Eco-distribution Mapping of the Priority Medical Plants of Southern India. *Current Science*.75(3): 205.

Verma, SK; Sharma, SK; Singh, C and Mehta, H. 2004. Breeding, Improvement and Germplasm Conservation of Medicinal and Aromatic Plants- A Review. *Indian Forester*. 130(3): 291-303.

Vishnoi A, Babbar SB and Gupta SC (1979) Induction of Androgenesis in Anther Cultures of *Withania somnifera*. *Z. Pflanzenphysiol* 94: 169-179.

Vitali G, Conte L and Nicoletti M (1996) Withanolide Composition and *in vitro* Culture of Italian *Withania somnifera*. *Planta Medica* 62: 287-288.

Waman, A.A., U. Konana, S.B. Narayanappa, A. Tholakalabavi and B. Gowda, 2011. Callus Culture and Plant Regeneration from Seedling Explants in 'Poshita' Indian Ginseng. *Horticulture & Environment Biotechnology*.52(1): 83-88.

Index

****